Night Music

THE
SEAGULL
LIBRARY OF
GERMAN
LITERATURE

Theodor W. Adorno

Night Music

ESSAYS ON MUSIC, 1928–1962

EDITED BY
ROLF TIEDEMANN

TRANSLATED AND INTRODUCED BY
WIELAND HOBAN

LONDON NEW YORK CALCUTTA

This publication was supported by a grant from the Goethe-Institut India

Seagull Books, 2019

ISBN-13 978 0 8574 2 709 0

British Library Cataloguing-in-Publication Data
A catalogue record for this book is available from the British Library

Typeset by Seagull Books, Calcutta, India
Printed and bound by Hyam Enterprises, Calcutta, India

CONTENTS

TRANSLATOR'S INTRODUCTION

Though Adorno's thought has over time established itself in the Anglophone world as a complex constellation of ideas that can be accepted or rejected, but must at least be engaged with, it is notable that his work is still very often presented via some form of editorial mediation. Several compilations or 'readers' have been published in recent years,[1] and several of the book-length works (for example *Aesthetic Theory*[2]) have been augmented by extensive explanatory introductions from editors or translators (this introduction is not intended to add to that list, merely to explain some of the ideas behind this particular publication). One could certainly argue that Adorno's ideas are sufficiently remote from most Anglophone schools of thought to merit some degree of contextualization and background; there is a danger, however, that both the urgency of his insights and the stylistic specificity of his writing may lose

[1] For example: Brian O'Connor (ed.), *The Adorno Reader* (Oxford: Blackwell, 2000); Theodor W. Adorno, *Essays on Music* (selected, with introduction, commentary and notes by Richard Leppert; new translations by Susan H. Gillespie) (Berkeley and Los Angeles: University of California Press, 2002); Rolf Tiedemann (ed.), *Can One Live after Auschwitz? A Philosophical Reader* (Stanford, CA: Stanford University Press, 2003).

[2] Theodor W. Adorno, *Aesthetic Theory* (Gretel Adorno and Rolf Tiedemann eds; Robert Hullot-Kentor trans.) (Minneapolis: University of Minnesota Press, 1998).

some of their force as a result of this perceived need for apologists. I believe that the ideas of Kant, Hegel or Marx are sufficiently established within the intellectual consciousness, and the music of Mahler and Schönberg now sufficiently historical, for the writings to stand on their own.

In spite of this, it is vital to acknowledge the significance of the mediating work that has been undertaken in recent decades. This is particularly evident in the context of Adorno's texts on music, which are by their nature destined to receive less public attention than his socio-philosophical studies. A volume such as Richard Leppert's compilation[3] is invaluable for any student of Adorno's musical thought, presenting a cross-section of considerable magnitude and breadth astutely arranged by theme and discussing each complex in some depth. In fact, it should be taken as a sign of my respect for such undertakings, Leppert's in particular, that the present volume makes no attempt to compete with them; there is neither a need nor any prospect of success. Its aim is a different, perhaps simpler one.

Though the essays collected in the cycle *Moments musicaux* were written throughout most of Adorno's career—between 1928 and 1962—the fact that Adorno himself chose and arranged them in a particular, non-chronological order indeed suggests that they should be read as a cycle, an integral work, rather than a disparate assortment. A number of them have been published in translation in various compilations over the years,[4] but this state of disunity—compounded by being

---

3 See note 1, p. *viii*.

4 These are: 'Late Style in Beethoven' (Susan Gillespie trans.) in *Essays on Music*, pp. 564–8; 'Schubert' (Rodney Livingstone trans.) in *Can One Live After Auschwitz?* pp. 299–313; 'On Jazz' (Jamie Owen Daniel trans.) in *Essays on Music*, pp. 470–98; 'Alienated Masterpiece: the *Missa Solemnis*' (Duncan Smith trans.) in *Essays on Music*, pp. 569–83; 'On the Score of "Parsifal"' (Anthony Barone trans.) in *Music and Letters* 76(3) (August

rendered by several different translators—struck me as unsat-
isfactory for an adequate reception. While the number of existing translations made me wonder whether it would be justified
to publish all these essays, I decided to do so nonetheless out
of the belief that they should be read together and made accessible to Anglophone readers by a single translator. I would not
wish to give the impression of being dissatisfied with any of
the existing translations, all of which are competent and faithful. It should be noted, however, that every translator, as much
as he or she may see themselves as a neutral medium rather
than a recipient who intervenes and interprets, differs in their
style and reading. This is especially significant in the case of
complex texts such as Adorno's, which not only deal with intricate ideas expounded in intricate language, but are also—to
varying extents—very much literary in their stylistic awareness. Beyond such basic concerns as semantic accuracy, choices
of phrase order or emphasis through punctuation constitute
stylistic decisions, whether a translator admits it or not. Even
semantic accuracy, however, is often impeded by Adorno's
idiosyncratic constructions, for example the use of multiple
pronouns at some distance from the nouns to which they
apply, which can easily lead to misattributions (that may seem
perfectly reasonable in their contexts) if they agree with the
genders of other nouns.[5] In short, though it is not usually

1995): 384–97; 'On the Contemporary Relationship of Philosophy and
Music' (Susan Gillespie trans.) in *Essays on Music*, pp. 135–61. The only
one of the 19 encyclopaedia articles to be published prior to collation in
the *Gesammelte Schriften*, 'Jazz', was originally printed (in English) in
Dagobert R. Runes and Harry G. Schrickel (eds), *Encyclopedia of the Arts*
(New York: Philosophical Library, 1946).

5 For more extensive reflections on translating Adorno's musical writings,
see my Introduction to Theodor W. Adorno, *Towards a Theory of Musical
Reproduction: Notes, a Draft and Two Schemata* (Henri Lonitz ed., Wieland
Hoban trans.) (Cambridge: Polity, 2006), pp. *xvi–xxii*.

possible for all an author's works to be translated by a single person (especially when the œuvre in question is so voluminous), it is at least preferable for a cycle of translated texts to be read in the language of a single translator.

As a cycle, *Moments musicaux* has a more pronounced literary character than many of Adorno's other writings. This expresses itself both in a tendency towards relatively aphoristic forms (such as the essay on Offenbach) and an occasional indulgence in extended metaphorical reflections (as at the start of the Schubert essay). There is a further quality that makes the collection remarkable, however, and recalls Adorno's admiring comment about Walter Benjamin that he managed to find philosophical and poetic depth in the most everyday matters: the coexistence of shorter texts on subjects that would generally be viewed as secondary in the wider context of Adorno's thought, for example 'Homage to Zerlina', with extended analyses of more obviously fundamental matters, such as the essays on Schubert or Beethoven's *Missa Solemnis*.[6] The juxtaposition of apparent lightness and emphatic gravity, of associative and methodical writing, reveals, to my mind, a wider range of ideas than is frequently associated with Adorno. This is one of my foremost hopes for the present volume: that it will introduce readers to previously unfamiliar aspects of his thought.

The second part of the volume is of a slightly different nature. Firstly, the essays all deal with the contemporary music of Adorno's time,[7] which, despite having been one of his most pressing concerns, is given less attention than his works of

6 Even the infamous and much-derided 'On Jazz', which displays a number of misconceptions about the genre, seems rather more perceptive if its ideas are applied to mainstream popular music.

7 In keeping with the orthography that has established itself in Germany since Adorno's death, I capitalize the initials of the phrase 'New Music'. Absence of capitals indicates music that is simply temporally new, not programmatically or substantially new.

social critique or more incendiary texts such as *Philosophy of New Music*.[8] This is ultimately inevitable; even the music of Schönberg does not enjoy a wide audience, to say nothing of later and more (at that time) anti-traditional composers such as Stockhausen or Boulez. It is here, however, that Adorno shows some of his sharpest analytical insight, as well as an ability to connect the past with the present—and the future—that was uncommon among advocates of radical music at that time. The connections to tradition, social conditions and cultural politics evident in these texts make them, despite their more esoteric subject matter, equally rewarding for readers who may not be so familiar with the music of the twentieth century. And for those who wish to increase their familiarity, the nineteen encyclopaedia articles that open this part of the book offer an excellent overview of the central musical tendencies in the first half of the century. They present unusually concise critical descriptions of phenomena that were significant for all his writings on modern music, succeeding at the difficult task of restricting detail without sacrificing content. In this sense, they provide a useful starting point from which to approach the more complex analyses that follow them.

This part of the book also differs from the first in its textual status: these essays, written between 1929 and 1956, were grouped together not by Adorno himself, but rather posthumously by Rolf Tiedemann, a former student and the chief editor of Adorno's collected works. The title *Theory of New Music* was thus not Adorno's own, and is perhaps slightly misleading. As becomes clear very soon, we are not dealing here with the exposition of a single unified theory; it is rather a collection of theoretical reflections on different aspects of New Music. The word 'theory' should therefore be understood

8 Theodor W. Adorno, *Philosophy of New Music* (Robert Hullot-Kentor trans.) (Minneapolis: University of Minnesota Press, 2006).

in a less specific sense more akin to a phrase such as 'music theory'—that is to say, as works of 'New Music theory'. I considered changing the title of this section a number of times to something in the vein of 'Studies on New Music', 'Reflections on New Music' or 'Towards a Theory of New Music'; in the end, however, I decided that this question was sufficiently secondary for me to retain the original title for the sake of equivalence with the German edition. Hopefully readers will not be disappointed to learn that this 'theory' is 'only' a collection of shorter texts; as *Philosophy of New Music* shows, a more rigid and clear-cut theoretical framework is not without problems of its own, such as the temptation to exaggerate differences for the sake of dialectical opposition. Nonetheless, it should become clear that these texts, though written separately, are closely related in their themes and perspectives.

Finally, I would like to extend my warmest thanks to Naveen Kishore, Publisher, Seagull Books, and Petra Hardt, Head, Foreign Rights, Suhrkamp Verlag. Without their openness for new projects and faith in my judgement, this volume would never have come into existence.

February 2009

I

MOMENTS MUSICAUX

FOREWORD

After including earlier studies for the first time in his two volumes of musical writings, the author considered it expedient to present a cross-section of his musical-literary output, to collect essays from entirely different periods not found in any of his books. They all originally appeared in journals; most of them are now difficult, in some cases impossible, to find. They have not been arranged chronologically but, rather, according to subject matter. Changes have been made only where the author was too ashamed of old inadequacies.

One criterion of selection was whether to preserve an essay on account of its effects; another, whether motifs would be introduced early on but developed later, taking on some of the intensity of an idea's first formulation. But such effects easily wear themselves out. Finally, the book also contains some texts that were typical of the author's intentions while he was editor of the Viennese journal *Anbruch*.

Almost everything he ever wrote about music was already conceived during his youth, that is to say before 1933. Numerous essays from that period, however, were lost during the years of emigration; they were later salvaged for publication by Rudolf Komarnicki in Vienna. With a dedication that the author considers undeserved and that thus moves him all the more deeply, Komarnicki collected and made available everything relevant to which he had had access since the 1920s.

This public word of thanks expresses only a small part of the debt owed him by the author.

A few words concerning the individual essays:

'Beethoven's Late Style', written in 1934 and printed in 1937, may attract some attention on account of the eighth chapter of *Doctor Faustus*.

The essay on Schubert was written on the hundredth anniversary of his death. Being the author's first extended study concerning the interpretation of music, it was let through despite some instances of clumsiness and the philosophical interpretation proceeding in too immediate a fashion, neglecting technical and compositional aspects. There is a glaring imbalance between its high ambition—also that of its tone—and what it achieves; as in 'Night Music', written shortly after it, much remains abstract in the bad sense. The only *captatio benevolentiae* the author can present is the fact that his later effort was centred on the correction of such flaws; in this sense, they are themselves an aspect of his thinking.

The next four essays, separated by a considerable number of years, tentatively explore some of the author's experiences with opera that have accompanied him since childhood.

'Night Music' was intended as a programme for the intellectual orientation of *Anbruch*. Many of the author's later efforts concerning the historical dynamics of music, the internal changes undergone by works and the theory of musical reproduction can be traced back to it.

The portrait of Ravel and 'Reaction and Progress' give an idea of what the author then sought to realize in *Anbruch*. The text on progress was the antithetical partner to an article by Ernst Krenek on the same subject. The idea of the command of musical material, a central category in *Philosophy of New Music*, can be recognized in it.

'New Tempi' is a model for those texts that combine aesthetic and historico-philosophical reflections with practical musical instructions. Most essays of this kind were published by *Pult und Taktstock*, a conducting journal, whose editor, Erwin Stein, a student of Schönberg, proved highly sympathetic to the author's endeavours from the outset.

The jazz study of 1936 is the first extended text that the author, following the paralysis of the first years under Fascism, was able to put to paper. It can be considered a breakthrough in several respects: it unites artistic, technological and social analysis. The unpublished additions written immediately afterwards show the author's will to find the substance not by looking at the matter from a distance but, rather, by getting extremely close to it. Both date from the author's time in America; some detail information was supplied by the composer Mátyás Seiber, who directed the jazz class at the Hoch'sches Konservatorium in Frankfurt until 1933 and recently fell victim to a fatal accident. The insufficient knowledge of the specifically American aspects of jazz, especially that of standardization, is as sensitive an issue as the obsolescence of some characteristics of European jazz in the 1930s. The more the genre remains constant in its essence, the more fans emphasize its historical changes. The author would be the first to admit that some elements he has described have meanwhile gone out of fashion, and that his interpretation of various aspects is too directly socio-psychological, with too little attention to institutional social mechanisms. The author has made up for his failure to address certain topics and to foresee others in the 'Fetish Character' essay in *Dissonances*, the jazz study in *Prisms* and the chapter on light music in *Introduction to the Sociology of Music*.

The articles on Krenek, Weill's *Mahagonny* and Zillig's Verlaine songs are more physiognomic than analytic in nature.

Concerning the essay on Schönberg's wind quintet (1928), the author would like to cite some lines from a letter written much later by the composer to Rudolf Kolisch on 27 July 1932:

You worked out the row for my string quartet (except for one small matter: the second consequent is: 6th note C sharp, 7th G sharp) correctly. It must have taken a great deal of effort, and I doubt I would have had the patience. Do you really think it is of any use to know that? I can hardly imagine it. I certainly believe that it can act as a stimulus for a composer who is still inexperienced in the use of rows, suggesting one way to approach a piece—a purely technical indication of the possibility to draw on rows. But this is not where we discover aesthetic qualities, at least not the primary ones. I cannot warn people often enough not to overestimate the value of these analyses, as they only lead to what I have always fought against: the realization of how it is *made*; whereas I have always helped others to realize what it *is*! I have attempted to make this clear to Wiesengrund on several occasions, and also to Berg and Webern. But they don't believe me. I cannot say it often enough: my works are twelve-note *compositions*, not *twelve-note* compositions: here people are confusing me once again with Hauer, for whom composition is only of secondary importance.[1]

In truth, however, the author was not at all interested in counting note-rows. Long before that point, he had been, in agreement with Schönberg, analysing the latter's twelve-note works as compositions, from the perspective of the musical context. The essay on the wind quintet, which presents the idea of the 'constructive realization of the sonata', was intended to serve this very purpose. The published text was only its introduction; the main part examined in detail the motivic-thematic and formal structure of the long scherzo in that work,

1 Erwin Stein (ed.), *Arnold Schönberg: Letters* (Berkeley: University of California Press, 1987), p. 164f.

Op. 26, without any consideration of the row. It was lost; it is not inconceivable that it may surface in the archive of *Pult und Taktstock* some day. It should be added that there can no longer be any doubt that Berg and Webern were equally remote from considering composition with note-rows as an end in itself; for them, it was purely a means of representing what was composed. At a time when the fetishism of methods overshadowed all other compositional questions, the controversy has taken on a currentness that could not have been foreseen thirty years ago.

'Alienated Magnum Opus', finally, forms part of the complex of the philosophical work on Beethoven projected since 1937. This has not yet been written, primarily because the author's efforts were foiled time and again by the *Missa Solemnis*. He has therefore attempted at least to point to the reason for those difficulties, to formulate the question more precisely, without presuming already to have found its solution.

Ralf Teidemann
Christmas 1963

BEETHOVEN'S LATE STYLE

The maturity of a significant artist's late works is not like that of fruits. They are not usually round but, rather, furrowed, even ruptured; they tend to lack sweetness, and are prickly in their refusal to be merely tasted. They show none of that harmony which the classicist aesthetic is accustomed to demanding of a work of art, and the marks they bear are more those of history than growth. The common explanation for this is that they are products of a subjectivity or 'personality' uncompromisingly articulating itself which, for the sake of its own expression, breaks open the roundness of conventional forms, twists harmony into the dissonance of its suffering, and scorns all sensual charms through the self-aggrandizement of the liberated spirit. This takes the late work to the limits of art, and closer to the document; and indeed, writings on Beethoven's last works seldom lack references to his life and fate. It is as if art theory, confronted with the dignity of human death, were willing to forfeit its claims and abdicate in the face of reality.

This is the only way to understand the absence of serious objections to the inadequacy of such a view. That inadequacy becomes apparent as soon as one pays attention to the formation itself, rather than its psychological origins. For it is its formal law that must be identified, provided that one does not cross the line to the document—once beyond this line, any of Beethoven's conversation books could be more meaningful than the C-sharp minor quartet. But the formal law of the late works, at any rate, is such that they are not fulfilled in the concept of expression. Beethoven's last works contain highly 'expressionless', distant formations; hence, there was an equal inclination to speak of a new, polyphonic-objective construction as well as that uncompromisingly personal component. His inner conflict is not always between the resolve to die and a demonic humour; often, it is the epitome of the enigmatic, palpable in pieces of a cheerful, even idyllic, tone. The immaterial spirit does not avoid such performance indications as *Cantabile e compiacevole* or *Andante amabile*. One should by no means invoke the cliché of 'subjectivism' to characterize his stance; for in all of Beethoven's music, subjectivity—very much in Kant's sense—acts less to break forms apart than originally to create them. This is exemplified by the *Appassionata*: it is certainly more compacted, closed and 'harmonic' than the late quartets, but in equal measure more subjective, autonomous and spontaneous. And yet those final works rise above it through their mystery. Where does it lie?

Only a technical analysis of the works in question could help to revise our view of late style. It would have to focus from the outset on a peculiarity that is studiously ignored by the popular view: the role of conventions. It is familiar from the works of the aged Goethe and from late Stifter but equally evident in Beethoven, that supposed representative of a radically personal stance. This makes the question more pointed: for the foremost principle of any 'subjectivist' approach is the rejection of all conventions, and the remoulding of those that prove inevitable in accordance with the requirements of expression. Thus it was precisely in the works of his middle period that Beethoven drew the commonplace accompanying figures into the dynamic of subjectivity through the creation of latent inner parts, through their rhythms, their tension and whatever other methods, and transformed them according to his intention, or even—as in the first movement of the Fifth Symphony—developed them from the thematic substance itself, wresting them from convention by virtue of their uniqueness. The Beethoven of the late works is very different: in his entire formal language, even where he makes use of so singular a syntax as in the last five piano sonatas, one finds sprinklings of conventional formulae and phrases. They are full of decorative chains of trills, cadenzas and fioritures, and often the convention becomes visible in a stark, unconcealed, unaltered form: the first subject of the Op. 110 sonata shows an innocently primitive accompaniment in semiquavers that would hardly have been tolerated in the style of the middle period; the last of the Bagatelles presents introductory and concluding bars like the distraught prelude to an opera aria— and all this amid the hardest rock layers of the polyphonic landscape, the most restrained stirrings of isolated lyricism. No interpretation of Beethoven's late style, or indeed any other, is adequate if it only explains the ruins of convention psychologically, with no attention to the actual appearance; for it is only in its appearance that art's substance lies. The relationship between conventions and subjectivity must be understood as the formal law from which the substance of the late works originates, if they are truly to amount to more than touching relics.

It is precisely in the thought of death, however, that the formal law manifests itself. If the validity of art wanes in the face of death's reality, it can certainly not enter the work directly as its 'subject matter'. Death is imposed only on creatures, not their creations, and has therefore always appeared in art in a broken form: as allegory. This is the stumbling block for all psychological interpretation. In declaring mortal subjectivity the substance of late works, it hopes to perceive death directly in the work of art; this remains the deceptive crown of its metaphysics. Certainly it recognizes the explosive force of subjectivity in the late work; but it seeks it in a direction opposite to that in which it is pushing, namely in the expression of subjectivity itself. In fact, however, this subjectivity, existing mortally and thus in the name of death, disappears from the work. The force of subjectivity in late works of art is the eruptive gesture with which it exits them. It breaks free of them—not to express itself but, rather, to discard expressionlessly the semblance of art. All it leaves behind are the ruins of the works, and it communicates—as if in code—only through the hollows it erupts from. Touched by death, the master's hand releases the heaps of material it had previously shaped; the tears and cracks in it, testimonies to the ultimate helplessness of the ego in the face of the existent, are its final work. Hence, the surplus of material in *Faust II* and *Wilhelm Meister's Journeyman Years*; hence, the conventions that are no longer penetrated and mastered by subjectivity but simply left to stand. With the escape of subjectivity, they splinter off. As splinters, disintegrated and abandoned, they finally transform themselves into expression; no longer an expression of the solitary ego but, rather, of the created being's mythical development and its fall, whose steps the late works strike symbolically as if in momentary interruptions of their descent.

In Beethoven's final works, then, conventions become expression in the act of their own naked self-representation. This is the purpose of the oft-noted abbreviation of his style: it seeks not to cleanse his musical language of formulas but, rather, to strip the formula of its semblance of subjective control. Once released and lifted out of its dynamic context, the formula begins to speak for itself—yet only in the moment when subjectivity, escaping, rushes through it and suddenly illuminates it with its intention; hence the crescendi and diminuendi, which, seemingly independent of the musical construction in Beethoven's final works, often send tremors through it.

He no longer gathers up the landscape, now deserted and estranged, to form a picture; he bathes it in the light of the fire ignited by subjectivity when, faithful to its dynamic idea, it strives to break out and crashes against the boundaries of the work. Even his late works remain processes; not in the sense of development, however, but as an ignition between extremes that will no longer tolerate any secure centre or harmony for the sake of spontaneity. Between extremes—in the most precise technical sense: on the one hand, monody, the unison, the meaningful formula; and on the other, polyphony, which suddenly raises itself above all these. It is subjectivity that forces extremes together in the moment, that imbues dense polyphony with its moments of friction, shattering them in the unison and fleeing, leaving behind the bare note; and that places the formula as a monument to what once was, a monument of which subjectivity itself, in its petrified state, forms a part. But the caesuras, that abrupt breaking off which characterizes Beethoven's last works more than any other feature, are those moments of eruption; the work is silent when it is left, and turns its lacuna outwards. Only then does the next fragment follow, rooted to the spot by the command of erupting subjectivity and sworn to its predecessor for better or worse; for the secret lies between them, and can only be invoked in the figure they form together. This explains the nonsensical circumstance that Beethoven's final works are deemed both subjective and objective at once. Objective is the brittle landscape, and subjective the light that alone can set it aglow. He does not bring about their harmonic synthesis. Acting as a force of dissociation, he tears them apart in time in order that they might, perhaps, be preserved for the realm of the eternal. In the history of art, late works are the catastrophes.

1937

SCHUBERT

> The whole useless body was consumed by transparency.
> Little by little the body turned into light, its blood into rays.
> The limbs froze in an incomprehensible gesture.
> And the man was no more than a sign
> among the constellations.
> *Louis Aragon*

When one crosses the threshold between the years of Beethoven's and Schubert's deaths, one must shudder—like one who climbs up from a heaving, opened-out, cooling crater into the painfully fine, white light; before the lava formations on the summit, spread so vulnerably, he notices a web of dark vegetation and finally makes out the eternal clouds, now close to the mountain yet still far above his head, as they follow their path. Rising from the abyss, he sets foot on the landscape that surrounds it and makes its bottomless depth visible at all by tracing its outline with the formidable silence of its contours, and by consenting to receive the light met previously by the blind, glowing mass. Though Schubert's music may not always contain the might of the active will that arises from the centre of Beethoven's nature, the pits and tunnels that run through it lead into the same chthonic depths from which that will originated and uncover their demonic image, which the act of practical reason managed time and again to control; but the stars whose glow is visible from there are the same ones whose unattainable light the zealous hand sought to grasp. Strictly speaking, then, one must refer to Schubert's landscape; for nothing would falsify the substance of his music more profoundly than an attempt to construct him—seeing that, unlike Beethoven, he cannot be understood in terms of the spontaneous unity of a person—as a personality whose idea, as a virtual centre, could integrate all its disparate qualities. On the contrary: the further the traits of Schubert's music move away from such an intra-human point of reference, the more they prove themselves as signs of an intention that alone can overcome the fragments of illusory totality of which human beings, as self-determined spirits, would like to believe they consist. Beyond the reach of any idealistic synopsis or hasty phenomenological exploration of 'unified meaning', and no more a closed system than a purposefully growing flower, Schubert's music acts as the scene of the coexistence of truth characters that it does not produce but, rather, receives—and which can only be uttered by humans once thus received. Certainly, one should not imagine that Schubert's music is utterly devoid of the personal element of composition. Just as the popular view that Schubert, the poet of his own self, expressed without hindrance or interruption what he, as an entirely psychologically determined being, happened to feel at that moment, misses the truth, it would be equally mistaken to attempt to erase Schubert the human being from his music and seek, following the model of Brucknerian phraseology, to make him the medium of divine inspiration or even revelations—as indeed the talk of artistic intuition, a murky concoction mixed from an inferior psychological interpretation of the production process and an arbitrary metaphysics of the finished result, can only ever encumber our understanding of art. Both notions are essentially the same, as great as their superficial contrasts may be, and from the disqualification of one the other's automatically follows. Both rest on a false notion of the lyrical which, in keeping with the blasphemous superelevation of art in the nineteenth century, they take for the truth—for a part of the true human being or a splinter of transcendent reality, while the lyrical, as art, still remains an image of reality; it differs from other images only in the fact that its appearance is tied to the irruption of reality itself into its possibility. Thus the respective proportions of the subjective and objective in the lyrical component that characterizes Schubert's landscape are determined anew. The lyrical essences are not produced: they are the smallest cells of existent objectivity, whose images they constitute now that the great forms of lasting objective substance have long since been deprived of their authoritarian validity. These images do not, however, enter the soul of lyrically receptive human beings as rays of light enter vegetation: works of art are never creatures. Rather, human beings strike them as if they were targets: if one hits the correct number, they are transformed and permit reality itself to shine through them. The force that strikes them is human, not artistic: they are touched by the feelings of humans. Only thus can we understand the indifference of the subjective and the objective in the lyrical creation. The poet does not offer an immediate representation of his feeling; rather, his feeling is the means of drawing truth, in its incomparably tiny crystallization, into the creation. Truth itself does not enter the creation; it represents itself within it, and the unveiling of its image remains the work of humans. The artist unveils the image. The image of truth, however, always stands within history. The history of the image is its disintegration: the disintegration of the illusion of truth with reference to all aspects of its intended substance, and a revelation of its transparency for the aspects of truth content which it implicitly invokes, and which emerge in their pure form only through its disintegration. The disintegration of the lyrical creation is above all the disintegration of its subjective substance. The subjective content of the lyrical work, in fact, consists only of its material content. The aspects of truth content depicted are merely touched on by them; the unity between the two belongs to the historical moment and dissolves. Thus the lasting aspect of lyrical creations is not, as static natural superstition would have us believe, that of unchanging, basic human emotions but, rather, the objective characters that, at the origin of each work of art, were touched upon by those emotions which are ephemeral. The subjectively intended and reproduced essences, however, suffer the same fate as only the great materially determined forms, which are softened by time. The dialectical collision of the two forces—the forms, which are found among the stars in deceptive timelessness, and the materials of consciousness's immanence, which posit themselves as the ultimate inderivable givens—shatters both, and with them the provisional unity of the work: it opens up the work as the scene of its own transience, and finally reveals what images of truth had risen to its crumbling ceiling. Only now has the landscape character of Schubert's music become evident, just as the Luciferian verticality of Beethoven's dynamics can only now be weighed up. The dialectical liberation of Schubert's true substance took place after Romanticism, of which he could hardly ever be considered an unequivocal part. It read his work as the symbolic language of the subjectively intended, suppressing the problem of his forms in banal critique; it dynamically outdid the psychological utterances it drew out of him, exhausting them as quickly as only the inferior type of eternity can be exhausted. But it left behind the work's remnants as its better part, and the lacunae from which subjectivity escaped, the cracks in the poetic surface, fill visibly with the metal that had previously enclosed itself beneath the intelligible utterances of the soul. The transformation of Schubert the man into that repugnant object of petty-bourgeois sentimentality whose embodiment Rudolf Hans Bartsch may have created in the figure of Schwammerl but which still secretly dominates all current writing on

Schubert in Austria, testifies to the decline of moving subjectivity in the truth character of the work—reaching its pinnacle, as the conclusion to all Romantic constructions of Schubert, in the obliteration of that subjectivity in *Das Dreimäderlhaus*.[1] For that is how small humans must become in order to stop obstructing the perspective they opened up, and from whose sphere of influence they should not be expelled altogether, rather livening it up as the tiniest of decorations on the periphery. And yet the figure of Schubert the misfit, a laughing stock among shop girls while partly one of them himself, gushing away in his erotic helplessness, is indeed closer to the genuine image of his music than the pre-revolution dreamer constantly sitting by the stream, listening to its murmuring. It is also highly fitting that *Das Dreimäderlhaus* uses Schubert, not Mozart or Beethoven, and the socially determined Biedermeier affinity for genre postcards, which gives any impulse to turn Schubert into kitsch free rein, identifies itself within the work as the continuance of the isolated, of that same quality which dominates the Schubertian landscape. Even if the continuity of Schubert's forms reaches an end, while those of Beethoven and Mozart continue mutely and unbroken—though one should not decide this until the question of form has been posed seriously—the confused, banal, skewed and, in terms of the existing social order, highly inadequate world of the potpourri, guarantees his themes a second life. In the potpourri, the traits of the work that are scattered throughout it move together to form a new unity; though it is unable to legitimate itself as such, it alone shows the incomparable nature of those traits by directly confronting them.

1 *Das Dreimäderlhaus* ['House of the Three Girls'] is a Viennese operetta, premiered in 1916, based on a semi-fictional account of Schubert's romantic life. The music is by Schubert, but rearranged by the Hungarian Heinrich Berté (1857–1924). The libretto, written by Alfred Maria Willner and Heinz Reichert, was adapted from the 1912 novel *Schwammerl* by Rudolf Hans Bartsch (1873–1952).

The continuance of the theme as a theme is guaranteed by the potpourri, which strings together one theme after another without having to react to any of them through changes. No theme, once past, could bear such emphatic proximity to another; one senses a terrible rigor mortis in the opera potpourris of the nineteenth century. In Schubert, however, the themes are compressed without congealing into a Medusan figure. It is only their blind compilation that clears the path leading back to their origin, and conversely also enables access to Schubert's form. For, as the jigsaws of music, potpourris wanted to take pot luck on rediscovering the lost unity of works of art. They could only be given a chance if that unity was not itself a subjectively created one, the kind that could never be summoned through such a gamble but, rather, through one arising from the configuration of the images captured. Admittedly, this now seems like a roundabout affirmation of that common view of Schubert which is mistaken in its attitude to the lyrical: the view of Schubert's music as an organically developing entity, growing purely from within itself without reference to any preconceived forms—perhaps devoid of any form at all—and blooming in the most refreshing way. The construction from the potpourri, however, is a strict rejection of precisely that organological theory. Such an organic unity would necessarily be teleological: each of its cells would necessitate the next, and the force holding it together would be the active life of subjective intention, which died out, and whose restitution would certainly not be in keeping with the idea of the potpourri. Wagner's music, founded on the image of the organic, fundamentally precludes the potpourri—unlike that of Weber or Bizet, who are indeed related to Schubert. The cells that are layered in the potpourri must have been interwoven according to a different law than the unity of living entities. Even if one concedes that Schubert's music, relatively speaking, is one that grew rather than being fashioned: its growth, very much fragmented and never content with itself, is not herbaceous but, rather, crystalline. By reinforcing the original configurative separation of Schubert's traits, and thus the constitutively fragmentary nature of his music, the conserving transition to the potpourri illuminates the entire Schubertian landscape. One should not mistake it for a coincidence that, in the nineteenth century, the potpourri developed as a surrogate musical form at the same time as the miniature landscape became popular for bourgeois consumer items of all kinds, culminating in the postcard. All those notions of landscape converge in the motif of suddenly leaping up from history to cut it off, as if with a snip of the scissors. Their fate still lies within history, but it only provides the setting: history never forms their subject matter. The idea of a timeless, mythical reality is represented in a demonically depraved form through them. In the same way, potpourris also lack any inner time. The complete interchangeability of all individual thematic elements points to the simultaneity of all events which move alongside one another without histories. It is in this simultaneity that one reads the contours of the Schubertian landscape, which find their infernal reflection in it. Any truly legitimate depravation of aesthetic content is inaugurated by works of art in which the unveiling of the image has been achieved to such an extent that the power of truth shining through them is no longer restricted to the image but enters reality itself. It is this transparency, which the work of art must pay for with its life, that the crystals of Schubert's landscape possess. There, fate and reconciliation lie joined; their ambiguous eternity is shattered by the potpourri so that it can be recognized. Before that, it is the landscape of death. Just as history does not take on a constitutive role between the appearance of one Schubertian theme and the next, life is not the intentional object of his music. The problem of hermeneutics, however, which is irrefutably posed by Schubert, has so far been pursued only in the polemic against Romantic psychologism and not with the necessary intensity. The critique of all musical hermeneutics rightly destroys any interpretation of music as a poetic reproduction of psychological elements. It is not, however, justified in eliminating the connection to the objective truth characters that have been pinpointed and in replacing the inferior subjectivist view of art with a faith in its blind immanence. No art is its own subject matter; it is simply that its symbolic intention is not abstractly separable from its material concretion. It is indivisibly bound to it in its origin, and can only break off from it through history. In history, the content emanating from the work changes and only the mute work exists purely for itself. Schubert's work, still more eloquent today in depravations than any other music of his time, did not have to petrify, as it did not draw its sustenance from the ephemeral dynamic of subjectivity. It is already imbued with the inorganic, erratic, brittle life of stones in its origin, and death is embedded too deeply within it for it to have any reason to fear death. This has nothing at all to do with the psychological reflexes of imagining the experience of death, and the countless anecdotes telling of Schubert's premonitions of death hardly amount to more than faint signs. There is rather more significance in the choice of texts whose power sets the Schubertian landscape in motion, even if that power is soon enough buried beneath its mass. It should especially be noted that the two great cycles use poems in which images of death return time and again to confront the human being, who wanders between them, as tiny as only Schubert is in *Das Dreimäderlhaus*. The stream, the mill and the black winter wasteland, stretching out timelessly in the twilight of the mock suns as if in a dream, are the signs of the Schubertian landscape, and dried flowers its sad ornaments; they are produced by the objective symbols of death, and their feeling returns to re-enter the objective symbols of death. This is the nature of Schubert's dialectic: it draws in the paling images of existent objectivity with the power of subjective inwardness, finding them once more in the smallest cells of musical concretion.

The allegorical image of death and the maiden is consumed within it; not to be released in the emotions of the individual, however, but to rise up, after its downfall, from the musical figure of sorrow. This certainly changes its quality. But the change can only succeed at the smallest level; the large scale is governed by death. Only in the cyclical character of the two song series could it become evident: for the circulatory behaviour of the songs is the timeless movement between birth and death dictated by blind nature. The one striding through it is the wanderer. The category of the wanderer has never been elucidated in its defining dignity for the structure of Schubert's work—even though it offers increasingly profound insight into his mythical substance the more thoroughly it avoids Wagner's overt symbolism, and understands in its true form what is quoted illusorily there. If psychoanalysis confiscates the categories of travel and wandering to the realm of the objective symbolism of death as archaic residua, both can reasonably be sought in the landscape of death. The eccentric construction of that landscape, every point equidistant from the centre, reveals itself to the wanderer, who circles his way through it without progressing: all development is its complete antithesis, the first step is as close to death as the last, and in circling, the dissociated points of the landscape are scanned but never actually left. For Schubert's themes wander in the same way as the miller or the one left by his beloved in winter. They know no history, only perspectival circulation: all their changes are changes of light. This explains Schubert's tendency to present the same theme two, even three times in different works and in different ways; the most notable example is probably the repetition of that still-present melody, which appears as the theme of piano variations, as the variation theme in the A-minor quartet and in the music for *Rosamunde*. It would be foolish to explain that recurrence with the insatiability of the minstrel, who could, after all, with his endlessly proclaimed wealth of melodies, have found a hundred other themes; it is the wanderer alone who encounters the same passages again, unchanged yet in a different light, which are without time and present themselves as unconnected, individual entities. This schema does not only concern the repeated use of the same theme in different pieces but, substantially, also the constitution of Schubert's forms in themselves. In them, the themes also remain devoid of any dialectical history; and if Schubert's sets of variations, unlike Beethoven's, never disturb the fabric of the theme, but rather encircle and evade it, then this circular wandering is Schubert's form most of all where it is not given any openly accessible centre—no, rather where this centre reveals itself only in the power to direct anything that appears towards itself. This is how the Impromptus and *Moments Musicaux* are fashioned, and the works in sonata form even more so. It is not only the underlying negation of all thematic-dialectical development that sets them apart from the Beethovenian sonata, but also the repeatability of unaltered characters. In the first A-minor sonata, for example, the music hinges on two individual ideas[2] that are not contrasted as the first and second subjects but are both contained in the first and second thematic groups; this is not due to any motivic economy that rations the material for the sake of unity but, rather, to the return of the same amid an elaborated diversity. Here, one can discover the origin of that notion of mood which remained valid for the art of the nineteenth century, especially landscape painting: mood is the changing aspect of the eternally self-identical—yet, without this change having any actual power over it. One need only loosen the bonds of that unchanging character, and mood is transformed at once into illusion. Hence, the authenticity of Schubert's perspectival

2 The original word is *Einfall*, referring to an idea in the sense of something arising in a moment of inspiration—from *einfallen*, meaning 'to occur to', a term commonly used in the context of German Romanticism. It is generally translated here as 'individual idea'. [Trans.]

moods is tied inseparably to the authenticity of the identical substance they circle; and if they managed to escape the decline suffered by mere mood art, this was due to the characters themselves that were captured by them. The individual being-in-itself is repeatable, but never what is subjectively produced, which by necessity unfolds in time. It is not the repetitions as such that endanger the forms of Schumann and Wagner, merely the repetition of the unrepeatable, whose existence is justified only at that point in the form where it rises up from the intra-temporal subjective dynamic. Not so in Schubert. His themes are manifestations of truth characters, and the artist's capacity is limited to capturing their image with feeling and then, once it has manifested itself, citing it again and again. Each citation occurs at a different time, however, and thus the mood changes. Schubert's forms are invocations of the singular manifestation, not transformations of the invented. This underlying *a priori* is absolutely constitutive for the sonata. There, instead of mediating developmental sections, one finds abrupt harmonic shifts as changes of light leading to a new area of the landscape in which processes of growth are as alien as in the previous part. The development sections do not dissect the themes into motives in order to ignite the dynamic fire with their smallest parts but, rather, offer a progressive disclosure of those unalterable themes; the music looks back, taking up themes that have been explored but are not yet past. And all this is enclosed by the thin, crackling husk that is the sonata, spreading itself over the growing crystals before its impending rupture. For a true formal analysis of Schubert, of a kind that has not been undertaken but is programmatically self-evident, one would above all have to examine the dialectic between the overarching schema of the sonata and Schubert's second, crystalline form. Only through this dialectic, in which the individual idea must assert and affirm itself to reach beyond the deceptive dynamic of the sonata, can that form ensue. Nothing could strengthen the themes more than the immanent compulsion to control a form that is not willing of its own accord to tolerate them as themes. With Schubert, the constitutive difference between the individual idea and invention, which should not be assumed to follow the line separating grace and will but, rather, crosses both, is given exemplary definition; for both have an equally dialectical relationship with the objective aspects of form. Invention suffuses them with constructive power from the position of the subject, and subsumes it within the assertion of the person which the form then freely brings forth again from within itself. The individual idea breaks the form's boundaries through dissociation by preserving its constitutive dignity, which was lost on the large scale, in the smallest remnants, where it communicates with the subjective intention. Invention builds in the realm of the infinite task and seeks to establish totality, while the individual idea reveals the figures of truth and is rewarded with finite success on the smallest scale. Only then does it become clear what is meant by hitting upon an image. It is hit in a dual sense: as the target is struck by the marksman, and as reality is captured by its representation. One speaks of a person's features being 'well captured' in a photograph if it resembles that person, and the same applies to Schubert's individual ideas with reference to their immortal model: often enough they still manage to preserve its traces, as if simply uncovering something that had always been there. At the same time, however, those ideas show a human being penetrating the realm of truth as confidently as only a sharp-eyed marksman can. In both cases, the striking occurs in the moment, a flash of illumination, not in extended time; its smallest part stands as a signal of its own sublation. The sign that the mark has been hit: a hole in the foreground of the form that was targeted, and at the same time a gap that offers a glimpse of the unattainable, true form; Schubert's themes are asymmetrical, an early mockery of the architecture of tonality. In their irregularity, the autonomy of the captured image asserts its primacy over the abstract will to pure formal immanence, but rightfully fractures the unity between subjective intentions and their historically posited stylistic correlates; and so the work must remain a fragment. It is in the Schubertian finale that the fragmentary character of his music reveals itself in the material. The circular motion of the song collections conceals what inevitably becomes manifest in any temporal sequence of timeless cells as soon as they strive simply to approach the developmental time of the sonata; the fact that Schubert was unable to write the finale of the B-minor symphony should be viewed together with the inadequacy of the finale of the *Wanderer* Fantasy. It is not a case of the passionate dilettante failing to master the conclusive ending; for it is the Tartarus question of 'whether not yet completion be' that dominates Schubert's region with its spell and causes music to fall silent. This is why those successful Schubert finales that remain are perhaps the most powerful symbols of hope in his entire œuvre.

This, admittedly, is not yet to be found in the *Wanderer* Fantasy. Even its light forest green contracts to a sinister Acherontic chasm in the referential adagio. The hermeneutics of death that pervades so many of the images in Schubert's music touches their objective character but does not exhaust it. The affect of death—for this is what is duplicated in Schubert's landscape, the sorrow for human beings rather than the pain within them—is the only gate to the underworld where Schubert leads us. The hermeneutical word, still able to follow the transition to death only a moment ago, is powerless before it. There is no longer any metaphor that can open a way through the forests of ice flowers, the crystals that suddenly shoot up, falling over like lifeless dragons; the bright world above that is always the starting point for the way into this realm is little more than a perspectival means of sending the first and second dimensions ahead of the third. As a herbaceous covering, it is as thin as the organic-dialectical sonata laid over Schubert's second form. His tendency to go blindly after mythological poems in his choice of text, making little distinction between Goethe and Mayrhofer, demonstrates in the most drastic manner the failure of all words in that deep space where the word merely casts off materials but lacks the power truly to illuminate them. It is the empty falling of these words, not their elucidated intention, that the wanderer follows into the depths, and even his human passion becomes a means of descending while observing; the descent does not lead to the base of the soul, but rather to the vault of his fate. 'I long to kiss the ground / burn through ice and snow / with my hot tears / until I see the earth below.' This downward pull comes from the harmony, the proper means of creating natural depth in music. Nature here is not, however, the fitting object of the intra-human feeling for nature; the images of nature are rather allegorical representations of the chthonic hollow itself, as inaccessible in this guise as the poetic word has always been. It is no coincidence that Schubert's moods, which do not merely circle but also drop abruptly, are tied to the sudden harmonic shift, the glimpse of a modulation that casts light on the same object from varying degrees of depth. Like blinds, those sudden modulations, never developing or mediating, block out the light from above; the introduction of the second thematic group in the first movement of the great B-flat major sonata, the violent chromatic progression in the first movement of the E-flat major trio (to name one example) and finally the beginning of the second subject in the C-major symphony—all these completely transformed the phenomenon of key change in the sonata model, making it a perspectival drop into harmonic depths; and the fact that the second thematic groups in those three major-key pieces appear in the minor creates, according to the symbolism of major and minor which Schubert still followed, the vivid impression of a step into the dark. The demonic function of depth is fulfilled in Schubert's altered chords. In this landscape, divided into

major and minor, they are as ambiguous as mythical nature
itself, pointing up and down simultaneously; their lustre is
wan, and the expression they are lent by the configuration of
Schubert's modulations is that of fear: fear of the lethal recognition of the earth and the annihilating recognition of the bare
human self. And so it occurs that the mirror image of the dop-
pelganger passes judgement on humanity on the basis of his
sadness. It is only because these instances of modulation and
alteration are sprinkled into the idiom of tonal order that they
take on such power in their historical moment. As the antithesis of the natural world above, they undermine it. Once it has
collapsed, modulation and alteration too are drawn into the
nondescript flow of subjective dynamics; it was only later, with
Schönberg's emphatic definition of chord degrees, that the
power of Schubert's harmonic principle was regained— before
being snuffed out for good. Schubert's harmonic language, followed on its descent by counterpoint as the palpable shadow
of melody, reaches its nadir in the pure minor of sorrow. If the
affect of death was the gateway to the depths, it is the earth
itself, finally reached, that constitutes the physical manifestation of death; looking upon it, the falling soul recognizes itself
as a woman, inescapably trapped within the context of nature.
In the last great allegorical poem written in German, Matthias
Claudius's image of Death and the Maiden, the wanderer
reaches the heart of his landscape; there, the essence of the
minor key is revealed. But just as punishment follows swiftly
for the child caught in the act, and invention follows necessity
in that stock saying, so here consolation follows sorrow. Rescue
is achieved through the smallest step: the transformation of
the minor into the major third. The two move so close
together that once the major third has appeared, the minor
reveals itself as its shadow. Little wonder, then, that the qualitative difference between sorrow and consolation, whose concrete formation contains Schubert's true answer, was passed
over through mediating procedures, or that the nineteenth

century thought it could encapsulate Schubert's basic stance with the term 'renunciation'. But the illusion of reconciliation created by resignation has nothing to do with the consolation found in Schubert, in which we sense clearly the hope that the compulsion of our entanglement in nature might somehow have its limits. As heavily as Schubert's sorrow may weigh upon us, and as much as the wanderer may long to be consumed by the waters of birth in his despair, consolation stands unshakeably above the dead man and guarantees: there is still hope, for his place will not be in the depraved magic circle of nature for ever. It is here that time catches fire in Schubert's music, and the successful finale already issues from a different sphere to that of death. Certainly, also a different one to Beethoven's 'must'; for compared to Beethoven's threateningly demanded, beleaguered, categorially palpable yet materially unattainable joy, Schubert's is the echo that is heard, confused yet ultimately certain and directly given. Only once does it lead to a great dynamic moment: during the build-up in the finale of the C-major symphony, whose wind melody—as if sung by real voices—bursts into the musical picture and breaks it open as almost no other music has ever been broken open from its true foundation. Normally, however, the attainment of joy in Schubert occurs in other, bizarrely confusing ways. In the great four-handed rondo in A major, the expansive sense of well-being sings with such a tangibly lasting presence that it suggests an everlasting physicality; it is as fundamentally different to Beethoven as good food differs from the immortality postulated in practical reason. The extended nature of Schubert's movements is also often interpreted as an expression of joy, and the talk of 'divine length' continues to be as popular as ever. If his themes stand side by side timelessly in the landscape of death, music consolingly fills that rediscovered time, so remote from the mortal end, with the anticipated constancy of the eternal. The repeatability of the individual element in Schubert stems from its timelessness, but changes through time into its material fulfillment. By no means, however, does that fulfilment always require long movements or even the pathos of a large form. It much prefers to dwell in a region far beneath the approved conventions of bourgeois musical practice. For that Schubertian world of genuine joy, of dances and military marches, of the lowly four-handed piano and of floating banality and mild drunkenness, is as ill-suited socially to bourgeois, even petty-bourgeois music-making as it is remote from any naïve affirmation of the existent. Whoever insists on classifying Schubert as a minstrel should at least take into consideration that the alleged minstrel in question would be of low social standing, closer to gypsies, storytellers, conjurors and their companions than to the metaphorical simplicity of the artisan. For the joy of Schubert's marches is unruly, and the time contained within them is not one of spiritual development but of the movements of crowds. In its unmediated expression, Schubert's joy no longer knows any form; ready for use, it approaches baser empirical reality and almost allows that reality to take advantage of it by breaking out of the domain of art. Only a dilettante could have found the music to accompany such anarchic joy; and what high statesman, after all, would not have found revolution dilettantish? That dilettantism, however, is the dilettantism of beginning once again, and its mark the independent organization that emerges from that beginning. Organization remains a compositional technique in Schubert's case, but the image trembles. Nowhere does it come closer to the truth than in Schubert's folk music, whose sense is completely different to that which any of his successors sought to write. Schubert did not undertake any correction of lost closeness by means of unattainable distance: for him, transcendental distance becomes attainable in the utmost proximity. This lies just beyond the gateway, like Hungary, yet is as remote as its incomprehensible language. It is the origin of the secret one finds not only in the Hungarian divertissement, the F-minor fantasy and the secondary themes of the A-major rondo, but in fact running in different directions through Schubert's entire œuvre, approaching tangibly before disappearing like a phantom in the C-sharp minor theme from the finale of the A-minor quartet. The language of this Schubert is a dialect—but one that has no native soil. It has the concreteness of a homeland, yet its only homeland is one remembered. Nowhere is Schubert further from the earth than where he refers to it. It reveals itself in the images of death: viewed closely, however, nature annuls itself. Hence, there is no path leading from Schubert to genre music or folkish art, only one leading to the deepest depravation and one leading to the barely mentioned reality of a liberated music for a changed humanity. At irregular intervals, like a seismograph, Schubert's music registered the message of humanity's qualitative change. The response, fittingly, is that of weeping —whether it is the weeping of the most impoverished sentimentality in *Das Dreimäderlhaus* or the weeping of a shaken body. In the face of Schubert's music, the tear falls from the eye without first asking the soul: it falls into us, so remote from all images and so real. We weep without knowing why; because we have not yet reached the state promised by the music and, in our unspoken joy, all we need is for it to assure us that we one day will. We cannot read it; what it holds up to our fading, overflowing eyes, however, are the ciphers of an eventual reconciliation.

1928

Between the affected gentlemen and tragic ladies, she is no more than an episodic figure. Now the irresistible gaze has fallen upon her—the dissolute grandee holds out his hand to her across the class divide separating them, and she would be too shy not to follow him to his castle immediately: it is not far from here. Because, however, the conventions of opera buffa do not allow the seduction of an innocent that could certainly not be avenged as stylishly by her Masetto as the decent Ottavio would avenge Donna Anna's, da Ponte foils the design of promiscuity, which attaches no importance to fair exchanges; he restores both the moral and social hierarchies, and, amid the stygian night, lets the lamplight of blessed intimacy shine on her reconciliation with the namesake of all fools and buffoons. In the postlude from Mozart's orchestra, it seems as if mankind's divisions had been reconciled.

Such reconciliation occurs in the name of freedom. Zerlina's music sounds as if it were wafting through an open casement window into the white and golden hall of the eighteenth century. What she sings are still arias, but her melodies are already those of songs: nature, whose breath lifts the spell of ceremonial conventions while still enclosed by them, is securely embedded in the fading style. The rhythms of Rococo and revolution pause in the image of Zerlina; she is no longer a shepherdess, but not yet a *citoyenne*. She belongs to the historical moment between the two, and in her we glimpse a humanity untouched by feudal oppression and protected from bourgeois barbarism. One finds an element of it in some of the poems and figures of the young Goethe. He offers a miniature portrait of her—'And so she steps before the mirror / in all her vigour'—and, like Friederike, she stands

> on the boundary between the rustic and the urbane. She walked slimly and lightly, as if she had no weight to carry, and her neck seemed almost too delicate for the tremendous blonde tresses attached to that sweet little head. She looked around very clearly with her lively blue eyes, and her well-behaved little snub nose pointed as freely into the air as if there could never be any anxiety in the world; her straw hat was hanging from her arm, so I was afforded the pleasure of seeing and recognizing her full grace and loveliness the very first time I laid eyes upon her.[1]

A girl who, without any malice, makes up for her infidelity by encouraging her lover to beat her, thus transforming rustic rawness into refinement—she anticipates the utopian state in which there is no longer a difference between city and countryside.

But does some reflection of this radiance not fall upon the seducer too, who is cheated of this sweetness in the end? For what would we have seen of her grace and loveliness had the nobleman, already half-powerless, not aroused them on his flight through the opera? Because he no longer has the power of the *jus primae noctis*, he becomes the harbinger of lust— rather odd for the bourgeoisie, who promptly reject it. They learned their ideal of freedom from this fearless man; as soon as it becomes general, however, it turns against him, the one

---

1 Johann Wolfgang von Goethe, *Dichtung und Wahrheit* [Poetry and Truth], VOL. 2 (Stuttgart: Cotta, 1819), p. 10. [Trans.]

for whom freedom had still been a privilege. Soon they will absorb despotism into freedom, thus perverting it into its own opposite. Don Juan, however, was untainted by lies; his despotism would be the freedom of the others, which he thus grants the same honour of which he robs it. Zerlina was right to like him.

As a parable of history, she is eternally static. Who-ever falls in love with her is enamoured of the ineffable, sounding from the no man's land between the battling epochs in the guise of her silvery voice.

1952/53

Der Freischütz is considered a German national opera, and is indeed a more fitting candidate than *Die Meistersinger*. For the German element here does not present itself as such and compromise itself through nationalist attitudes. Though the first thing one thinks of will not be the forest, which, as Canetti showed in *Crowds and Power* (1960), is not as innocent as one would expect of plants: 'The mass symbol of the Germans,' Canetti writes,

> was the army. But the army was more than the army: it was the marching forest. In no other modern country in the world have people maintained such a strong emotional connection to their forests as in Germany. The rigid, parallel nature of the upright trees, their density and number, fill the German heart with profound, mysterious joy.[1]

This would have been a factor of no small significance in the early pre-revolution period.

Musically speaking, the specifically German quality of the Romantic opera is to be found more in relation to the Austrian. It does not, as even Schubert largely did, speak in the idiom of Viennese Classicism. *Der Freischütz* does not have

---

1 See Elias Canetti, *Crowds and Power* [*Masse und Macht*] (Carol Stewart trans.) (New York: Farrar, Straus and Giroux, 1984 [Hamburg: Claassen Verlag, 1960]), p. 173; translation modified. [Trans.]

the pure formal immanence or the self-enclosed, integral character of great symphonic music; it is less binding, more open.
A breeze comes wafting in through windows and openings,
bringing in air that is normally kept out by our dense cultural
life. This lends the score a freshness that, without much tone
painting, turns it into the imaginary language of the forest.
Nowhere is this done more beautifully than in Agatha's recitative on the words 'How lovely a night', where she steps out
onto the balcony. While the starry sky above the castle grounds
in *Figaro* forms a safe canopy above the confused lover, *Der
Freischütz* comforts through a sigh of relief: out in the open.

The work has an exterritorial, almost traditionless quality
also found in Gluck. Both composers paved the way for the
emancipation from the constraining logic of art music. This
emancipation was then achieved by Berlioz; it is no coincidence
that Gluck and Weber were his favourites. *Der Freischütz* is
extremely bourgeois in its union of intimate familiarity and
foreignness to tradition, which is probably why the rising
German bourgeoisie considered it more directly related to
its cause than Beethoven or Mozart. One could say that *Der
Freischütz* was the first major work of music that no longer
existed within a pre-established style.

Compared with Mozart, the characters—both in their
personal profiles and in purely musical terms—are far more
drastic. It is very informative to compare couples from each:
the Countess and Susanna in *Figaro* and Agatha and Ännchen
in *Der Freischütz*, playing the roles of the sentimental and the
naïve. In Mozart's case, the individualization of the two
women occurs through the subtlest of nuances within his
formal language, which takes priority throughout. In Weber,
they are contrasted in a more cheeky, loose fashion. Ännchen,
the *serva padrona* turned little Biedermeier cousin, reaps the
benefits of bourgeois emancipation by saying exactly what
comes into her head, coquettishly sharing her admiration of

the slim boy with her female listeners, while Susanne, on the distant quasi-ancient pinnacle of an erotic ritual, wreathes her beloved with roses. Such elements as the impudent tone during the gruesome ballad or the spluttering line 'Let the wild hunter hound there, and whoever sees him will flee', which sings of the spirit world with the importance of a small sensation, were completely without precedent. But progress has its price: this pithiness of characterization, which was continually heightened in musical drama until Berg, was initially accompanied by a noticeable simplification, the mark of the bourgeois victory over the feudal aristocracy of Europe, whose rudiments are still preserved in the Viennese tone of revolutionary humanity.

The qualitative leap of *Der Freischütz* becomes most evident in Weber's treatment of the orchestra. What is new is the way in which the instruments begin to break off from the classicist totality; their renewed synthesis only occurred with Wagner's consistently applied principle of orchestral mixture. The sonic palette of the classical orchestra shows independent colours in *Der Freischütz*; at times it glistens, and at times it grows cloudy. The clarinet, making use of all its registers high above the string tremolo in the overture, arches over it like a vision; low clarinets and bass pizzicati merge into a colour blacker than Beethoven would ever have dared to demand of his instruments, even in his darkest passages. The trombone exits the three-part chordal texture, aping the final part of the passionate love theme in a marvellous episode during the development—the echo as infernal laughter, the first musical distortion of expressive effect. This imitation pulls the voice of passion down into the pure depravation of myth. Mockery becomes a productive force: the 'he-he-he' chuckling of the farmers begins on the weak beat as if it were strong, undermining the entire rhythmic order. No composer before Weber had compositionally formulated the power of disintegrating music as one encounters it at the sinister conclusion of the waltz; Mahler paid tribute to it in the trio of the First Symphony, even in the scherzo of the Ninth, and one finds echoes of it in Stravinsky. This is not the Bohemian Forest in which the cradle stood,[2] but rather incipient horror, a realm of enchantment from the early days of the disenchanted world.

The historical status of *Der Freischütz* is that of a more refined German Singspiel. The colourful, relaxed alternation between dialogue and music and the small scale of many of its numbers were significant in helping to establish a rapport with the audience in Romantic opera. Whereas *The Magic Flute* builds on the legacy of the Singspiel and turns it into world theatre, however, a theatre in which the high and the low, opera seria, couplets, songs, decorative singing and enlightened mysticism come together in the great round cosmos as if for the last time, without any divide between Sarastro's realm and Papageno's, *Der Freischütz* draws on the Singspiel for the force of the sudden and the disparate. Because the music is intermittent, rather than filling out the whole of the action, its freedom from specific models becomes a stylistic principle in its own right; in lacking a foundation in a given style, *Der Freischütz* is also the first opera that created a style, modestly and involuntarily. This balances out the formal power it lacks in comparison to Mozart or *Fidelio*, and determines the quality of the individual pieces. Caspar's brief strophic song about the earthly vale of tears, with the whistling piccolo and the abrupt ending on the weak beat, is far superior to the lengthy triumphant aria of the obligatory villain, and the hermit, whose intercession against retributive justice displays an excellent dramaturgical conception, does not have the same musical worth as Sarastro; whatever aspects of the work do not fit into its formal scheme become conventional. The

2 This is a reference to the nostalgic folk song 'Tief drin im Böhmerwald' ('Deep Inside the Bohemian Forest'). [Trans.]

less pretentious the individual pieces are, the better they work—and the more enigmatic they are. This applies in particular to the most popular one, the song of the bridal wreath. It is generally interpreted as a jovial folk song, and the tempo marking *Andante quasi allegretto* tends to be forgotten. If one has the courage to let the choir sing at a more leisurely pace, the song suddenly takes on a pale, ominous quality, and its cheerful etiquette is exposed as a lie, just as the libretto intends. The viola figure that joins it, with the A flat in the final verse, then helps this character to appear, and the waning orchestral postlude is the heartbreaking image of melancholy. A neighbouring note and a few dissonances are enough to infuse the harmlessly catchy melody with a trace of the ominous. Musically too, the bridal chorus is a symbol of death. All this has the colour of old children's books, the inextinguishable red of the sunset.

The richest piece is perhaps Agatha's aria, which secularizes the chorale into an intimate song in a recurring adagio; in the recitative sections, it comprises a series of little images that combine utter simplicity with an air of experiencing something for the first time. The rushing of semiquavers, only hinted at before, leaves all opulent forest murmurs[3] far behind, while a few horn staccati give an impression of listening for distant steps. On the word 'clouds', in anticipation of a storm, there is a dissonance. Although it is no more than a diminished seventh chord over a secondary dominant pedal, it sounds like something one has never heard before—so replete with expression that barely any later extended chord can compete with it. Such little images, almost going past like the frames of a film, also form the basis of the wolf's glen scene where each accompanies a situation or an apparition. It is precisely this restraint through a restriction to stage music, abstaining from the idea of a great continuous finale like that in the second act of *Figaro*

3 A reference to '*Waldweben*' II.iii, Wagner's *Siegfried*. [Trans.]

or in the dungeon scene, that lends the central piece in *Der Freischütz* its compelling originality. It fearlessly trusts in the disappearance of images. Symphonic ambitions would be out of place in a Singspiel, and conflict with the colours of the changing moments—an infernal vision made of Biedermeier miniatures. The kaleidoscope was invented around the same time *Der Freischütz* was composed; part of the need that spawned that invention manifested itself as music in the wolf's glen.

One can observe how the element that supplied unity in classicism broke off from the rest of Weber's pictorial world, so to speak, becoming independent and thus changing its character. The principle of integral thematic work, of developing variation, was replaced by that of momentum; a compositional method turned into the gesture with which the music presents itself. It reminds one of the piano virtuoso that Weber was, of the wide spread of his hands which reached daringly beyond the octave. The gesture has something brilliant and illusory that also contains expression; momentum and dazzlement are never far apart in *Der Freischütz*. While classicism sought to justify the whole as meaningful through the unity of thematic work, Weber's momentum already has a certain blindness akin to the later ideas of will and life, and hence reinforces the demonic character of the accusation; it unrolls itself without reason or direction, like the wheel in the wolf's glen. In fact, it is Weber's momentum that characterizes the reaction form used by Richard Strauss a century later. Beethoven, the epitome of the dynamic composer, did not really have anything similar. Life, as an unconscious urge, is constantly exceeding its limits; its great leaps already contain the fall. While great Viennese music constructed its meaning, this revels in the autonomy of its own vigour. Certainly, this vigour is still feared as a state of godforsakenness; the question in Max's great aria 'Is there no God?', which refers not so much to hell as to the immanence of chance, goes beyond mere operatic rhetoric—it points out what Weber's expansive arc, from the introduction of the first chorus to the allegro parts of Agatha's and Max's arias, had contained all along.

This arc is the path from the parlour to the prehistoric world—perhaps the image that lies at the heart of the entire Biedermeier period as its riddle, and also Jean Paul's. The mustiness of the interior glows in the same way as in Poe's 'The Fall of the House of Usher' not long after that; the forester's lodge is built above chthonic caves. Any production, if it is to avoid cheating the children of what their *orbis pictus* promises them, must take this into account; only once the lodge, without any precocious artisanal stylization, is as clearly recognizable as the spirits and animals of the wolf's glen, can that arc materialize. What is good enough for the rhinoceros should be good enough for the wild boar. The images are archaic and modern at once; the director must pay attention to this, and sooner make all the hunting men colourful clones of each other than sacrifice an illusion that here forms the medium of the alienated.

In the spirit of the work, it is gender that mediates between the parlour and the prehistoric world. The fate of Agatha, the personified cavatina, contains an unresolved sexual symbolism, and it is precisely its cut-off, unrecognizable nature—the shot represents defloration—that creates the overshadowed secret in which the music finds its refuge, as when a girl cries in her sleep. Confinement itself is the demonic nature she fears like a threat from without; hence she can scarcely escape it. As in the fairy tale, the metaphysics of *Der Freischütz*, in whose time the only significant German literary fairy tales were written, is that of the hair's breadth. The allusions to sexuality are at once references to the decline of that same bourgeois way of life which—as if under censorship—the work confirms. *Der Freischütz* narrowly escapes catastrophe; the caesuras of the

Singspiel are no other than those placed into the myth by the fairy tale. The quality of redemption does not shine into that Godforsaken immanence but is, rather, fulfilled within it, the highest echo in the glen—reconciled nature.

1961/62

Usually, the question of what drew Offenbach, that magician of parody and parodist of myths, to the late Romanticism of the German Hoffmann is answered with a reference to the elective affinity of the demonic character. Though one can hardly deny this, it also says very little. The figure formed by Offenbach's first and last opera with the poet is of a far more definite nature; it is no coincidence that the man himself is called onto the stage in it. He is made to inhabit, physically, the scenic framework he set up, the fables he created. For, the demonic character whose dark name this music calls is not that of abstract forces from the underworld but, rather, originates from the domestic interior, just as Dr Miracle comes through the walls of Crespel's room. If spirits and ghosts have always been tied to the hour and the place, that hour and place are now themselves spirits and ghosts. Humans live trapped within them until they suffocate. They are as foreign to them as churchyards and crossroads were in former times. The mechanical cabinet whose formulae unroll lives of their own from within themselves, followed unsuspectingly by the duped senses; the courtesan in Venice, drifting away on the gondola as if conjured up by the magic lantern—a costly phantasmagoria; Antonia's music salon with the coughing piano and the transparent painting of her mother, the deathly model of all family portraits. Whereas the Offenbach of the operettas abandoned all magic from prehistoric times through the world of objects as the mumbo-jumbo of profanation, he had now dazzlingly illuminated the mumbo-jumbo of the profane object world as the true magic of prehistoric times—'electric and galvanic', as Lintorf calls it, using words that belong to the archaism of the technical age. It was Hoffmann, however, whom he invoked as the lord and master of the object world. Now, the one who called up the spirits cannot rid himself of them; as the unlucky lover, he will be haunted in this scenic setting by the doll Olympia, the courtesan Giulietta and the corpse Antonia— he who was once strong enough to summon them unseduced from the display case, the tabouret and the swivel chair—until the end of time. The prostitutes in Vienna are called 'dollies' [*Pupperln*], and, in her pale afternoons, Antonia leads a phantom life that singing forces her to lead, like Eurydice, and in which she wastes away as she sings. The estranged objects are the spirits, trapped in the interiors without access to active life; their semblance mimics the lover and music captures him as it does us, those who hear it 'in sweet melody from afar'. Distance is nearness. This is why Offenbach's 'Romantic' opera is one of the few from the nineteenth century with a modern subject. Here, the glasses at the extravagant buffet strike the hour of death; and the shapes that step from the walls to enter the frozen groups of people are no angels.

The objects are diabolical because they have broken out of any context in which they could serve the living. The physical cabinet is a curio collection of 'enamel' figures; Giulietta's pillows are arranged for show in order to steal the shadow or mirror image of fools, and one could almost think that the Grand Canal was lying here under glass, that there was not a hint of a breeze to alleviate a humidity belonging not so much to the senses as to the decor; finally, when we get to Crespel, the objects from the past have united in conspiracy—together with the servant Franz, a neuter factotum sung by a tenor buffo, a powerless bringer of disaster. The objects all around are as senselessly solitary as the deaf servant, who lets in the one person he is supposed to keep away from everyone; and, as their outward existence no longer knows any function, a second, mad one, awakens within them. Offenbach has captured this superbly in the deepest structure of the form. The fact that the opera remained a sketch, and a piano reduction that almost seems to have been written for the domestic setting which comes to the fore in it, is not due simply to the biographical fact of the master's death. Rather, the very law governing the opera is that of the sketch. No overarching context is permitted to stand between the particular life of the objects and the listener's fear. One finds individual ideas in it, like the very first bars, that would have been adequate for a symphony, and another composer would have composed the whole of Venice from the introduction to the barcarolle without hesitation. Here, however, it remains unique and without consequences, as scattered as the objects and without causality like the spirit world. The motives are as short as names and where leitmotifs do appear, they undergo hardly any variation: spirits do not develop, and forever obey the same call. One finds no counterpoint, no polyphony, no further-reaching forms moving towards some endpoint: the music is a rigidly, abruptly changing marker of events, never their reproduction, let alone interpretation—what counts here, more than any interpretative sense, is to find and sing the right sign. But what writing is *not* to be found there! Those first bars: an embodiment of the *ominous*, disappearing for ever before the code can be deciphered. The students' song of mockery about Luther: in a danger zone where merriment can turn into base cruelty at any moment. The ballad of Kleinzach: the beloved's duplets and triplets wind like the precious monogram of memory. Or the barcarolle itself: how it shines forth from the puddles

outside the cafes, huts and machines—and yet, could one not
say that it truly needs them, in order to shine so genuinely
amid the false that no melody can match it? Dapertuttos's aria
is an enigmatic partner piece to Wagner's Venusberg; since
Busoni's well-chosen words, the melodrama—whose text is by
no means inferior, and should be taken literally: 'You have no
sword, take mine.'—'I thank you'—has been known as one
of the masterpieces of musical dramaturgy. Deceitful and
unmoved, fate moves on past its victims, already prepared for
the next betrayal, as these are just about to die. And then the
introductory bars of the final act: they seem to be saying 'So
it is serious—let events take their course.' No deceit answers;
yet in the next bars we are already lost, with the delicate quavers of Antonia's piano and the song of the dove, which pauses
while the quavers keep ticking: a quiet, imperceptibly quiet
clock that measures the time for which Antonia is allowed to
sing. The corpse Antonia—her cheeks are red only from the
sunset shining through the curtains, and it is almost the terrible silence that she is singing crazily at the harpsichord; she is
to be set upon with inexorable swiftness by the shadows on
the walls, which Hoffmann vainly seeks to dispel with the
flickering lamp of delayed emotion. And the figures of the
shadows! The great invocation through Miracle's ostinato has
only one precedent. It is uncertain whether Offenbach knew
it: it sounds like the terrible scherzo from Beethoven's last
quartet. The mother's song: an aria from great operas that we
carry about with us from early childhood, borne on broad
waves, down into the sea of origin, fluorescent with the aura
of decay. The servant's song: it almost seems to take too much
time, but when its rhythm returns—now distraught, with the
expression of horror—we know that this was in truth the most
valuable time; it remained unused, because it too was at the
mercy of the singing interior as a parody of the mistress. If he
had not tarried, all might have turned out for the best; but

now it is too late. The closing passage does not dare pause for air: it races along as if fleeing from the worst of dreams, so as not to be for ever trapped in it.

Nonetheless, this room of death is where everything in the opera that rises above its demonic character flourishes. The duet of Hoffmann and Antonia: as if even the illusion of love wanted to last and console in the face of death; the two search in vain to find words for their love song, but can only call upon the mild, sweet arc of its melody—passing rapidly, yet everlasting. If the motives in *The Tales of Hoffmann* are the burning script, melodies are the sound of release. The barcarolle rises from the murderous depths of the lagoon to resound as the utterance of the one who, because she is beautiful, comes where there is humiliation, guilt and depravity as the promise of the right human being. When Nicklausse drags Hoffmann away with the call 'the guard': how, for all the shame and lies, could joy not be near? Joy that the two strangers, the poet and the courtesan who deceived him, were in agreement after all for a second: when Hoffmann stabbed the disgruntled client. The moment rejoices eternally, and is invoked by the barcarolle, Hoffmann's peculiar hymn of praise, even though Giulietta has long since become the prize of the hunchback. The spirits into which all the objects of the bourgeois world are transformed here—they simultaneously exceed the objects by breaking out of them. The catastrophe that haunts *The Tales of Hoffmann* is not simply that of man amid the world of objects; it is also that of the objects themselves in transformation.

Artist, doll and courtesan—where have I heard that before? Was it merely childhood that took over the three beloved images with that formula? Or does the word 'courtesan' not also evoke the memory of a priceless amulet—a depiction, in metal form, of something that had always been? Should three words from Hoffmann the narrator, together with this music, not cause the encapsulated world of objects to burst open, that world whose scars are inscribed upon them?

1932

Of all Wagner's music, it is that of *Parsifal* which has entered the public awareness least, and accordingly little of great insight has been said—aside, perhaps, from the formal analyses of Alfred Lorenz—about its peculiarity. The 'lex Parsifal', which was intended to grant the *Bühnenweih-festspiel* copyright protection beyond the thirty years that were customary at the time, never came about; it is, however, surrounded by a manner of protective layer that probably comprises, in equal parts, an awe of the cultic element and a fear of boredom. This fear, at least, is unfounded; the same heaviness that shocks the unsuspecting operagoer contains what will always make the work disconcertingly new. Wagner always had a certain roundabout quality; it is connected to his suggestive gesturality, the tendency to talk the listener to death. The broad musical current of *Götterdämmerung* sometimes recalls that swimmer in Uhland's poem who is pulled under by his own armour;[1] the framework of leitmotifs throughout the tetralogy cripples all development. In *Parsifal*, this is intensified and

1 Adorno is referring to the poem 'Die Rache' ('The Revenge'), in which a knight is murdered by his squire. Having submerged his master's corpse in the river, the squire attempts to cross a bridge on the former's horse, but it bucks and throws him into the water, where he drowns on account of the armour's weight. Ludwig Uhland, *Gedichte* [Poems] (Stuttgart & Tübingen: J. G. Cotta, 1829), p. 353. [Trans.]

thus transformed: the master of transitions ends up writing a *static* score. But the art of listening that the work demands, and which must be learned by any who seek to understand it, is of an investigative kind: an eavesdropping on the work. To understand *Parsifal* one must understand its excess and extravagance, its peculiarity and particular manner—as evident already at the beginning of the prelude, with those woodwind chords that float devoid of melody, and in which the first stanza of the communion theme only fades away four bars after its actual ending. It is as if the style of *Parsifal* attempts not only to present the musical ideas, but also to compose their aura to accompany them; this aura forms not in the moment of the event but in its aftermath. One can only follow the intention by submitting even more to the music's echo than to the music itself.

In compositional terms, the static nature of *Parsifal*, created from the idea of an unchanging, repeatable ritual in the first and third acts, necessitates an abstinence from fluid development and propulsive dynamism for long stretches—with the notable exception of Kundry's scene in the second act. The number of motives is smaller than in the other works from Wagner's mature period. Most of the incantations and formulae in the manner of 'You must never ask me' are to be found in *Lohengrin*, and the approach taken in *Parsifal* in fact draws upon that work in certain respects for the sake of its subject matter. Because of their allegorical content these motives are consumed from within, so to speak; they are ascetically thin and drained of sensuality; they all—like the *Parsifal* idiom as a whole—have something broken, inauthentic; the music wears a black visor. Wagner's force draws on the legacy of primary imagination to create the virtue of a late style which, in accordance with Goethe's phrase, steps back from the phenomenon. This character becomes clear if one compares the sinister, almost dimmed fanfare motive from *Parsifal* to the

Siegfried motive: it is as if the former were already a quotation from memory. At the same time, however, those fragmentary motives are much more naked than in *Tristan*, for example, much less interwoven, less drawn into the course of the composition and also subjected to less variation. Often they are simply strung together with a deliberate nonchalance, like little pictures. Admittedly the turning point of the whole work, Kundry's call of 'Parsifal', breaks away from the sound of the flower- maiden ensemble, with two sustained middle voices, and reveals itself—precisely through its identity with what precedes it—as non-identical. Most of the time, however, the music avoids that quality of momentum that normally defines Wagnerian forms.

The mere accumulation of motives, the ascetic abstention from musical combination and free *Abgesang*, consistently corresponds with a tendency towards simplification. When the spear floats above the hero's head towards the end of the second act, the miracle is made musical not through the fabric's splendour and opulence but, rather, by an extreme reduction of means. The Faith motive in the trumpets and trombones, a harp glissando, tremolo octaves in the violins— that is all. In his treatment of the orchestra, Wagner eschews division of melodies, soloistic differentiation and the ideal of the smallest difference throughout. The approach is far more choral than in the previous music dramas; more Brucknerian, one might say. Tutti passages alternate with recitative-like sections featuring only a hint of accompaniment. But the refinement of this simplicity is unprecedented; the subtleties are sparse, not forgotten. The choral approach is based on doubling; it barely allows any instrument or group to be recognizable as such. A mixed sonority such as the opening one, where the Communion motive returns with accompaniment in the violins, oboes and a 'very delicate', i.e. not soloistically prominent trumpet, is unique. The art of mixed wind textures, limited to the woodwind in *Lohengrin*, is now also applied to the brass: both trumpets and trombones are often doubled by the horns, which are used to the maximum. This softens the bright sharpness of the sound; it becomes fuller and darker at the same time, like the overall colouring of *Parsifal*. This dimmed orchestral sound with its muted forte has, from late Mahler through to Schönberg, gained the greatest significance for New Music.

In the compositional material, these tendencies towards simplification become a tendency towards the archaic: there are hints of church modes. Wagner's most mature compositional experience seeks to defuse the old contradiction in his œuvre, that of fanfare-like diatonicism and craving chromaticism, by banishing the latter to hell—the Tristan chord, in the low register of the woodwind, now symbolizes Klingsor's world—while the diatonicism is warped and darkened through modal chord sequences, conspicuous secondary chords in the minor. They lead to the oft-noted resemblance between the *Parsifal* style and Brahms, which actually lies in the most external aspects of the harmonic reservoir and scarcely relates to the inner fabric of the composition. This fabric, aside from a few thematic combinations, is almost devoid of polyphony, even thematic fragmentation ['*durchbrochene Arbeit*'].[2] The harmonic language, on the other hand, displays an element that is extremely advanced, even compared with *Götterdämmerung*: the unresolved dissonance. The prelude closes with a dominant seventh chord in A-flat major. Following the rules of harmony, one can interpret the subsequent F flat in the trombones that opens the first act as a false progression—but the seventh chord is rather understood, during the caesura that accompanies the rising curtain, as absolute, as a question extending into infinity.—And the diminished seventh chord

2 Adorno places the German phrase in quotation marks. [Trans.]

with the added minor ninth already used in the *Ring*, which sounds upon Parsifal's great outburst in the second act— 'Amfortas! The wound!'—is not given any harmonic continuation at all; instead, the Kundry motive which that chord accompanies drops as a single voice. The magnificent process of erosion applied to the musical language, which—mirroring Kundry's expressionistic stammers—is dissociated into unconnected expressive moments, threatens the traditional harmonic structure. *Parsifal* marks a historic point: for the first time, the multilayered, unstable sound is emancipated and allowed to stand alone.

Certainly the immediate effect of *Parsifal* on its composer was far smaller than that of *Tristan*, *Die Meistersinger* or the *Ring*. Of all the operas, it can least comfortably be assigned to the New German School; *élan vital* and affirmative gestures are so drastically absent that the redemption at the end is no more credible than a fairy tale. The third act in particular is dominated by a tense mood that makes Parsifal's act of salvation seem illusory and powerless; ultimately Wagner remained more faithful to his beloved Schopenhauer than those who degrade him to the apostle of renewal would like. This, however, made the subterranean effect of *Parsifal* all the more lasting. Whatever rejected false splendour in fact formed itself through it: sacred opera is an early form of objectivity. One passage in the Bell Choir from Mahler's Third Symphony contains an undisguised reference to the funeral music for Titurel; and the Ninth Symphony would be inconceivable without the third act, especially the pale light of the Good Friday Music. The work it influenced most, however, is Debussy's *Pelléas et Mélisande*; the opera of that French anti-Wagnerian is musically akin to the dreamlike shadow of Wagner's music drama. The bare outline, the static juxtaposition of sounds, the veiled colours, the intermingling of archaism and modernity—the Middle Ages as a prehistoric world: all this can be traced back to it, and the rhythm of the Parsifal motive haunts the structure that marked the beginning of a new Western music, and really also neoclassicism. Wagner's power extended through *Parsifal* into the generation that renounced him. With *Parsifal*, his school went beyond itself.

What *Parsifal* and *Pelléas* have in common, however, is the element of art nouveau, which Wagner inaugurated in Germany long before the name existed. The aura of the pure fool corresponds to that of the word *Jugend*[3] [youth] around 1900, and the 'quickly dashed off' flower maidens resemble the first art nouveau ornaments; one such ornament became a heroine in the figure of Mélisande. The idea of the *Bühnenweihfestspiel* is precisely that of an art religion—the word, incidentally, is much older, coming from Hegel—as in art nouveau. Through the discerning consistency of its style, the aesthetic structure is intended to invoke a metaphysical sense whose substance is untainted by the demystified world. It is the production of such 'consecration' [*Weihe*] that *Parsifal* aims for; the auras of both the clear shapes and the composed reverberations serve this purpose. The artistic expression of that which, according to Schopenhauer's dogma, is the nature of the world, of blind will, and the glorification of the quietus, the negation of the will through sympathy, is chimerically ascribed the power of salvation by the work. It is from the vanity of this hope, however, the untruth of *Parsifal*, that its truth stems: the impossibility of invoking the departed sense through spirit alone. The saviour of art requires salvation as a secret Klingsor. What survives in *Parsifal* is its expression of the frailty of invocation itself.

1956/57

---

3 The German term for art nouveau is *Jugendstil*, 'youth style'. [Trans.]

NIGHT MUSIC

For Alban Berg, in admiration

It could easily happen: the socially prefigured question of how music from the past should be rendered today, as there is no one to listen to it—this doubtfulness could be reinforced by the presence of the same sentiment among the music-makers themselves. The absence of those able or willing to receive such offerings is not the only reason why the impossibility of interpreting historical works adequately is becoming increasingly evident; nor is it merely because the musicians lack the necessary grounding in tradition. The works themselves are starting to become uninterpretable. For the essences which interpretation seeks to access have been wholly transformed in reality, and thus also in the works, which are located in history and participate in living history. History has unlocked the works and revealed the original essences within them, has made them evident; they become visible only through the disintegration of their morphological unity in the form of the work, when it was only the inviolable unity of the two that created the necessary space for an adequate interpretation—and this interpretation now wanders aimlessly between fragments and recognizes their essences, but can no longer draw them back into the material from which history expelled them. Now they shine visibly and distantly: they no longer warm the closer shells they left behind. Hence, we recognized the character of Bach—in terms of its aesthetic structure, which supposes itself perceived and simultaneously points questioningly beyond itself—at a time when the reason for that objectivity was radically foreign to us. Perhaps in earlier times that objectivity was locked inside the works to such an extent that, bound to the material as its irremovable form, it regulated the freedom of their interpretation—the objective characters of the work simply mirrored those presupposed in reality before the work even originated, and, in the safety of such agreement, the performer could presumably approach the work as an enclosed self and share productively in its present.[1] Today we consider the objectivity of the work necessarily reduced to a stylistic principle: abstract, because the bond between the recognized, past essences and the musical material that is left no longer exists. The preludes and fugues have remained in their own company, and the only way we can reproduce them is to retrace the contours of their form, which have long since withdrawn into enigmatic silence. Because they no longer bear the measure of interpretation within themselves, it must either be posited from without as a rational schema or accepted by the questioners as a mystery to which they will never find the answer; freedom of interpretation is distorted into private wilfulness. The present of the works refuses to show itself to humanity.

It would be conceivable for the history of the interpretation of works now receding into the past to find its continuation in the history of their derivatives. While interpretation is inexorably being supplanted by the fidelity of mechanical means of representation, which create the petrified image of their dead forms, the dying works themselves are beginning to

---

1The noun 'present' is used here in the sense of a 'nowness', a state that would be valid and authentic at the current moment. [Trans.]

decompose. Light and serious music separated long ago; Sarastro and Papageno only shared the same opera stage when, in the revolutionary moment, the bourgeoisie believed that in attaining human rights, it had also attained joy itself. As bourgeois society neither achieved happiness nor realized human rights, however, the classes of music separated just like those of society; while any true joy among the ruling classes became implausible in the face of society's fractured state, the semblance of joy conversely became its means of deceiving the oppressed classes about their situation. When joy was unreal in society, its unreal form was ideologically enlisted by society, and, in any art that strove for truth, there was no longer any place for it. Now that the pathos-laden loneliness characterizing the art music of the nineteenth century has itself become questionable, light music is taking hold of its declining counterpart—not least because a distorted image of the great essences vainly invoked by the latter remains present within it. At the same time, however, the depravation through kitsch that displays the powerlessness of the great works also reclaims their leftovers for society, which, because its own order is no less illusory than kitsch, is only capable of experiencing them as such. One sees the lilac-wreathed gate of the *Dreimäderlhaus* being entered by a ballet of smashed forms whose volatile, strung-together state perhaps reveals for the first time what was captured in those works beneath the dynamics of creator and personality. The Toreador embarks on a second career by dancing the shimmy, just as he sacrifices the bull to the irate deity; José's fate theme accompanies the futile seduction of the chaste Joseph by Frau Massary, in the same way that the only remaining form of true astrology is found in the magical, secret amorous choices of bad women; Lehár's boring Frasquita is an exemplarily strict transformation of Carmen as a whole, who, as kitsch, finally separates the traits of opera from human experience as fully as those traits had lain hidden within its authentic form. Chopin's music, which—like that of Schubert's and

Bizet's—fed directly off collective sources and had a more lasting power in the fragmentarily individual than in the totality of forms, proved amenable to transformation for this very reason—and because the *grandes dames* he flatters are the ideal of the little girls of today; and so, in the sport of dancing, the *grandes dames* who forgot him may encounter him once more in the dances he had been persuaded to write for the sake of the little girls. Not only the waltzes, but also the *Fantasie Impromptu* proved workable and yielded up their last substance to the poverty of popular composers, who became rich through it. Meanwhile the slumber theme of *Die Walküre* is already accompanying the magic fire of bars. The second act of *Tristan* has become ripe for Boston; one need only leave out the syncopations, replace them with jazzier ones played by a saxophone, and the Night of Love can come down upon us once more. It was only the rudiments of the European faith in education that once protected Mozart and Beethoven, who have now been integrated into cinema, from more energetic use. Surrounded by noise, the works preserve themselves in silence.

It is vital to remain mindful of the fact that changes take place within the works, not simply in the people who interpret them. The state of truth in works corresponds to the state of truth in history. This is the only convincing way to disprove the objection that one need only change people sufficiently, reawaken their lost sense of scale, form and inwardness, and works that bore them today will bloom once more for them, inducing them to turn away from kitsch in favour of the true originals. In the here and now, the objectors say, we have reached a point at which a great artist is not only able to produce but also to reproduce at will, in so far as he unifies an original idea and the power of representation and is completely validated by some tradition. This argument presupposes freedom of choice;

yet one must realize that artistic freedom is never freedom of choice, is least of all freedom of choice. Certainly, an insistence on the lasting substance of the work is justified in the face of cheap aesthetic historicism. Yet this must not be seen in some ahistorically timeless, constant natural reserves within the work that can be drawn upon at will, any failure in this operation— at least, a failure measured against the work's continuance— being purely coincidental. The freedom of the artist, whether a reproducing or a producing one, unquestionably lies alone in the fact that he has the right to realize, beyond the constraints of what happens to exist at the time, what is recognized by him in accordance with the most advanced state of historical development as the current truth of the work—not recognized in the sense of some abstract reflection, but as a content-based insight into the nature of its material which is always historically preformed. All that is timeless about the work is that which manifests itself forcefully here and now, and which breaks open everything that is mere semblance; the seemingly unchanged natural qualities are at best the location of the dia-lectic between the form and the substance of the work, and often enough merely a lazy borderline concept of idealistic aesthetics: the 'work in itself', which can in reality never be separated from the work in its historical manifestation; and if, one day, nothing remained but this 'work in itself', the work would be dead. For depending on something unchanging in any music and fighting against current changes in interpretation can never mean saving the eternal work from expiry but, rather, playing off the past against the present. Denying the disintegration of works into history is reactionary in its purpose; the ideology of education, as a class privilege, does not ever want to suffer the disintegration of its noble treasures, whose eternal nature is supposed to guarantee its own eternal continuance. And yet the truth character of the works is tied precisely to their disintegration; it can be identified in the history of Beethoven's works in the nineteenth century. It is not the temporal and individual difference between observers—the contemporary critics, E. T. A. Hoffmann, Schumann, Wagner, the psycho-hermeneutical exegetes of the pre-war years and finally those of today—that dictate the differences between views, as if the disconcerting richness of thematic shapes, the poetic wealth of the secret within it, the depth of personal inwardness, the heightened dramatic dialectic, the extensive property of the heroic mindset, the graded abundance of spiritual content and, finally, the formally constructive imagination of Beethoven were preserved, albeit in an arbitrarily changing light, as eternally identical items that are discretely contained in the work and can alternately be appropriated at will. In reality, those essences separate from the work, layer by layer, when their hour has come, and none can be restored to the work once gone. There is no choosing between them, and all that our power of insight can do is ensure the realization of those essences which form part of the full currentness of the work. Once these essences have been entirely revealed, the works become unequivocal and are no longer current; their interpretability comes to an end.

The end of interpretability cannot be predetermined theoretically; it is decided in the present. The uninterpretability of works can only be asserted in current and polemical terms once they have discharged their secrets long enough to become secrets themselves. Uninterpretability as a critical category does not, however, prevent works whose validity is questioned from being performed, factually and not even entirely senselessly. It is impossible to foresee whether the industry of classics maintained by concert organizers and music festivals will continue unhindered as long as those in a position to pay necessarily desire safe, non-current interpretations as ceremoniously darkened wall decor for their comfortable listening rooms. Many a pianist will still be roused to passion by the Medusa stare of the ossified *Appassionata*, instead of mournfully developing the image of its tremendous head or turning his stricken eyes away from it; and it will not be clear that his passion has objectively turned into a deceit that is silently mocked by the petrified, inaccessible edifice of the work. Many a female pianist will, her hair flying about her, pour out the private longings of her soul into the blind alleys of Schumann's forms, not realizing in her vanity that her own echo is audible only to herself; she may find the trace of the soul's halting, lost utterance within, but can no longer bring it back to life. The only truly current mode of reproduction in this phase, the completely manifest, constructively transparent one advocated by Schönberg, has yet to take over the full breadth of musical life—though it is beginning to affect that breadth through Klemperer and Scherchen, and perhaps its sound will demonically force the continued presence of those works that threaten to fall silent. Now, however, it is time to take into account that all talk of the immortality of works has reached its limits.

We are still accustomed to viewing all music too impartially and only from within. We believe we are inside it in the same way as a safe house, whose windows signify our eyes, its corridors our bloodstream and its door our sex; or that it actually grew out of us, the plant from the seed, and that even the finest offshoots of its leaves are bound by law to imitate that inner cell. We posit ourselves as its subject, and, even if we dilute ourselves into the general, transcendental subject in order to rescue it from the disintegration of the merely organic, it is still we who impose our rule upon it. The crisis of subjectivist music that is apparent today in both perception and practice does not spare the works, which originate from the immanence of consciousness by acknowledging that the development of other music is becoming necessary while ensuring that the earlier subjectivist variety remains unchallenged. This is how it would be if we continued to view it merely from within. But the decline of musical subjectivism, historically speaking, is such that the subjective component disappears in works that were originally subjectively constructed. There is in fact no such thing as purely subjective music, and the subjective dynamic has long been used to conceal forgotten, threatening, objective qualities that are now finally breaking through. For the disintegration of the works is above all the disintegration of their interiority. The essences that escape from them stand above others as the personal ones, and together with others as the constitutively subjective ones whose very structure removes them from the fluctuations of privately psychological subjectivity. The autonomous spontaneity of the moral human being issues forth from Beethoven's works as their formally constitutive basis; it can no longer be reached by interpretative realization. What remains, however, is the external shaping of its forms; it is apparent that autonomous subjectivity is its driving force, yet the two are clearly separate. With the departure of the transcendental substance, critique also leaves the realm of subjective immanence: its position becomes transcendental. Certainly it cannot undo the muteness of the remaining work; by viewing the work and its substance as separated through time, however, it looks upon the muteness of the work itself, and the contours of the mute work are of a very different nature from those of the speaking work. While the living work automatically presented itself through the semblance of life, the disintegrating work becomes the scene of a dissociation of truth and semblance. No work lies within truth, and the disintegrating work is far removed from it. But the essences that were once embedded in the work now illuminate it brightly from without, and in their light its external lineature forms figures that may be ciphers of truth. Thus the entities of muteness and consolation, suprapersonal elements of all things operatic, only became knowable when the music that aimed for them fled to the realm of subpersonal usage after they had spent a deceptively long time submerged in inwardness. They are not meant any more personally than the intention of a popular song is the content of the cabaret singer's soul.—Or the sonatas of former times are now entering the stage of their constructive analysis, and thus the problem of the sonata will have to be posed anew—as already in Schönberg's quintet—in the same way that the pure form underlying all that is subjectively intended presents itself within it. The constitutive foundations of music have shifted to a state of audible externality once more; the disintegration of the semblant interior has reinstated the true exterior of music. At the current historical moment, it seems more legitimate and profound to speak of musical materialism than to claim that music is materially determined in any ahistorical sense.

1929

Not Strauss, who always returns swiftly to his vital naïveté; not Busoni, who conceived of it and undertook it, but never gave it a purely musical form himself: no, Ravel alone is the master of creating masks in sound. No piece of his is meant literally as it stands on the page; none, however, requires anything outside itself to explain it—his work shows a reconciliation of irony and form to produce a contented illusion. People call him an impressionist. If the word is intended more strictly than as a mere analogy to the preceding painting movement, it refers to a music that dissolves its natural material completely through the infinitely small unit of the transition, yet remains tonal. At the outermost historical threshold of that region stands Ravel; the fact that he did not pursue the impressionistic functionalization to its logical conclusion is precisely what places him on that threshold. He is already too knowing to practise impressionism in its pure form, as he no longer trusts in its foundations; at the same time, however, he belongs to it so fully that he can never wish to negate it. The sworn enemy of all dynamic nature in music, the last anti-Wagnerian in a situation where the spell of Bayreuth had completely worn off, he gazes upon the world of forms in which he himself is trapped; he sees through it like glass—but does not shatter the panes, instead settling into his confinement with the cunning of a prisoner. Through this, the style and location within society are defined. His music is that of a *grand-bourgeois*, aristocratic upper class that realized its own nature; that also sees the dangerously undermined foundation beneath itself; that takes the possibility of catastrophe into account and yet must remain what it is, as it would otherwise have to eliminate itself. The fact that this stratum of society does not predominantly enjoy Ravel as much as Strauss's erotic flair, or today perhaps Stravinsky's baser tricks, does not testify against Ravel— if anything, it speaks against that society, demonstrating that it is either less knowing than its manifestation in Ravel's music or has already lost the aesthetic power to recognize the portrait which Ravel's music, flatteringly enough, presents it. Or is his music the dream image of some *high life*, fairy tale or *mondanité* as alien to that society as a liberated one—and perhaps even related to the latter? It certainly has little directly in common with solid accumulation, and, as soon as mastery distances itself so far from its social origin that it barely echoes this origin any more, one can ascribe better secrets to it than those which keep it under their spell.

Any talk of mastery inevitably leads to Debussy. Despite the stupidity of the clichéd ideas under which people subsume the two French composers, this is not unjustified. For nowhere in the music of today—with the possible exception of Schönberg's school—are the stylistic similarities greater, yet the divergences between the actual compositions more radical, than between these two. The question of whom to assign priority leads nowhere. It is inarguably Debussy, though only a few years separate the first truly individual pieces of Debussy from the earliest of Ravel's, in which his personality is already fully explicit. But the question of priority is of no consequence, for no category could be more inappropriate to Ravel's intentions than that of originality. He does not wish to express his personality, to begin from inwardness; he confidently records the vanishing figures of his historical moment, as Degas—with whom he has a great deal in common—recorded the figures of his racehorses and ballerinas. He did not make the uncompromising choice of musical material that Debussy did; he does not define his motives in the quasi-mathematical fashion of his senior but surpasses him in sweet, soft opulence. His approach to the means found by Debussy in his faith in their historical dignity is lighter, more sceptical and more extensive. What makes him remain incomparable, however, is the fact that he never degraded them to facets of the language of his time, or even of the national music movement—to which he belonged—but, rather, preserved the exclusive succinctness that Debussy gave them. He has nothing in common with Florent Schmitt, not even with Dukas. His impressionism was never as immediate as Debussy's; *La Valse* forms its apotheosis in a quotation of the musical pluperfect. The early piano pieces, for example *Jeux d'eau* or *Gaspard de la nuit*, give impressionism access to the full wealth of pianistic resources, which Debussy, still involved in a fresher reaction against the New German School, avoided. Ravel was very clearly different from the start. His impressionism simultaneously understands itself as a game; it lacks the pathos of limitations and programmes. Its richness goes against the polemical idea of the *musicien français*; it is no coincidence that his piano writing shows not only the influence of his teacher Fauré but also of Lisztian virtuosity, something that would be inconceivable in Debussy. The respective developments of the two masters— in so far as one can speak of development in Ravel's case— progressed in strictly opposite directions. Their paths cross in the domain of children's music. Ravel muffles the virtuosity of the first piano works to produce the Sonatine, and even the sparseness of the four-handed suite *Ma mère l'Oye*, which can certainly be considered one of his principal works. The crisis of poetic Impressionism, whose lack of immanent formal power could only be paralysed with considerable effort through sufficient knowledge of artistry, becomes acute as infantilism; like Debussy, like Stravinsky later on, and not unlike Laurencin in the field of painting. Nowhere are the natures more sharply separated, however, than where they come closest to each other. For all its charm, Debussy's *Children's Corner* has the affectionate bonhomie of secure bourgeois existence. This child has a good life; it has an entire toyshop to itself—'*La boîte à joujoux*'—just like the one we wish we had. Stravinsky's infantility is a tunnel leading from modernity to the prehistoric landscape. The children of *Ma mère l'Oye* and the Sonatine—especially the minuet—on the other hand, are sad, illuminated *plein air* children; dabbed with sunlight in the colourful avenue but looked after by English governesses. Debussy's childlike quality was the game of a man aware of himself and his own limitations, and Stravinsky's was a lateral attack on the adult world of objects; only that of Ravel was the aristocratic sublimation of sorrow. 'And children grow up with deep eyes'; Ravel could have set Hofmannsthal—if he had needed him, already having Mallarmé. His sorrow chooses the imago of the childlike because it remains in nature, and hence, in concrete musical terms, within the natural material of tonality and the harmonic series. He certainly breaks it up into its flickering particles of solar dust; as infinitely divided, however, his music remains in the sphere of what has been. He never exceeds the preconceived form that is implicit in the choice of highly qualified material—and the construction never infiltrates its herbaceous surroundings. The elements we hear in his music are established ones.

Ravel's music as a whole preserves the features of the sad child: the prodigy. Perhaps this is the origin of his masquerade: he masks himself as if out of a shame, a shame which those forms from which he draws his life force do not allow him to break through; the shame of the prodigy who has all these things yet is hopelessly trapped within natural limitations. His music takes us on a tour leading through the illusory regions

of *noblesse* and *sentiment*, through the haughty children's landscape and, finally, to the ancient. Not the primitive; not to the
pathos of awakening that guides Debussy; rather, into sorrow
without faith. It is no coincidence that his archaist magnum
opus, with the withered fragrance of the Forlane, stripped of
its layers by its own harmonies, and its most tender of min-
uets—that the great *Le Tombeau de Couperin*, composed over
many years, became a music of mourning. The ancient quality
in Ravel does not have the same gravity as in Debussy, whose
Hommage à Rameau seems to have been lifted from the depths
of the submerged cathedral. Ravel's melancholy is the bright,
glass melancholy of time rushing away, which it is so unable
to halt that it cares little whatever might slip away from it; if
its tenderness is lost for words, it can fall back on the old G
major, which is no more real to it than the ephemeral tenderness itself. And so an aspect of questioning, intentionless fortuity enters Ravel's music, an element that it would be both
foolish and unjust to denigrate as mere artistry, aestheticism
and experimentation: before the boundless knowledge of his
music, all things are truly equal, and it is through chance that
he realizes the fate of what he sees prefigured. Debussy gains
both compositional opulence and constructive support
through the exclusivity of his choices in his last works, *En
blanc et noir* and the piano études; Ravel becomes narrower
the less he, the younger composer, allows himself to go on
believing in that impressionistic brilliance which had begun
to move beyond itself: it ends, for the meantime, with the frail
Lydian opening movement of the violin sonata and the
dynamic-colouristic illusionist act of *Bolero*. Here we find the
elimination of all immediacy that, being alien to the spirit, fell
prey to technical mentalities—while Ravel, occupied with his
own concerns, can no longer allow himself either to be dominated by foreign material or to set the familiar aglow through
foreign intentions. The landscape has disappeared; its air and

its subtle trembling, the only remnants, are what define the music. Debussy dissolved the substance of his immediacy in the compositional attack, in the cruel splitting of his material, which enabled him to produce works as coherent and well-formed as the greatest paintings of their time. Ravel lost faith in the substance that belongs to the world of Romantic semblance from the start; hence, he does not even try to atomize it but, rather, to bypass it, to circle it, to reinterpret it—and, finally, makes it vanish into nothingness like a conjuror. This is why, in truth, his music knows no development. Once his ear had grasped impressionism, each new work became a new trick, and tricks have no historical continuity. The artistry thus posited, however, draws its validity from history. This is the only way for a music to present itself that trusts wholeheartedly in the dignity of its forms after their power has faded, even in France. This is precisely why German musicians, especially the best and strictest, love Debussy, yet are almost always suspicious of Ravel. His music concludes the Romantic age by invalidating that personality which had always posited musical forms.

Wunderkind music has the best literary taste; in Ravel's case, one can finally read the texts without embarrassment—especially the libretto by Colette. Going by the notes of the score and a knowledge of Ravel's being, *L'Enfant et les sortilèges* must be considered his masterpiece. Every bar of the music is possessed of childlike enchantment, but a single word from the maternal earth—and how maternally France still behaves towards those who have renounced their origin—is sufficient to give back to nature, concealed a thousand times, its former prerogative. One cannot foresee what will survive. But perhaps later, in a different order of things, one will still hear in the minuet of *Sonatine* how beautifully one used to compose at five o'clock in the afternoon. The table is set for tea, the children are called, now the gong is already sounding, they hear it and play one last round before joining the circle on the veranda. By the time they are excused, it has grown cool outside and they must remain indoors.

1930

Even if one believed, like Pfitzner, in the unchanging nature of works, that eternity invented by the nineteenth century to deify the creator-artist, the actual texts of those works would refute such a notion. As they stand, they do not offer any concise rules for interpretation, and the possibility of interpretative changes in the works within the framework of their respective texts is so radical that it must ultimately attack the texts themselves. The older the work, the clearer its changes. In the case of works whose origin lies in objectively binding forms and a closed tradition of musical practice, the sign language of subjective intentionality is in an imperfect state of development; that sign language alone was able to spawn the illusion of a work unchanged by time. Unchanged works from the seventeenth century would already be hieroglyphs, just as in all mediaeval music, for all the talk of reviving its polyphonic principles, the unfathomable, hieroglyphic character cannot seriously be denied. While the unchanging works fall silent, the others disintegrate through change. And yet this process of change, as it objectively affects the work, grants—for a certain time—a rule of interpretation that cannot be sought in the ahistorical work. This does not, admittedly, mean that history renders the work powerless as a work and simply acts as its fortuitous location. Rather, recognition of the currently valid interpretation of a work occurs strictly between the text and history. Interpreting a work in a current manner, that is to say according to the objectively contemporary state of truth within it, interpreting a work more fittingly and correctly, always also means: interpreting it more faithfully, reading it better. History allows latent essences that are objectively but not subjectively implicit to rise up in the work, and the guarantee of their objectivity is the gaze that focuses more closely on the text and becomes aware of those aspects in it which previously lay concealed and scattered within the work, and now identify themselves in the text itself—though they can do so only at their historical moment. If one goes about bringing musical interpretation to a current state in the right way, it is not a wilful approach to the work but, rather, a better form of fidelity; a fidelity that understands the work as it is transmitted to us concretely through history, instead of presupposing an abstract thing in itself when the work is still entirely caught within the historical constellation of its original time. When the work is called upon as ahistorical, it falls prey to history as an ideological monument of something past; the eternal element within it can only be recognized in its historicity. The necessity of looking upon works as new and foreign is dictated by the works, not by people. This is to be carried out as prefigured by the historical state of the works in relation to our possibilities of insight.

It lies within the awareness of all fluctuations and empirical contradictions, yet can also be supposed with a degree of general determinacy, that works must be played ever faster in the course of time. The reason for this lies in the works, not in psychology. The works shrink in time; the manifold elements existing within them move closer together. This may be indicated by the functionalization of music—not the music alone—in the way one can follow through history since the establishment of the harmonic principle: the manifestations of music's existential content become smaller, and they distance themselves

ever further from the great self-enclosed surface shape, ultimately becoming monadic power centres that present themselves in the transition from one existent to another, yet no
longer directly in the existent itself. The authenticity of music
is transferred to incomparably small cells and their allocation.
This pinpoints as the genuine sense of the process of functionalization in music a shifting of its substances in such a way
that they gain their true, illusionless layer only after the disintegration of their arbitrary surface, and in complete miniatur-
ization. Calling the progressive subjectification of music its
progressive demythologization would amount to the same.
That process informs the sequence in which works emerge;
the task of a recognizant interpretation is to show it in the
works themselves. The history of musical writing mediates
between the sequence of works and their history. It has become
ever smaller since the Middle Ages. The potency of the longa
and the breve shrinks; the former is long forgotten while the
latter leads a pitiful existence in compositions with an archaist-
sacral stance. The semibreve as a whole note has been viewed
with suspicion since Beethoven, though the reactionary neoclassicist movement is now attempting to talk us into accepting
it again. Where our music realizes its historical status most sin-
cerely, it can be notated with demisemiquavers: a glance at
Schönberg's *Erwartung* testifies to this. Conclusions must be
drawn from this for interpretation, as has long since occurred
and been taken for granted. Even if one supposes absolutely
identical tempi, older music must be played faster today in
relation to the notated values, as we now at least indicate the
same duration with different symbols. Certainly this would
not amount to a demand for a change in the tempi as absolute
units, but it would show how stringently history forces interpretation; the meaning of notation varies through history, and
even the realization of identical tempi now calls for the same
notation to be executed at different speeds. The categorical
validity of the texts has been broken.

This validity disappears completely as soon as one decides to conceive of the change in the symbols not in isolation but, rather, in connection with the works' own changes. When Handel wrote his sarabandes, for example, chord degrees held such power through the harmonic principle, defined only a hundred years earlier, that the progression from the tonic to the dominant seventh chord in second inversion on the dominant, connected through a suspension, meant a tension that wanted to be felt and required time to be felt—making sure to avoid a dissolution of the stable tonic triad and thus the form, instead of enabling this triad to proceed in a meaningful way. For us, however, progress through history is so worn out, so hollow and used up, that as such, illuminated via tempo, it would no longer be bearable. If there were a realer interest in Handel today than that of music-philological rehashing, it would have to follow the flow of the melodic line which was certainly only possible historically in such calm steps through the marvelling attainment of the harmonic principle but which we could recognize more fittingly once liberated from that long-disintegrated harmony, which only inhibits our far more harmonically functional consciousness instead of setting it in motion as it was originally supposed to. This results in the necessity of playing Handel at a faster absolute tempo, even faster than he was probably played in his time. This provokes loud objections and protests: that it takes away his dignity, as well as a unity in his work that encompasses all elements inseparably. First of all, one must respond to this by pointing out that dignity as a form of truth character no longer means anything to us. Just as it is not binding for us in reality, it can equally not be so in art, which does not contain the real past but is relevant to us only to the extent that we are forced to recognize its content as truth content. Today, art could assert dignity only as semblance. It would have to simulate an expression of unimpaired richness of being that is unattainable and not worth attaining for us, and whose aesthetic postulation

thus lacks any legitimacy; dignity could be bought only by sacrificing our current state of musical awareness—and moreover
at the price of boredom. Even if it is revealed in the work and
in reality, the unity of the work is by no means canonical. It
disintegrates into history; fragments are the only reality that
remains of the work, while its unity transpires as mere semblance and separates off from such reality. Seeking to assert
such unity after it has become questionable in the light of the
work's immanent historical state means galvanizing a condition divested of life, and its living ruins are of more use to us
than the dead whole. The space of the dead whole is antiquarian, and has an antiquarian validity; not, however, that of
immediacy. One serves it better by preserving it silently than
by seeking to create the semblance of something living. We
know how works from the seventeenth and eighteenth centuries were rendered in certain towns within the tradition of
central German church music; how solemnly slow in slow
tempi, and how moderate and deliberate in fast ones. The layer
of sanctity encasing that interpretation stems from the fact
that the work can no longer be directly interpreted as such;
one must stylize it in a sacral and ultimately aestheticized fashion, transpose it into an artificial, as it were ahistorical aural,
space in order to reproduce it with any fidelity to tradition.
Someone who recognizes such distinctions cannot fail to hear
the didactic moralism, the unreal and ideological-reactionary
character, of such interpretations, where every strong beat is
emphasized as if it were an instance of true and indissoluble
being while the ear is already sixteen sequential bars ahead. All
interpretation of such historical fidelity has an 'as if' quality:
it interprets as if the works were still unchangingly present in
their original state, when they have in fact changed to such a
degree that their original guise is no longer accessible at all—
or only in gloomy holy places. This is exemplified by the tendency towards exaggeration. Handel probably did not need to
spell out his metres, as his strong beats were already powerful

enough as bearers of harmonic progression. Now that this power has faded; it has to be replaced through an overemphasis of the accents simply to conserve that past effect, which can no longer be adequately gained from the material itself. And so it is precisely the desire to preserve the work ahistorically that leads to a mode of musical presentation that comes from without, from the reactionary ideology of the performers, and goes against the concrete musical nature of the work through its starkness and rigidity. This shows the impossibility of such interpretation, and, simultaneously, once one has conceded the decisive fact of functionalization in its consequences for individual works, the necessity of performing those works more quickly.

The newer, faster tempi gain their specifically current quality through the crisis of expressive pathos—first of all, in relation to Beethoven. Being substantially part of the Romantic reaction against the total process of functionalization, which they were unable to halt nonetheless, the pathetic tempi were consistently slower. The force of expression in music always lies in the individual element; only what is perceived in immediate musical terms can be understood in an analogous fashion to the 'experiences', but the total progression of a movement is of a completely different nature to the psychological experiential context of humans. The musical context objectifies the individual musical phenomena in the way that, in the context of human experience, they can be objectified through the forms of conceptualization but certainly not through the merely intuitive experiential context alone. This is why all psychologically oriented musical practice dwells on the individual at the expense of the totality, which sublates expressive immediacy. In terms of formal analysis, such pathos could almost be viewed as a means of eliminating the formal difficulty resulting from the predominance of the singular by attempting to pass off this insistent representation of the individual as an actual formal intention. By contrast, interpretation becomes ever faster the more consistently it follows the formal construction and grasps the particles as formally constructive. The connections between large formal sections, often even the establishment of a partial whole, can only become clear at a tempo that no longer presents these parts as autonomous entities but, rather, in such a way that they are incomplete at the moment of sounding, and can only be understood as components of the whole. Or conversely, from the perspective of the whole: the notion of a formal whole only comes about when the parts move close enough together that they must inevitably be perceived in direct relation to one another. This poses completely new interpretative problems with regard to the individual element, which is not meant to disappear but, rather, to become recognizable in its constructive location within the whole, and thus also to be thoroughly constructed in itself: the individual shape is now no longer exhibited in slow motion and thus set apart from the whole as something self-enclosed but, rather, drawn into the whole. Thus its vivid representation now becomes a task that can no longer be solved through the tempo but through an altered representation of the part itself. This involves phrasing and metre, conscious emphasis—above all, an emancipation from schematic four-bar groups—and dynamics, as dictated by the formal construction of both the whole and the parts. This leads to the connection between the new tempi called for and the changed style of interpretation as a whole. To avoid making the musical shapes become worn out in the new tempi and turning the whole into mere empty movement, it is necessary to find a different mode of interpretation, a metric-rhythmic and dynamic interpretation largely emancipated from the strong beat and thus from tonal cadences. On the other hand, in order to succeed in presenting the formal parts as elements of a whole—with a constructive abandonment of withered rhythmic-harmonic symmetry—that move purely according to their own formal categories, not any preconceived schema, yet avoid descending into anarchy—to solve this central problem of contemporary interpretation, it is necessary to up the tempo and move the particles closer together. It remains uncertain whether such a reconciliation of the part and the whole can always succeed in the phase of the works' disintegration. It cannot, at any rate, be presupposed as directly given, and, in those cases where it is realized, it will prefer this to happen as a rational configuration of parts that have already separated, rather than as an 'organic' totality. Perhaps the true purpose of the tempo increases that can no longer be avoided today is to recreate the lost organic unity of the works by constructive means, by enabling the dissociated parts of the disintegrated work to move close together and seek refuge in one another. Tempo modification, which stems from the historical changes undergone by the works, only finds its purpose by capturing the works in their historicity. It is inaugurated by the disintegration of the works—and proves its value through the disintegrated works. One could see a prototype in the approach of the virtuoso, whose intense practice and extreme repetition already made the works crumble while they still seemed historically intact. And indeed d'Albert, in those interpretations of Beethoven's middle-period works which are still astounding today, especially the *Waldstein* sonata and the *Appassionata*, found through improvisatory anticipation the new tempi that constructive insight now renders compulsory. It was only with Schönberg, through the construction of the musical material and all its further-reaching consequences for the overall presentation, that this insight was gained. It is no coincidence that his discovery was based on a precise knowledge of the originals—that is to say, that the change in the work resulted dialectically from fidelity to it. He had Beethoven's F-minor quartet, for example, played with the original metronome markings; this revealed not only the nature of the individual movements but also the form of the whole, especially the correspondence between the first and last movements.

The battle taking place over the works under the problematic heading of 'technicization' has not been imposed from without, through the discovery of new material for presentation. The fact that such material could be found corresponds to an objective historical state of the works in themselves, which makes it impossible to interpret them other than in a thoroughly new fashion whose drastic representation is technicization. This necessity reveals itself in the need to choose new tempi and play all music at a faster pace than traditionally, thus inevitably modifying it overall, quite independently of the respective technical means; it comes from the works themselves. At the notional level, the interpretation demanded by the works in accordance with their historical state and the interpretation that technicization can render possible are moving closer together. Admittedly, the technical means must be assessed with reference to the most advanced stage of interpretation itself, and interpretation must proceed on the basis of an understanding of the work—not in helpless analogy to current technical practice.

1930

The question of what is meant by jazz seems impossible to answer with a clear definition. Just as the historical origin of the genre loses all clarity in the haze of recent developments, its boundaries become uncertain in the ambiguous usage of the present day. To give some approximate idea, one could say that it refers to the realm of dance music, whether used directly for that purpose or slightly stylized, since the war, which stands apart from the previous kind through a decided, but still highly ill-defined, character of modernity. This is perhaps shown most vividly by the attacks—which incidentally differ greatly according to region—on jazz, whose accusations are polarized to the extremes of the soullessly mechanical on the one hand, and the indecently decadent on the other. Musically speaking, that 'modernity' essentially revolves around sonority and rhythm, without breaking fundamentally with the harmonic-melodic convention of traditional dance music. The main rhythmic principle is syncopation. In addition to its elementary form—as used in the cakewalk, the precursor to jazz—it appears in a variety of modifications, which always remain permeable to that basic form. The most widespread modifications are: erosion of the strong beats through omission (Charleston) or ties (ragtime); the use of metric illusion, for example 'secondary rag', where a 4/4 bar is treated as a series of 3 + 3 + 2 quavers, with an accent on the first note of each group, which is removed from the primary rhythm as a 'false metre'; and, finally, the 'break', a quasi-improvised cadence normally found at the end of the middle section, two bars before the return of the main chorus. With all these syncopations, however, which sometimes appear extremely complicated in virtuoso pieces, the basic metre is retained with the utmost rigour; it is always marked by the bass drum. Rhythmic events concern the music's accentuation and phrasing, but never the overall course of a piece; and even accentuation, through the bass drum and the group of continuo instruments assigned to it, always remains tied to a fundamental symmetrical pattern. Hence, symmetry, especially in the 'overall rhythm', is completely respected. The validity of the eight-bar period, even the four-bar half-period, remains unchallenged. In correspondence to this, one finds equally simple harmonic and melodic symmetries, divided into perfect and imperfect cadences—the sound of the music is characterized by that same simultaneity of eruption and rigidity. It combines expressive and continuo-like, objectively constant elements: the violin and the bass drum are its extremes. Its life force, however, is that vibrato which makes a single note, rigid and objective in itself, seem to tremble; that injects subjective emotions into it which are, nonetheless, powerless to break this rigidity of the basic sound—just as the syncopations are unable to shake the basic metre. In Europe, the saxophone is considered most representative of that sound, and, accordingly, bears the brunt of the widespread resistance. This instrument, however, which has taken on such modernist infamy and allegedly exposes the overstrained occidental nerves perversely to Negro vitality, is in fact of venerable age. One already finds it discussed in Berlioz's writings on instrumentation; it was invented in the nineteenth century, when the emancipation of the art of orchestration led to a demand for subtler transitions between the woodwind and brass sections, and is used—not obbligato, admittedly—in

Bizet's *L'Arlésienne Suite*, a work that has long since taken on classical status. In many countries it has been used in military music for generations, and is thus hardly able to shock people anymore. Its significance for jazz as actually practised today is perhaps less than that of the trumpet, which has a far greater variety of playing techniques at its disposal than the saxophone, and whose functional employment is therefore much more convenient and independent of the overall sound than the former. The jazz sound itself, however, is not determined by a single conspicuous instrument but, rather, functionally: through the possibility of setting something rigid in vibration, or more generally through the possibility of creating interferences between the rigid and the eruptive. The vibrato itself is an example of interference in the precise physical sense, and the physical model can be considered suitable to represent the socio-historical phenomenon of jazz.

The technological fact of this function can be understood as a symbol for a social one: the genre is controlled by the function, not by any autonomous formal principle. As dance music, it seems to avow its own social use. But one can also observe its ardent striving to declare its function merely abstract, simply subsumed under the formula of dance music, only to practise it all the more unchallenged in secret: hence, the function of jazz presents the dialectician with a riddle. Just as there are few elements of material that could contribute to its solution, there are equally few formal types developed by jazz. Much of what passes for jazz among the general public, though perhaps not for jazz experts, does not even attempt to fulfil the most rudimentary criteria of rhythmic or sonic interference. This applies first and foremost to the tangos, which are rhythmically very primitive and only draw on the elementary form of syncopation without ever making it a principle of the musical fabric. It also applies to that intermediate form between jazz and the march that emerged as the 'six-eight' after

'Valencia' of 1925 and spread uncommonly rapidly, its march-
like aspects becoming ever more explicit—syncopation was
replaced by a constant rhythm running all the way through,
and sonic interference abandoned in favour of a homogeneous
and 'melodious' tutti sound. It never separated itself clearly
from jazz in practice, however, and is played by orchestras in
alternation with consistently syncopated 'hot music'. On the
other hand, a great deal of music is considered jazz or jazz-
related purely on account of its sound, without any consideration of the rhythmic principles of jazz: the widespread success
of Weill's songs was very much a success of jazz, even though
the rhythmic characterization of their melodies, based on the
declamation of lines of text that have been set, is completely
opposed to the methods of jazz; the only manifestations of jazz
are the continuous basic rhythm and the sound of the saxophone. Jazz is not what it 'is'—in its own context, it is bare
and its aesthetic structures can be seen through with a single
glance—it is what it is used for; this raises questions that
would require thorough examination to answer. Not questions
such as those raised by the autonomous work; they are far
more like those of the detective novel, which, like jazz,
doggedly maintains a strict stereotype while doing everything
in its power to make the recipient forget this by adding individualizing traits which are themselves exclusively determined
by the stereotype. Just as, in the detective novel, the question
of the criminal's identity mingles with the question of what
everything means, we find in jazz the question of what this
strange subject could be, trembling and marching at the same
time, mingling with the question of what purpose it serves,
why it is there in the first place—while it asserts its existence
as something completely natural, only concealing how difficult
it would find its self- justification.

　　For if, as has often enough been the case, one wished to
view the usability of jazz, its suitability as a mass item, as a

dialectically advanced corrective of the bourgeois isolation of autonomous art, and even to accept its usability as a motive for the abolition of music's object-character, one would be lapsing into that latest form of Romanticism which desperately seeks to escape the fatal character of capitalism by affirming the object of fear itself as some ghastly allegory of imminent freedom, and by sanctifying negativity—a sanctity in which, incidentally, jazz would like to make us believe. Whatever the situation of art might be in a future order of things, whether its autonomy and reity will survive or not—and the economic perspective supplies various reasons why the right form of society will not be centred on the creation of pure immediacy—this much is certain: the usability of jazz does not negate alienation but, rather, reinforces it. Jazz is a commodity in the strict sense: in musical production, its suitability for everyday use establishes itself in no other form than its saleability, which stands in the most extreme opposition not only to the immediacy of its use but also to that of the work process itself; it is subject to the rules—as well as the arbitrariness—of the market, just as its distribution is subject to those of competition or even its heir. And those characteristics of jazz that seem to show an expression of immediacy—namely, the supposedly improvisatory traits of which syncopation is taken as representative—are, themselves standardized, used to supplement the standardized commodity character in blank parrot fashion in order to conceal it, though without gaining power over it for a second. Through different intentions—whether that of elevated 'style', individual taste or even individual spontaneity—jazz seeks to improve its sales and cloak its commodity character, which, through one of the system's fundamental contradictions, jeopardizes its own success on the market if it appears undisguised. However ardently jazz might don the mantle of New Objectivity, it is the very thing that all objectivity claims to battle most furiously, namely artisanship; and its objectivity amounts to no more than a tacked-on ornament designed to fool us that it is more than a mere object.

Such deceit is initially in the interests of the bourgeoisie. If it is truly granted the prerogative to enjoy its own alienation, the pathos of distance—which Nietzsche was still well-disposed towards—is of little help in attaining this enjoyment in the present antagonistically advanced situation. Just as communal ideologies of the most varying kinds make that distance smaller in the consciousness the more inexorably it grows in actual being, that which is alienated is bearable only as long as it purports to be unconscious and 'vital': the most alien is presented as the most familiar. For the function of jazz should initially be viewed in relation to the upper classes, and its more consistent forms are still, at least for any more intimate reception than simply being at the mercy of loudspeakers and orchestras in mass establishments, essentially reserved for the dancing and highly initiated upper class. For its members, jazz represents—rather like the gentlemen's evening attire—the inexorability of the social authority that the class itself constitutes but which is glorified in jazz as something primal and primitive, as 'nature'; in its individual or style-specific aspects, however, jazz appeals to their 'taste' whose complete freedom of choice is legitimated by their position. But the fact that jazz, both because of its rigidity and its individualizing taste, is 'not kitsch' helps those who are thus disciplined to keep a clear conscience. The effects of jazz, however, are no more restricted to the upper class than the latter's consciousness differs greatly from that of the dominated class: the mechanism of psychological mutilation on which the continuance of the present conditions depends also holds power over the mutilators themselves; and if these are sufficiently like their victims in the structure of their drives, the victims receive the compensation of being allowed to share in the rulers' goods, in so far as these are fashioned for a mutilated drive structure. As a superficial effect and a diversion, albeit not a serious leisure ritual, jazz pervades the whole of society, even the proletariat; if there are any exceptions in Europe, then only specifically agrarian communities. Often, the dependants identify themselves with the upper class through the reception of jazz; they consider jazz 'chic', and it allows the ordinary employee to go to the beer cabaret with his girlfriend and still feel that he is something better. Yet here it is probably only the 'primitive' elements of jazz, that is to say the danceable strong beats of the basic rhythm, that are perceived; highly syncopated hot music is tolerated without entering the consciousness more directly—especially as the cheap dance halls cannot afford virtuoso jazz orchestras, and the indirect rendition through the radio remains far less affecting than that of the genuine musicians at their own time and place. It is characteristic for jazz as a form of interference, however, that one can easily dispense with its more differentiated elements without eliminating it, or even preventing it from being recognizable as jazz. It is pseudo-democratic in the sense that characterizes the consciousness of the time: its attitude of immediacy, definable through a rigid system of tricks, hides class differences. In the ideological realm, as in the current political one, such democracy is closely accompanied by reaction. The deeper jazz strays in society, the more reactionary traits it assumes; the more completely it is enslaved by the banal; the less it tolerates freedom and outbursts of the imagination; until finally, as the musical accompaniment to the modern collective, it simply glorifies oppression itself. The more democratic jazz is, the worse it becomes.

The fact that its democratic air is a mere pose becomes clear from its reception; nothing could be more wrong than to think of it as plebiscite. The financial power of the publishers as well as the music's distribution via the radio and, above all, the cinema develop a tendency towards centralization that restricts freedom of choice and, for the most part, barely permits genuine competition; the irresistible propaganda machine belabours the masses with the songs it likes, which are usually the bad ones, until their tired memory is defenceless and at their mercy—and this fatigue of the memory in turn affects further production. The pieces that are decisive for the large-scale effect of jazz are precisely not those which develop the idea of jazz as interference most purely, but quite technically backward, coarse dances that only contain those traits in a fragmentary manner. These are considered 'commercial':[1] if the banal hit pieces sell enough, the publishers tend to add a 'modern', i.e. reasonably consistent, hot piece, for free. So even for mass consumption, hot music cannot be dispensed with entirely. This testifies to a certain surplus of musical productivity in relation to market demand. The orchestras want hot music—partly to show their virtuosity, partly also because the endless repetition of the simplest things becomes unbearably boring for them. At the same time, however, this artisan hot music, the relatively progressive form of jazz, is also necessary in order to elevate mass consumption. If an understanding of hot music gives the upper class a clear conscience for their taste, then the incomprehension of the majority in the shock of the uncomprehended, if it is related to hot music, gives them the vague satisfaction of being 'up to date',[2] perhaps also a confirmation of their erotic emancipation through the dangerously modern or 'perverse'. All this is mere decorum; only the most obvious and rhythmically trivial melodies end up being hummed. In their wider reception, the hot pieces are at most comparable to pseudo-modern painters such as van Dongen, Foujita, Marie Laurencin, or—better still—to cubist advertising pictures.

1 English in the original. [Trans.]

2 English in the original. [Trans.]

The objection to these arguments is obvious: that it is wrong to speak of centralism or false democracy because the propagandist mechanism is not sufficiently effective. Hits cannot be 'made'; hence, one cannot propose adequate theoretical conditions for success. One of the greatest hits of recent times, for example—'Capri'—was brought out by a small publisher after being turned down by the larger ones, and achieved success purely under its own steam. If one asks jazz experts why some pieces enjoy such great success, they will usually reply—the more business-minded they are, the more eagerly they will respond—with depraved magical formulae from the vocabulary of art: inspiration, genius, creativity, originality, mysterious power and other irrational expressions. As transparent as the motives of that irrationalism may be, the irrational component of hit successes cannot be overlooked. Which pieces will be successful and which will not cannot be predicted with apodictic certainty, any more than one can know the fate of a security on the stock market. This irrationality, however, is not so much a suspension of social determinacy as something that is itself socially determined. First of all, theoretical examination can arrive at numerous necessary, if not adequate, conditions of 'success', i.e. social effectiveness. Proceeding further, the analysis may then stumble on the 'irrational' aspects; when asking, for example, why of two quite similarly formed and equivalent pieces, one was successful and the other was not. But it cannot suppose any creative miracle where nothing has been created. Assuming that such irrationality is not simply reduced to unequal opportunities of propaganda and distribution, fortuity itself is an expression of an overall social character, one of whose hallmarks is, no matter how precisely larger tendencies may be determined, the toleration of and even demand for anarchic randomness in all concrete details. Likewise, in the realm of ideology, monopolism by no means amounts to an elimination of anarchy—just as the reality in which a hit is heard is not neat and orderly. In the same way that time and place may determine the fate of a work more than its own merits, the consciousness of its recipients is not systematic and the irrationality is first of all that of the listeners. This is not a creative irrationality, however, but a destructive one; no originating force but, rather, a recourse to false origins dictated by a force of destruction. Perhaps in a right society there could be a correlation of quality and success; in our wrong one, however, the lack of correspondence testifies not so much to an occult quality as to the falsity of society.

If jazz in fact takes recourse to false origins, then both the talk of the irrationality of its success and that of its intrinsic irrationality, its archaic upheavals, or whatever phrases zealous intellectuals might use to justify the industry, lose their meaning. The belief in jazz as an elemental force, as something that could enable the regeneration of our supposedly decadent European music, is a mere ideology. It is actually questionable how much jazz even has to do with genuine Negro music; the fact that it is very often performed by Negroes and that the public demands Negro jazz as a branded product proves little, even if folklorist research were to confirm the African origin of many of its practices. Today, at any rate, all formal elements of jazz are completely abstractly preformed by the capitalist demand for its exchangeability. Even the much-vaunted improvisations, the 'hot' parts and breaks, are of purely ornamental, never constructive or formally constitutive significance. Not only is their location—even down to the bar number—stereotypical; not only is their length and harmonic structure exactly predetermined as a dominant chord effect; even their melodic shape and their possibilities of simultaneous combination can be attributed to very few basic forms: all essentially the circumscription of the cadence, a harmonically figurative counterpoint. The connection between jazz and Negroes is similar to that between the salon music of the cafe violinists—which jazz is confident of having supplanted—and the gypsies. As Bartók has shown, the latter is brought to the gypsies from the city; like the consumption of jazz, its production is also urban, and the skin of the Negroes is as much a colouristic effect as the silver of the saxophones. By no means do blank musical commodities herald the rise of triumphant vitality; the onetime heroes of the European-American leisure industry have since been engaged by it as its lackeys and advertising figures, and their triumph is merely a baffling parody of colonial imperialism. To the extent that one can speak of Negro elements in the earliest examples of jazz, perhaps in ragtime, these would be not so much archaic-primitive utterances as the music of slaves; even in the indigenous music of Africa, the use of syncopation with tied beats seems only to be found in the lower classes. Psychologically, the structure of jazz's precursors is most reminiscent of a maid singing to herself. High society acquired its music of vitality—assuming it did not have it tailor-made from the start—from domesticated slaves, not savages. This could certainly explain the sado-masochistic traits of jazz. The archaism of jazz as a whole is as modern as the 'primitives' who produce it. The improvisatory immediacy on which half its success hinges is strictly a part of those attempts to break out of the fetishized world of commodities that desire to withdraw from it, yet not change it, and thus serve only to entangle even further. Whoever flees to jazz from a music that has become incomprehensible, or from the alienation of everyday life, becomes caught up in a system of musical commodities whose only advantage, compared with others, is that of not being immediately transparent; but which, in its decisive aspects—namely the unimprovised ones—crushes precisely those hopes for humanity with which the fugitive comes to it. With jazz, powerless subjectivity leaps from the world of commodities into the world of commodities; the system permits no escape. The element of ancient drives that resurfaces with it is not the freedom longed for but, rather, regression through oppression; the only archaism in jazz is that which modernity has created using the mechanism of oppression. It is not old, repressed drives that are liberated in the standardized rhythms and standardized outbursts: instead, we find new, repressed, mutilated drives freezing into masks of what has long since passed.

The modern archaism of jazz is nothing other than its commodity character. Its elemental aspects are those of the commodity: the rigid, almost timeless immobility within movement, the mask-like stereotypes, the union of wild agitation as the illusion of dynamism and the inexorability of the power controlling that agitation. Above all, however, it is the rule that an element of the market is as good as one of myth: jazz must therefore always be the same while always feigning novelty. This becomes clear through the expectation, both paradoxical and crippling for any genuine creativity, that composers should only ever write 'just like x', yet 'originally', drawing on originality for effect. Someone capable of achieving both at the same time would fulfil the ideal of the 'commercial';[3] the irreconcilability of these two expectations, however, as they apply to all commodities, may contain one of the most deep-seated contradictions of capitalism itself: the contradiction of a system that simultaneously has to develop and constrain productive powers. In jazz practice, the familiar usually dominates. The cards of jazz all seem to have been played; nothing new has been added to the basic elements since the foxtrot and tango—there have only been modifications of existing ones. Even the individual 'idea',[4] the concept of which is both socially and aesthetically problematic, remains largely dependent on an adherence to successful models; it is as thoroughly preformed by convention as only the basic types

14 English in the original. [Trans.]
15 See Adorno, 'Schubert', note 1 in this volume, p. 17. [Trans.]

themselves are. Only occasionally does the new, seemingly as an individual nuance yet purely fortuitous from the actual perspective of the individual, make an appearance: when, always almost unconsciously, it characterizes objective social tendencies—and is thus precisely *not* an individual nuance. Sometimes, albeit not remotely in the majority of cases, innovation leads to a piece's great success, for example with the first six-eight—'Valencia'—or the first rumba. Such pieces are mostly printed against the will of the publishers, as they involve a clear risk. The musical correlate of the demand for both the 'just like' and 'original' aspects, however, is that a successful jazz hit must combine an individual, characteristic aspect with complete banality in all others. By no means is this always vividness of melody; precisely this aspect is remarkably lacking in all cases. Any kind of detail is sufficient—in 'Valencia', for example, it is the slight irregularity of metre, something that eludes the consumers. This is why the publishers, like every propagandist, are concerned most of all with the title, the start of the lyrics, the first eight bars of the chorus and the end of the same, which is usually anticipated in motto-like fashion in the introduction. Everything else, in other words the musical development, is unimportant. The old principle of the rondo, which perhaps genuinely refers back to cult forms—namely to contrast the memorable round dance itself with the less independent or conspicuous secondary element—is used by jazz to ensure longevity, and thus sales: as a contrast to the chorus, the verses[5] are deliberately kept bland.

5 Adorno uses the words *Couplet* and *Refrain* for 'verse' and 'chorus', except where quoting English usage (the more common term for 'verse' is *Strophe*, but *Refrain* is the standard German word for 'chorus'). To avoid misleading connotations, they have consistently been translated, rather than retained as possible references to the rondo tradition or political cabaret in Germany and Austria. [Trans.]

The unity of the characteristic and the banal that provides the model for jazz does not only concern the shape of the jazz pieces in themselves. Rather, and most importantly, it is realized in the relationship between production and reproduction, the very factor to which jazz owes its reputation of spontaneous immediacy. The piece as such is—to exaggerate somewhat—banal; its rendition, which often disguises it to the point of unrecognizability, is characteristic, striking and virtuosic. Remarkably enough, it is the composer who has to vouch for convention in jazz; the one who modifies it is the arranger, sometimes connected to the publisher or the orchestra but always in close collaboration with the reproducers. And if one compares the performance of a good ensemble with the score of the piano reduction, for example, one could easily believe that the arrangers, not the composers, are the qualified musicians. It almost seems that completely indifferent material is best suited to being turned into jazz. One of the best known virtuoso pieces in jazz—'Tiger Rag', which orchestras like to use for a demonstration of their skills—is extremely simple as a composition. It would seem, then, that jazz has progressive tendencies in two directions, both different to intra-musical developments: firstly, through the reintroduction of the reproducer into the composition. Whereas the two are hopelessly estranged in art music, and the expressive markings in New Music leave no room for reproductive freedom—and, in fact, interpretation threatens to disappear entirely—it seems that in jazz, the reproducer can assert his rights anew in relation to the work, and hence man in relation to the object. That, at least, is how jazz has been understood by its more conscientious apologists: the ethos of Krenek's *Jonny spielt auf* testifies to this. But this ethos is Romantic, and it was only consistent when Krenek followed *Jonny* by composing his Romantic one-acters as epilegomena. For the intervention of the arranger or performer in jazz cannot, unlike the improvisation of a great actor, genuinely alter the material, make it a mere vehicle for subjective proclamation. Charm and showmanship, the new colours and the new rhythms, are simply inserted into the banal—just as the jazz vibrato is merely inserted into the rigid note, and syncopation into the basic metre; in fact, this interference in jazz is the achievement of the arrangement in its treatment of the composition. The contours of the latter, however, remain the same. Even in the most extravagant breaks of an arrangement, one can still hear the schema. The reproducer may pull on the chains of his boredom, he may indeed rattle them but he cannot break them. There is no more reproductive freedom than in art music. Even if composition were to permit it, the establishment of a jazz practice with a specific name for every minute subjective nuance would not be tolerated. If the human being cannot break through in the composition itself, he will certainly not do so through a reproduction that respectfully decorates that composition's bare walls to disguise their inhumanity—but, in so doing, helps that very inhumanity to continue in secret.

Secondly, however, one could see a progressive element in the disposition of the work process in jazz, which is based on an interplay between production and reproduction. It presents itself as a manifest division of labour that forms its 'material' in technical freedom and rationality without being dependent on its fortuity, the fortuity of production conditions or the people involved. One person has an 'idea', or what passes as such; a second person harmonizes it and makes a composition out of it; then the lyrics and the rest of the music are written, with the composer, or sometimes the arranger, further spicing up the rhythms and harmonies; then the whole thing is finally orchestrated by an expert. This much-touted division of labour, however, by no means takes place in accordance with the plan of rationalization—any more than it does in film production, for example. Its true reason is the need of the producer, of which he later makes the virtue of a collectivism that does not in fact apply. Whoever supposes a high capitalist rationality in the production process in jazz is believing in an illusion similar to that created by the flashing machinery which the jazz orchestra, with its metal instruments and raised piano lid, seeks to imitate, and which is designed to romanticize the commodity of jazz in the sense of a vague sophistication, a 'tempo of the times'. This rationalization, which declares itself so eagerly in the multiple authors' names on the title pages of piano scores, functions very inadequately; there is no trace of systematic collective work, and the contradiction between the 'material' and its technicization is self-evident— which shows the failure of this technicization. The division of labour essentially stems from the fact that the ideas often come from amateurs, in many cases from 'outsiders'[6] to jazz practice who are not able to orchestrate in a manner appropriate to jazz, and often cannot compose or even notate a piece; at the other end of the production process stands the consideration for the ensembles associated with the publisher, each with their particular economic interests. The fortuity of the initial material is by no means the result of this technical control but, rather, shows the intrusion of anarchy into the production process. The latter does not so much control the initial material as remain dependent on it and its fortuity: this limits the rationality of both the procedure and the result. Jazz experts obey the audience and its representatives in the production process; this process, however, is fundamentally antithetical to all technical consistency. If a piece's initiator were an expert, its success would be endangered from the outset. The division of labour in jazz is no more than a parody of future collective compositional procedures.

The most extreme case of the audience representative in the production process—which, as such, is alienated from the

---

6 English in the original (*Outsidern*). [Trans.]

individuals—is the amateur. He is the textbook example of a social factor that may have real effects on musical practice today; and is hence of exemplary significance, even if one does not estimate the number of amateurs involved in jazz as very high. This significance, admittedly, should not be understood as it is posited by jazz ideology itself. The amateur is not the fresh character without baggage whose originality has asserted itself against the routine of the industry; this belongs to the realm of the Negro myth. Nor is it the case that social reality intervenes in the work of art without images or illusions through him, or that through this intervention the work itself transcends into reality. As the advocate of society in jazz, he is rather the advocate of its extreme illusory nature. His function in the production process is to guarantee the apperceptibility of the product. His ideas are the precipitate of internalized conventions. Just as the businessman who is inspired to poetry on the occasion of a birthday celebration will not express himself with immediacy and urgency as a result of his literary naïveté but, rather, however uneducated he may be, will serve up an imitation of Heine, Scheffel or Busch—likewise the amateur duplicates the template of current jazz music, perhaps even taking the commercial chance of debasing it further. What entitles him, and not some other, to present this imitation to the public that has supplied him with it, is not so much the individual qualification of his ideas as the fact that he summons the hysterical lack of inhibitions to utter something he has not suffered through. He invests in the production of that very reservoir of unconscious musical and extra-musical associations, expectations, categories and errors that are eroded or made visible to musicians as they learn their craft, and, once lost, could never be reconstructed. Yes this reservoir constitutes a substantial, perhaps even the decisive, condition for audience appeal: an inestimable contribution to commercial success. The helplessness of the one who is excluded from the specialized craft, who is almost afraid of music as if it were some social power and seeks out of this fear to adapt to it, but without succeeding—this helplessness is as essential an ingredient as the normal experience and awareness of the regular listener. For helplessness—the whimpering vibrato—and normal consciousness—banality—belong together as constituents of jazz itself as a form. The nature of the amateur is the subjective correlate of that objective formal structure. His mistakes are a part of jazz's *a priori* in the same way that, as shown by Karl Kraus and thoroughly confirmed by everyday experience, printing errors belong to that of newspapers. Errors of musical orthography, grammar and syntax can be identified in the piano versions—i.e. the originals—of many of the most successful hits; they are continued in the more subtle discrepancies that inevitably appear in elevated jazz pieces; for jazz is fundamentally inconsistent. If the cracks in the musical surface are starting to close up in newer, especially American literature, if there are fewer obvious mistakes and dilettantes are being excluded, this does not constitute any 'progress' in jazz. While it is gradually separating out towards extremes—'sweet music' and marches—the jazz core, namely hot music, is becoming stable on an artisanally intermediate level of care and taste that tames those improvisatory elements of eruption still sometimes at work in the original conception of jazz, resulting in symphonic simplicity and grandeur. Stabilized jazz is the kind that presents itself as 'symphonic', as autonomous art, but in so doing dispenses once and for all with those intentions that previously seemed to lead to collective immediacy. It makes itself subject to the standards of art music, but this only reveals how underdeveloped it is by comparison.

For the 'taste' of jazz and the ferments of its modernity, which is the opposite and corrective of the amateur, are as artistically fraudulent as, conversely, its immediacy. The expert

taste, which assesses and refines the conventional, has itself
long since become conventional; its modernity rests exclusively
on methods of the most recent musical modernity. They are,
simply put, those of musical impressionism. The coloured
composer Duke Ellington, a trained musician and main representative of the current 'classical', stabilized jazz, names
Debussy and Delius as his favourite composers. Except for the
'hot' rhythms, all the more subtle characteristics of jazz refer
back to that style, and it is hardly an exaggeration to say that
the latter only gained widespread recognition via the detour
of jazz: in Parisian night clubs, one can hear Debussy and
Ravel played between the rumba and the Charleston. The
impressionist influence is most obvious in the harmony. Ninth
chords, added sixths and other mixtures such as the stereotypical 'blue chord',[7] parallel chord movements and whatever vertical attractions jazz has to offer, are all borrowed from
Debussy. But the treatment of melodies, especially in the more
consistent pieces, is based on impressionist models. The dissolution into tiny motivic formulas that do not develop
dynamically, but are rather repeated statically, only being
altered rhythmically and apparently circling some immovable
centre, is specifically impressionistic. But it is robbed of its
formal sense in jazz: impressionism is adopted and simultaneously depraved. In Debussy, melodic commas form spaces of
time and colour from within themselves, according to the constructive command of subjectivity; in jazz, however, they—
like the false metres of hot music—are subsumed under the
metric-harmonic schema of the 'normal', cadential eight-bar
period. The subjective-functional division of the melody
remains powerless, as the imposition of eight-bar units almost
relegates it to the status of a melodic upper-voice figure that
merely plays with its particles, instead of composing a new

7 English in the original. [Trans.]

figure with them; the same occurs with the complex harmonies, which are caught once more by the very cadence from which their floating sonorities seemed about to escape. In jazz, even older elements must first be made harmless and taken out of their historical development before they can become marketable. On the market, the impressionistic ingredients function as an attraction. Previously isolated within the concert hall and artist's studio, they seem modern; in their crude schema, they seem subtly nuanced; and for the wider audience, as difficult as it may be to comprehend, even daring and subversive; they feign an advanced character abstractly. But the individual element that, with impressionism, is inserted into jazz, is not there by virtue of itself and does not belong to itself. It has long since become rigid, formulaic, exhausted—now the individual no less than the social convention before it. It is so easy to rid of its formal sense because it had already left it, in epigonal post-Debussy music as well as in jazz; being conventional, it can now be inserted seamlessly into convention. The individual modern element in jazz is as illusory as the collective archaic element.

Jazz shares the illusory character of the individual with salon music, to which impressionism itself tends in the works of its lesser representatives. The roots of jazz extend far into the salon style; it is from that style, drastically put, that it takes its espressivo and all those aspects in which some spiritual quality seeks to convey itself. The jazz vibrato is probably taken first of all from the cafe violinist who is resurrected in tango. Impressionist harmony always has a tinge of the sentimental harmony of the salon. The peculiar style of the whispering jazz singers, who are the most difficult to classify according to the norm, largely mirrors that of the *café concert*. The subjective pole of jazz—subjectivity itself taken strictly as a social product, a reified commodity—is salon music; it is from its stirrings that jazz trembles. If one wished to define the interference phenomenon in jazz in concrete, general stylistic terms, one could call it a combination of salon music and the march. The former represents an individuality that is not one in reality, merely its socially produced illusion; the latter is an equally fictitious community formed only by forcing atoms to move in a common direction. The effectiveness of the march principle in jazz is evident. The basic rhythm of the continuo instruments and bass drum consistently coincides with that of the march, and jazz could—since the six-eights—very easily change into the march. The connection is based in history: one of the bass wind instruments used in jazz is the sousaphone, named after a composer of marches. And it is not only the saxophone that came from military bands; the entire division of the jazz orchestra into melody, bass, 'obbligato' accompanying and mere filler instruments is identical to that of marching bands. This is why jazz is well-suited to fascist uses. It is especially popular in Italy, like the products of cubist artisanship. The ban in Germany is connected to the facade of resorting to pre-capitalist, feudal forms of immediacy and labelling them socialist. But, typically enough, this ban has no power. The battle against the saxophone has been calmed by the music organizations and the instrument industry; jazz itself continues unperturbed under other names, even in the radio; only the more advanced, neo-objectively upper-class hot music, which is difficult for the layperson to understand, has fallen victim to it. Not only is march-like jazz tolerated. The new marches, of the kind made especially well known through the cinema, are in fact descended directly from jazz.

The relationship between salon music and the march, which mingle in jazz, results from the demythologizing tendency of dance itself: the transformation of dance into bourgeois walking—possibly that of individuals out of the salon. The forerunners of jazz, before the war, were known as 'steps': they took their name from the stepping movement, that is to say from a component of walking. The social function of jazz, the tendency towards a demystification of dance whose history still needs to be written, must be transformed into its own opposite, the new magic, through the force of its own consistency. Once it is commanded rhythmically, the walking of the bourgeois individuals, now no longer magically bound, turns into marching. To the extent that dancing means synchronized movement, the tendency towards marching is present from the outset in walking dance; hence, jazz is originally a continuation of the march, and its history simply conceals the relationship. Certainly, the casual walking that jazz accompanies seems, at first sight, to be the opposite of marching. It seems to release the dancer from the captivity of precise gestures into the fortuity of everyday life which not even dance can enable the dancer to escape; in reality, however, it playfully glorifies it as a hidden order. With jazz, it believes, the contingency of individual existence wins out over its social rules, asserting that this is desirable. Jazz syncopation seeks to make the measured ritual a thing of the past; at times, it sounds as if the music were sacrificing its distance and aesthetic pictoriality in favour of the incarnated empiricism of the ordered yet fortuitous life. In films, jazz seems best suited to the accompaniment of events that are contingent and, in a twofold sense, prosaic: when people are shown strolling and chatting at a coast, or a woman is struggling with her shoe. At such moments, jazz fits the situation so well that it barely even enters the consciousness. Hence, also the significance of the hits of contingency, in which a chance word, as a scrap of everyday reality, becomes a shell from within which the music unfolds. Often enough, bananas and cheese at the train station or Aunt Paula eating her tomatoes have beaten out the erotic and geographical competition.

One can certainly not trust this contingency very far. The hits of contingency all too readily offer a—by no means unconscious—sexual meaning: they all tend towards the dirty joke. The cheese appeals to anal regression, the bananas mock the woman's substitute gratification; the more absurd the nonsense, the more palpable the sex appeal.[8] Walking itself—as evidenced by different languages—is directly related to coitus: the walking rhythm resembles the sexual, and if the new dances have demystified the erotic magic of the old ones, they have—showing a more advanced side, at least here, than one would expect—replaced it with the drastic insinuation of the sexual act. This is taken to the extreme by some dance academies where taxi girls are supplied with whom to carry out walking dances, such that they occasionally bring the men to orgasm; hence, the dance becomes a means of sexual gratification while simultaneously respecting the ideal of virginity. It is the sexual element in jazz that has incurred the hatred of ascetic petty-bourgeois groups.

This sexual element, however, is deliberately underlined by all jazz. In contrast to what psychoanalysis is accustomed to, one is inclined to deem—using its concepts—the symbolic representation of sexual union the manifest dream content of jazz, which is intended to be reinforced rather than censored through the suggestions in the text and the music. One cannot help but suspect that the crude and rather transparent sexual secrecy of jazz is only meant to conceal a second, deeper and more dangerous, secret. The first would be no different from that which gave early operettas such as *Ein Walzertraum* their title and plot; this would not affect the character of modernity found in jazz. The second secret, however, can be presumed a social one. In the light of the connection between jazz and contingency, one could well insist on finding the latent dream idea. For, as something social, it is not exhausted in sexual meaning: the social meaning must be wrested from it, even in

8 English in the original. [Trans.]

the sexual. Socially too, jazz initially offers a simple solution: the rondo-like combination of verse and chorus that it shares with traditional forms of light vocal music. With the terms 'verse' and 'chorus', the names and their content invoke the old relationship between the leading singer or dancer and the collective. The individual speaks isolated, as it were, in the verse; narrating modestly and unobtrusively, and not in the tone of a communal hymn, in the chorus—which answers a question posed in the form of the imperfect cadence—before receiving affirmation and being objectified as a part of society. The ritual is directed at individuals as its audience. The unconscious process intended for, and probably carried out by, the audience is thus initially one of identification. The individual in the audience experiences itself primarily as the verse ego, then feels secure in the chorus, identifying itself with the refrain collective, joining it in dance and thus finding sexual fulfilment. This is the well-known dream layer of jazz; it resembles that in films which, under the heading of the wish-fulfilment fantasy, has been dealt with time and again in all its trivial wit. At least, like the corresponding films, it already shows the primacy of society over an individual, even though the individual experiences itself as the defining factor. The process of production is particularly characteristic: it realizes the primacy of the chorus over the verse through the fact that the former is always written first and as the main element, whereas the verse is only sought afterwards; the individual, the 'hero' of the verse, is immaterial in the song's production. Often the verse relates some hare-brained background to the chorus, simply in order to connect the two at all. In orchestral arrangements the verse steps back entirely: the piece begins with the chorus and the verse is only heard once, like a rondo episode; repetitions and variations are only applied to the chorus. And only the chorus is actually sung. The piano editions, on the other hand, which are directed more at the private person, contain the full text as well as the music for both the verse and the chorus.

If theory is to penetrate to the centre of the social function of jazz behind such findings, or, in psychological terms, to the latent dream thought, namely the concretely and historically determined constellation of social identification and sexual drives for which jazz forms the scene, it must address the problem of contingency in relation to hot music—even if the latter, at least in Europe, has not established itself among a wider audience. For compared with the minima of the march and salon music, hot music stands as the attainable maximum; it is from hot music, if at all, that the 'idea' of that maximum can be constructed. The range of hot elements extends from artfully executed improvisation through breaks and false metres to the most fundamental case, the syncopation that seems to stumble out of the basic rhythm. These are contrasted with the norm, namely the consistent beat. They certainly have a better claim to signifying the jazz subject than its archaic rudiment, the verse: individual contingency embodies itself in their deviations. The jazz subject is clumsy, yet tends towards improvisation nonetheless; it stands as the self in opposition to the abstractly superordinate authority, but ultimately remains interchangeable; it lends it expression without moving it through expression. Thus its nature is paradox. The fact that it is itself preformed by convention and only seemingly belongs to itself, like the musical expression of the hot passages, forces one to conclude that the subject is not a 'free', lyrical one elevated into the collective but, rather, constrained in its origin: a victim of the collective. In this, however, jazz simultaneously re-establishes the prehistoric meaning of the fixed verse-chorus relationship anew at its own moment: for the leading dancer or singer is barely more than a human sacrifice, replaced or not. It is perhaps very helpful for the illumination of jazz in this context that the only significant composer at all close to jazz, namely Stravinsky, made the sacrifice of a human being—and the leading dancer, no less— the subject of his central work *Le Sacre du Printemps*, which became famous precisely for its artful syncopations; a sacrifice that is not so much dramatically interpreted as ritually accompanied by the music. The jazz subject's sense of being a victim is admittedly, now truly subject to dream censorship, weakened. It deviates from the collective as the syncopation deviates from the accents on the strong beats; it refuses to follow the given majority, which existed before it and is independent of it—whether out of protest, clumsiness or both—until, in a peculiar election of grace, it is received into the collective or, rather, assigned its place within it. It resists until the music proves, ironically and after the fact, that it was part of the collective from the outset; that the subject, itself a part of this society, cannot actually deviate from it at all; that its apparent clumsiness is in fact virtuosity of integration; and that—in every sense, and first and foremost the sexual—being unable precisely means being able, being able like the rest and even being *more* able than the rest.

The most precise forerunner of this jazz subject was developed in pre-war vaudeville; this historical question of whether the first tap-dances came from vaudeville would therefore be of the utmost factual importance in an elaborated theory of jazz. One can presume the eccentric to be the model for the jazz subject: one of the oldest and most famous jazz-like pieces of art music, a Debussy prelude written before the war, bears the title 'Général Lavine, Excentric', referring to tap-dance with the expressive marking 'Dans le style et le Mouvement d'un Cake-Walk'. The eccentric can first of all be understood as the exact opposite of the clown. While the clown is the one whose anarchic and archaic immediacy does not fit into reified bourgeois life, becomes laughable to it, but simultaneously—

sporadically—makes it appear laughable itself, the eccentric certainly also deviates from the purposeful regularity—the 'rhythm'—of bourgeois life; he is as much of a misfit and a loner as the clown, and may indeed tend towards the laughable at times. But his deviation is immediately apparent: not as powerlessness but, rather, as superiority—or at least the semblance thereof. The eccentric is met with laughter, but this laughter dies in shocked silence; and with the disappearance of his ridiculousness, that of society also elegantly vanishes into obscurity. The rhythm of his wilfulness is integrated seamlessly into a larger, ordered one, and his failure is located not beneath but, rather, above the norm: he obeys the law but is still different. This behaviour, with a gradual abandonment of the traits of playful superiority and liberal otherness, is adopted by the hot subject. The surface aspects of the best bands' performances already show traits of the eccentric. The juggling skills of the drummers, lightning-fast changes of instrument, improvisations that sound ridiculously wrong in the first bar only to prove right in the last; deliberate stumbling, meaningfully meaningless spinning around—all this is common to the more virtuoso kind of jazz performance and the eccentrics. The rhythmic categories of hot music itself are the categories of the eccentric. The syncopations—unlike the opposite variety, those of Beethoven—are not expressions of an accumulated subjective force directing itself against the given until it produces the new law from within itself. They are aimless; they lead nowhere and are arbitrarily revoked by an undialectical, mathematical resolution within the main beats. They are simply instances of coming too early, just as fear leads to premature orgasm and impotence expresses itself in early and incomplete orgasm. Syncopation in jazz is heavily relativized—and, once again resembling impotence, even mocked—by the basic rhythm, or rather the basic metre, which is absolutely fixed from the outset and maintained strictly in tempo and modified only through stresses. It expresses mockery and suffering equally in bleak ambiguity. The hot ego starts off as a clown, too feeble to follow the unproblematically posited collective norm, tottering insecurely in a similar fashion to some figures in American film grotesques, such as Harold Lloyd or sometimes even Chaplin. The decisive interventional tendency of jazz lies in the fact that this subject of weakness integrates itself precisely through its weakness—as if it were actually being rewarded for it—into the collective that made it so weak in the first place, and whose standard it cannot meet in its weakness. Psychologically speaking, jazz squares the circle. The contingent ego, as a member of the bourgeois class, is itself fundamentally and blindly at the mercy of the social law. In coming to fear the society's authority and to experience it as the threat of castration—in immediate terms: the fear of impotence—it identifies with the very authority that it should fear, but now suddenly belongs to it too and is allowed to join in the dance. The sex appeal[9] of jazz is a command: parry and you can take part too, and the dream thought, as full of contradictions as the reality in which it is dreamed, is: I can only be potent if I allow myself to be emasculated. The relationship between the jazz subject as represented by the hot elements and the social authority, the given metric law, is ambivalent in both musico-material and socio-psychological terms. The subject steps out of line and opposes the order out of fear; but its opposition, as that of an isolated individual which transpires as merely socially determined precisely in its isolation, is illusory. It relinquishes its individuality—namely syncopation—out of fear, but this individuality itself is nothing but fear; it sacrifices an individuality it does not possess, and, in its mutilated state, it feels one with the mutilating power, projecting it upon itself in such a way that it thinks it has 'ability' of its own. The deviating ego remains a piece of the total society, only one that is initially concealed, and the practice of jazz is

9 English in the original. [Trans.]

not so much its dialectical transformation and 'sublation' in the true sense as, rather, the rigid ritual of exposing a social character. The traits of weakness are implicit in the 'parodistic' or comic ones that are clearly found in hot passages, though no one really knows what is being parodied. At the same time, however, they present—in the spirit of the eccentric—the playful superiority of the individual over society; it is because it knows the rules of the game precisely that it can dare not to keep strictly to them. It is only this ironic surplus that makes jazz suspicious, and this is what is meant by those who hate it for its squawking and cacophony but not its adaptation of syncopation; fascism only leaves out the ironic surplus, not the model of rhythmic progression. For the specification of the individual in jazz is never, and never has been, that of an advancing productive power, only that of neurotic weakness—just as the basic musical models of the 'deviating' hot subject itself remain entirely banal and conventional. This is perhaps why oppressed peoples are particularly qualified for jazz: one could say that they demonstrate the mechanism of identifying with one's own oppression to those liberals who are not yet sufficiently mutilated themselves.

Jazz, the amalgam of the march and salon music, is a false one: that of a destroyed subjective element and a social power that produces, destroys and, through destruction, objectifies it. This applies both to the unity of the pseudo-free and pseudo-immediate with the march-like collective metronome and also at a colouristic level: to subjective-expressive sounds; to a subjective utterance that always cancels itself out by revealing itself as mechanical. Of all instruments, it is the unbearable Wurlitzer organ that shows these colours most faithfully—its sound exposes the nature of the jazz vibrato once and for all. It is functionally equivalent to the other sonic characteristics of jazz—distortion through mutes in wind instruments; the chirping, and thus vibrating, note repetitions on the plucked

instruments banjo and ukulele; the drawing of the harmon-
ica—in the sense that they all modify an 'objective' sound but
only so far that it remains inevitably manifest. It may be subjected to irony, but usually it itself subjects to irony the whimpering that helplessly seeks to survive in it. The objective
sound is veneered with a subjective expression that cannot
dominate it, and is thus constitutively ridiculous and pitiful
in its effect. The comic and grotesque elements in jazz, as well
as the anal, can therefore never be separated from the sentimental ones. They characterize a subjectivity rebelling against
a collective power which, however, it itself 'is'; thus its rebellion
appears laughable, and is suppressed by the drum as the syncopation is suppressed by the beat. Only in situations where
irony—regardless of its object—and the expression of subjectivity —whichever it might be—are considered suspicious can
this sound no longer be tolerated. Then it is replaced by the
militarily noble, devilishly euphonious sound of symphonic
jazz marches, whose blank unanimity does not even leave
room for the illusion of humanity anymore. When this occurs,
jazz has divided itself into the two poles from which it originated, while hot music, damned to premature classicism, leads
its meagre specialist existence in the middle. By that point,
however, jazz is beyond remedy in any case.

1936

OXFORD ADDITIONS

The title of Debussy's prelude 'Général Lavine, excentric'
seems to anticipate the idea of jazz programmatically. If one
gives the name its German meaning[10]—which is admittedly

10 The German word *Lawine* means 'avalanche'. [Trans.]

only accessible in French through *avalanche*—it refers to something breaking away and falling uncontrollably, something frightening; but the avalanche, being identical to destructive social authority, is a general. At the same time, the general is mocked by being named like an avalanche, just as, during the same time (around 1910), when the first teddy bears and the diabolo made their appearance, the rank of consul was mocked through the fact that uniformed monkeys were called 'Consul Peter'. They used to be put on show riding bicycles. The paradoxical creature that is mocked for being mutilated by society while being glorified as its sovereign is the eccentric. At the end of the prelude, he is presented in the spotlight, as it were, and the music's movement comes to a halt; this could easily be the model for the jazz subject, which, compulsively invariant, repeats the same tableau.

The truly decisive feature of the jazz subject is that, despite its individual character, it does not belong to itself at all; that the individual traits with which it protests against the social authority are in fact the very scars of mutilation left by it. This true identity reveals itself in the fear with which it identifies with society: this lends the jazz ritual its peculiarly affirmative character. Only because it is actually identical to the social principle can it identify with it psychologically and relish its own mutilation.

Jazz and pogroms go together. Zez Confrey, the author of the artful virtuoso piece *Kitten on the Keys*, named a different one *Poor Buttermilk*, evidently as a depiction of a Jew presented in a comical pitiful manner by the music. This motif already appeared in Mussorgsky's *Pictures at an Exhibition*. In the case of a pogrom, this combination of sentimental and comic elements is reversed as the joke that turns into cruelty. It is the gesture of someone in sudden, unbearable pain starting to dance because they 'cannot stand upright any more'. It lives on in the shrugging of shoulders.—Benjamin says: in jazz, one sees the gestures of people who might appear in a pogrom: clumsy people who are forced to be skilful.—I remember clearly my shock upon reading the word 'jazz' for the first time. It could plausibly be derived from the German word *Hatz* [hunt],[11] conjuring up the pursuit of a slower victim by bloodhounds. At any rate, this collection of letters seems to contain the same thread of castration that the jazz orchestra represents with its open piano lid. There can be no doubt about the symbolic character of this piano lid; whenever a grand piano is shown in American films, even in the most intimate duets, the lid is open—in obvious contradiction to the acoustic demands of the situation. The name for the last of jazz's precursors falls into the same context: ragtime. Jazz wants to do the same to fixed time as to a fixed body: to tear it to rags. *Tiger Rag.* 'Ragging time' through syncopation is ambivalent. It simultaneously expresses that opposing but illusory subjectivity which rebels against the regularity of time, and the regression dictated by the objective authority, which suppresses the historical experience of time in which the dancing body could share, undertaking to keep the powerless body in the realm of the timeless—what has been—and mutilating the body *itself*.

Concerning the relationship between jazz and salon music: when the ostensibly free, unfettered jazz subject moves from the salon to the march, this does not relate only to the—fundamentally illusory—expression of its subjectivity, but also to the rhythmic relationship with the norm itself. The dialectical precursor to the breaks is the rubato of salon music—though

11 The word 'jazz' is sometimes pronounced by German-speakers as if it were a German word (thus rhyming with *Hatz*), and this would have been much more widespread in Adorno's time. [Trans.]

they do not share its dialectical nature. For in the rubato, subjectivity, at least, claims to have some force, as illusory as it
may be. It consists essentially in the lengthening of notes, like
the long breath for which singers are praised. Accelerations in
salon music are always like the 'elegant', albeit devalued bows
of an equal in society. He keeps the time he has gained as a
possession; the basic rhythm cannot take it away from him.
The gesture corresponding to the rare cases of an accelerating
rubato in salon music would be that of a lady gathering up
the train of her dress. The jazz rubato is always simply the pre-
maturity of weakness; the subject flees from the system into
the system. There is no gained time left over: the atom and
the totality add up completely. Even the integration into the
whole, that is to say the confirmation, still has the character
of powerlessness. The rhythms added to complete the metre
are usually shorter models than the false metres, and thus further accelerations; this perhaps supplies the precise technical
correlate for the interpretation that integration occurs precisely
through castration. If one were looking for the appropriate
illustrative gesture, one could think of Claudette Colbert and
the enigmatically sad smile with which she lifts her skirt in *It
Happened One Night*. Even where jazz erupts, even where sexuality seems affirmed, it occurs with the coquetry of weakness;
the woman who is abandoned to eroticism becomes the ideological glorification of the socially abandoned human being.

If the jazz subject had a German name—and its internation-
ality surely permits the bestowal of one—it could only be Peter.
Consul Peter; poor, clumsy Peter; Peter Schlemihl, black
Peter;[12] the lonely, helpless man left by the girls: he in particular

12 The card game *Schwarzer Peter* is a German version of Old Maid, in
which the player left holding the odd card out—named *Schwarzer Peter*,
'Black Peter'—loses. The phrase is used metaphorically to indicate the
shifting of blame or responsibility; *jemandem dem Schwarzen Peter*

has changed his function to such a degree that a journalist wrote that every man with erotic chances could now stake a claim to the name Peter. The Bohemians Hille and Altenberg, outcasts and darlings at once, were the first to embody the fate of poor Peter. Perhaps the figure is based on the theological model of St Peter, whom Jesus chose as the foundation of his church even though he denied him three times. Today, there may be millions of girls who call their lovers Peter in moments of intimacy; for all men have become Peter, and, once the secret is out, there no longer seems to be any shame in it—in fact, this disclosure occasions his reception, and his other-ness holds the last trace of immediate, incommensurable individuality as an illusion. One finds a brutal expression of this in pre-war Berlin operettas, whose greatest hit was called *Puppchen* [Dolly]: both Peter and the jazz subject *in statu pupillari*. 'Everyone calls me Puppchen, I just love it': simul-taneous mockery and enjoyment of the name as a brand of social commodity. Puppchen is a man. When the song goes: 'Puppchen, you're my shining star, Puppchen, you're good enough to eat'—is this oral love not the literal archetype of love in jazz, integration as absorption and extermination? The music of *Puppchen* came from the Metropol-Theater[13] at the turn of the century; it was wiped out by the war. But all light music after it was a commentary on that same text.

The fulfilment of jazz's function, as a constitutively uncon-scious one, becomes possible through the fact that it is not generally perceived in its full momentary presence but, rather,

zuschieben, literally 'giving someone (the card) Black Peter', is equivalent to 'passing the buck'. *Schwarzer Peter* was the nickname of the famous German outlaw Johann Peter Petri (1752–1812), and it is possible that the name originates from him. [Trans.]

13 This was a theatre in Berlin, founded in 1898, that was renowned for its cabaret and operetta productions. It closed in 1997. [Trans.]

as an accompaniment to dancing or a background to conversation. It does not claim the status of a synthetic unity of apperception of the kind that, in the case of an autonomous work of art, makes the recipient forget the partial aspects forming it. Because the listener is not confronted with the objectification of the work, and listens at a completely different level to the one on which such unity constitutes itself, he can easily enough identify with the partial jazz subject and will be all the more able to do so the less he 'listens'. There is truly, as the saying goes, a world of difference between the listener and the identification of the subject in a Beethoven sonata: that of the work. It calls for an attentiveness that, precisely through taking hold of the work actively and subjectively, distances itself from it at the same time. An inattentive reception of jazz does no work on the music—and hence does not distance itself from it. If people actually listened to jazz properly, it would lose its power; rather than identifying with it, they would identify the music itself. This is expressed precisely by the frequently aired opinion that jazz is extremely pleasant to dance to but repulsive to listen to, though this also testifies to the false consciousness of those who dream what they dare not think.

It is in keeping with the stabilization of hot music on a medium artisanal level that the most effective ferment of jazz's ironic surplus in relation to existing circumstances, its true clown element, namely the scandalous use of 'classical' music as its starting material, has steadily decreased in the last ten years. This respect for cultural artefacts is at par with the fiction that the starting material, whose contingency was reinforced by the choice of classical models, is substantial and meaningful in itself—that the jazz subject is not a clown, hardly even an eccentric anymore but, rather, a hero. The somewhat amorphous concept of swing music,[14] which at least

14 English in the original. [Trans.]

emphasizes the melodic character of the individual 'idea' rather than rhythmic escapades, and uses a triplet rhythm that, in relation to the actual beat, is always somewhat irrational, falls into the same category as the repeated declarations of the German Reichsmusikkammer against the jazzing up of classical music.

The social function can perhaps be studied best in the behaviour of the dancers. They follow the objective rhythm without ever 'dancing out' the break; and one of the keys to the success of Mickey Mouse is the fact that he alone converts all the breaks into visual elements. The only ambition of the dancers in relation to the syncopations, however, is not to let themselves be driven mad by them. If they succeed, this offers them the pleasure gain of identifying with the objective authority and the oppression of the jazz subject at the same time. They do not realize that they themselves are this subject, any more than they comprehend the rhythmic form of the breaks. They simply identify with it in the possibility of erring or stumbling; all more explicit references in the dance moves have increasingly disappeared, becoming the domain of specialized 'step dancers',[15] the equivalent of the hot orchestras. Now the originally improvisatory element of protest is perceived only as a contestation of weakness.

One element of the interference character of jazz would seem to be the ambiguity of the 'eruptive' timbres of the saxophone or the muted trumpet. It is the ambiguity of the feigned mating call and the parodied cry of fear. Fear is ridiculed at the same time as being presented as sensuality—sexual inability as ability, even just in the singular figure of the break. For the jazz subject, this historical figure contains the ambivalence of libido and fear. While psychoanalysis understands fear as

15 English in the original. [Trans.]

repressed libido, jazz asserts that the utterance of fear is itself libidinous. *Tiger Rag*: it presents the mating call of the tiger at the same time as the fear of being eaten or castrated by it.

The socially unconformed element of jazz may lie in its position between the sexes. In undermining genital sexuality, the mechanism of mutilation and integration undermines the primary gender differences. While the sound of the jazz instruments approaches that of the human voice, and while the whispering of the jazz singers becomes similar to the timbre of the muted trumpet, it loses its specific gender character. It is impossible to agnosticize a muted trumpet as masculine-heroic; it is impossible to describe the anthropoid tone of the saxophone as the voice of a noble maiden, as Berlioz still did with that of the clarinet (which is still its relative). The reactionary aesthetician Waltershausen already referred to the bisexual character of the saxophone in a polemic. The mutilation of the genitally centred subject, of which jazz represents the ritual implementation, releases the partial drives at the moment of regression. Certainly they are immediately repressed through false integration and only then—in their social configuration—become pernicious: homosexuality turns into sworn collective, sadism into terror. But they resurface to oppose patriarchal genitality; for a moment, they are inflammatory. This is precisely what the dialectic of jazz has in common with the most advanced art music. In *Die glückliche Hand* or *Wozzeck*, the music calls on the partial drives by their names: this, not some Romantic element of 'espressivo', is what defines the expressionist phase of New Music. The actual timbres with which they present themselves, however, the colours that are initially hissing and garish but then muted once more—which, to use Schönberg's own phrase, one could call the 'muffled forte'—are the same ones that appear in jazz as 'parodistic'.

One can study the functional change of technical musical means especially intensely in the way that the different approaches to playing become similar in jazz. By introducing the jazz orchestra, commodity music first of all catches up with some of the results of art music—in a comparable fashion to its adoption of impressionist harmonies and colours. Following the tendency towards a functionalization of chromatic harmony, Wagner's orchestra had tended towards making the various techniques and timbres so similar to one another that they could be seamlessly connected: composition became an 'art of transition'. The most important connecting instrument, the French horn, served this purpose explicitly. But the invention of the saxophone, which is certainly quite characteristic of jazz, can be attributed to the same tendency. It was intended to mediate between brass and woodwind instruments; in its material it belongs to the former, in its mode of playing to the latter. This is the technical reason for its 'intersexual' character. One could relate it to that manner of psychological differentiation which, as something 'decadent', was considered by Nietzsche to be the most conspicuous of Wagner's traits: powerless men filled with yearning, like Tannhäuser, Tristan or Parsifal, suffer from it and are saved by it; Amfortas is unquestionably a monumental jazz subject. The initiative is passed on to the women. The functionalized sound of jazz introduces all these tendencies into light music. At the same time, however, they are deprived of their meaning. Whereas the sound of the smallest transitions and 'relationships', in Riemann's sense of functional harmony, leads to the music of a 'functional' society in Wagner, and equally serves the expression of social interdependence as much as that of the differentiated, internally functional individual, the same instrumental means in jazz—though fundamentally different, namely static, in their harmony—correspond to the tendency to turn and accordingly degrade individuals into interchangeable elements in the face of the governing totality. 'And in the end it's all the same whether I do it or you do'—this applies as much to the impotent lover, the heir of the 'sickly' Tristan and Amfortas, as to the muted trumpet and the saxophone. The jazz singer, reified, becomes like them; even externally, as Haselberg observed, through the use of the megaphone. At the same time, the element of 'progress' that still defined Wagnerian totality as its temporal telos is cut off. All the totality does is reproduce itself; it posits all relationships, only to absorb them immediately once more and hold on to them. Jazz, like the walking dancers in the crowded hall, does not go anywhere; its dynamism is absorbed by the very schema that produces it. It is precisely this change that 'functional' society itself has gone through. It went from the 'totality' as which Hegel still perceived it to a 'system' at the very moment when the irrationalist trend to which jazz belongs banished those systems, one of which is jazz.

1937

Ernst Krenek became famous as a very young man around 1920, at the time of the Donaueschingen music festivals and those in Salzburg, when the latter city and its International Society for Contemporary Music were identified with the avant-garde. Alongside Hindemith, Krenek was the most striking exponent of the second generation of radical composers following Schönberg, his closest students, and also Stravinsky and Bartók. His talent, supported by such performers as Scherchen, Schnabel and Erdmann, an eruptive and highly original force, was plain to see. From the day he completed his studies, however, it had been accompanied by something disconcerting and shocking, something that resisted understanding—far more than Hindemith, whose wildest pieces still remained comprehensible if only through their assured instrumental realization. Today, when all New Music is listened to with fatally respectful ears and scarcely unbalances its well-informed audiences, it is difficult to imagine the aggression radiated by the young Krenek's works—his first two symphonies, the First String Quartet, or the Toccata and Chaconne for piano, which led to a scandal. The world premiere of the Second Symphony under Laugs, which took place in Kassel in 1923, was probably no less potent in its effect than the legendary premieres before the First World War, such as Berg's *Altenberg-Lieder* or *Le Sacre du Printemps*. The final movement, an adagio, ended in that performance with a fortissimo that went beyond all acceptable standards, a dissonant chord progression in the brass analogous to a gaping black abyss threatening to swallow the earth from the outside. Such panic has surely not been caused by any music since—not even, strangely enough, by later performances of that symphony. And yet, if one reads the scores again today, Krenek's pieces from that time were by no means excessively complicated or extreme in their compositional make-up. Yet I remember a package of sheet music I received from Vienna around that time, containing the freshly published scores of Anton Webern's Five Movements for String Quartet and Krenek's First String Quartet. Though the Webern pieces were far more fragmented, detailed, masterful and advanced in their treatment of the material, Krenek's piece, which was somewhat primitive by comparison (though without any of the conventional motoric primitivism), showed an aspect of modernity— that modernity whose compelling and forceful nature lies in the fact that it takes where others give—that was absent from Webern's far more authentic short pieces.

One can only understand Krenek if one understands this ferment of the incomprehensible. Benjamin's concept of aura may be helpful:

> The definition of the aura as a 'unique phenomenon of a distance, however close it may be' represents nothing but the formulation of the cult value of the work of art in categories of space and time perception. Distance is the opposite of closeness. The essentially distant object is the unapproachable one. Unapproachability is indeed a major quality of the cult image. True to its nature, it remains 'distant, however close it may be'. The closeness which one may gain from its subject matter does not impair the distance which it retains in its appearance.[1]

Or: 'Experiencing the aura of a phenomenon means bestowing upon it the ability to raise its glance.'[2] Now music is surely the auratic art *par excellence*, and herein lies its specific difficulty today: a musical context only comes about if the individual phenomenon is more than simply itself, if it transcends into the non-present, the distant; and this context of meaning, the medium of musical logic, inevitably forms some kind of atmosphere around music. The old Romantic thesis that music is the ultimate Romantic art refers to this. Though music can never escape from this, that of the young Krenek—in sharp contrast to the other neo-objectivist and neoclassicist composers—was the first that sought, on its own strength, to break through musical aura to which even the most extreme works of Schönberg, Webern and Berg had still clung, and which was certainly not questioned by semi-progressive composers, even those who adopted the disdainful tone. His early music attempts to draw the musical dimension of distance into the music; it does not raise its glance any more than a floodlight. It does not float away, and one cannot listen attentively to it; rather, it moves towards the listener like some gruesome vehicle—too close for dreaming but too hard for playing. Here the music seeks to disrupt its own atmosphere; its whole manner is a revolt against musical transcendence. Its magical effect was precisely the horror at that demystification, at an unconscious will to rid the music of its last semblance of meaningful content that is no longer secure yet is the only thing holding it together. The music rebels with magnificent unhelpfulness against meaning for the sake of objective—negative—truth. Hence the threatening element, repressed since then and still not reawakened. To feel this today, one need only

1 Walter Benjamin, 'The Work of Art in the Age of Mechanical Reproduction' in *Illuminations* (Hannah Arendt ed. and introd.; Harry Zohn trans.) (Glasgow: Fontana/Collins, 1977), p. 245.

2 Walter Benjamin, 'On Some Motifs in Baudelaire', in ibid., p. 190.

play through the songs from various works published by the young Krenek in one volume, which abolish everything one formerly associated with musical lyricism through the naked literalness of their musical progressions, dispensing with any reference to the idiom that would grant them meaning. Long before the possibilities of total construction—let alone electronic ones—could even be foreseen, and coupled with a certain chaotic irrationality from the sphere of Dada, Krenek's early works dreamed the technical work of art. Through its dreamlike anticipation, their ego-alienated abstinence from all expression, they expressed that which all music since then has been labouring away at: universal reification, the sole power that still holds sway over it, and which it can oppose only by taking on its burden.

Krenek registered all this with the deafness and blindness of a historical chronometer. He obeyed a dictate, perhaps without having a precise sensual idea of the matter himself; rarely has music been so indifferent to sound. Nonetheless, those musical meteors did not simply fall from the sky. He was, in sharp contrast to Hindemith, the first young composer who no longer had a substantial involvement with tradition. This does not, of course, mean that he was not a true Viennese; but, polemically or not, he was not moulded by the past in the way all other exponents of New Music before him had been. Perhaps the reason for this can be traced back to his student days. Franz Schreker unquestionably had a rare talent for bringing out of his students the specific qualities of their disposition, but at the same time teaching them compositional manners, a certain self-assured air, as well as a certain level of formal ability. But all of his students, after a brilliant debut, ultimately paid the price for this. Though Schreker himself is said to have been very adept at composing in the style of Palestrina, learning with him not only occurred at the expense of a genuine control over conventional means but he also failed to insist on a fully responsible shaping of the larger compositional picture. It was a pedagogy of facades. He unleashed his students upon the world like neophytes. In the case of Krenek, the most talented of them, this led to his productive lack of tradition—reinforced by contempt for the slightly woolly sensuousness of his teacher's musical language, whose aura struck him as a mere sauce. The attitude of composing against the grain remained one of his most characteristic traits; a compulsion to suspend the contexts and connections supplied by musical idiom. Berg, who was very fond of him but reacted in completely the opposite fashion, once said that when one expects a sequence in Krenek's music, none appears, but when one does not expect one, it appears. Paradoxically, however, this very quality is secretly a part of Austrian tradition: one could identify numerous examples in Bruckner, as a resistance of compositional intention to the hierarchies of musical language that has long been as odious to composers as, to refer to the libretto of a Krenek opera, the triangle in the orchestra. Listening to Krenek in the right way means appreciating this approach of composing against the grain, and feeling, as it were, what is negated by the abruptness of his style, especially his phrasing.

The task Krenek set himself as soon as he awakened from the dream of the dreamless was therefore nothing more or less than catching up with himself. Eruption cannot be immortalized; the hand that no longer writes as if obeying a dictate must—and now with the tensest effort—acquire its own means. Working through the conflict with tradition demands taking it on in spite of everything. The numerous changes in what, to use the conventional idea, one calls Krenek's style are anything but the expression of a protean nature or one blessed with a frivolous affinity for donning masks. It stems from an almost desperate striving to gain conscious control over those elements that are normally, as language, unconsciously given.

Even in those of Krenek's pieces whose material, a polemically revived tonality, seems to have nothing in common with the early works, one can find the same inner constitution. Even tonality is pursued against the grain; it too rejects the meaning of unhindered flow. Finally, in a highly individual fashion, he arrived at a reception of the twelve-note technique. For him, its function was to restore the imaginative space of his youth at the same time as infusing it with a form of construction marked by the logic of musical tradition, though his approach is still a wayward one. The high point of this phase, perhaps even of Krenek's entire œuvre, is the large-scale opera *Karl V* in which he incorporates techniques from epic theatre. It is not a central work in the usual sense of the *chef d'œuvre* but, rather, as the most comprehensive effort to combine the incommensurable, the absurd in the grand sense, with the thoroughly crafted.

1957/58

The town of Mahagonny is a representation of the social world we live in, conceived from the bird's-eye view of an actually liberated society. No symbol of demonic avarice, no dream of desperate fantasy—nothing at all that means something other than itself but, rather, the exact projection of current conditions onto the untouched white surface of the state that is supposed to ensue, in the image of flaming banners. There is no classless society that becomes manifest in *Mahagonny* as a positive measure of those aspects of contemporary life which have been discarded. At times it barely shimmers through, as faint as a cinematic projection overlaid with a different one; this is in keeping with a form of insight that, compelled by the vision of a coming state, can certainly split the darkness of today with beams of light but is not authorized to fill in the outlines of a future world. The power of what is to come is manifest rather in the construction of the present. Just as the intermediate bourgeois world appears absurd and distorted in Kafka's novels because it is viewed from the secret position of redemption, the bourgeois world in *Mahagonny* is exposed as absurd in comparison with a socialist one that remains silent about its own existence. Its absurdity is real, not symbolic. The present system with its law, order and customs is seen through as an anarchy; we ourselves are in Mahagonny, where everything is allowed except for one thing: not having money. Imagining this clearly requires transcendence into a closed bourgeois world of consciousness in which bourgeois social reality is likewise considered closed. But one cannot stand outside: in fact, at least for the German consciousness, there is no non-capitalist space. Hence, the transcendence must, paradoxically, take place within the space of the existent. What does not reveal itself to the straight view can perhaps reach the skewed view of the child, for whom the adult's trousers to which it looks up seem like mountains, with the face as their distant peak. This slanted infantile vision, fed on books about Indians and nautical tales, becomes a means of demystifying the capitalist order, whose courtyards are transformed into the fields of Colorado, whose crises become hurricanes, and whose power apparatus is turned into revolvers in holsters. In Mahagonny, the Wild West transpires as the fairy tale immanent in capitalism, the kind seized on by children in the action of playing. Projection through the medium of the child's eye changes reality until its reason becomes clear; it does not make it disappear into the metaphorical, however, but grasps it at once in its immediate historical concretion. The anarchy of commodity production, the target of Marxist analysis, appears in projected form as the anarchy of consumption—reduced to a stark horror that no economic analysis could bring forth in the same manner. The reification of interpersonal relationships is moulded into the image of prostitution, and whatever love is only arises from the smoking ruins of boyish fantasies of sexual power. In a scene highly reminiscent of Kafka, the absurdity of class rule is demonstrated through a court process in which the prosecutor sells tickets as his own porter. Everything is subjected to a systematic optic shift that distorts the surface nature of bourgeois life into the grimace of a reality that is normally concealed by ideologies. The mechanism of displacement, however, is not the blind one of dreams, but operates precisely according to the insight that forces the Wild West and the world of exchange value together: namely that violence is the basis of the present order and the relationship between order and violence an ambiguous one. In *Mahagonny,* the spirits of mythical violence and mythical justice are roused from the stone masses of the big cities. Brecht points out their paradoxical simultaneity. Upon the foundation of the city, that mighty parody of all treaties, the matchmaker Leokadia Begbick gives her infernal blessing: 'But this whole Mahagonny is only there because everything is so bad, because there is no peace or unity, and because there is nothing one can hold on to.' When the rabble-rouser Jimmy Mahoney, the man driving forward the latent anarchy that is consuming him along with the city, loses his patience with it, he utters the same curse in reverse: 'Bah, no one will ever be happy with your whole Mahagonny, because there's too much peace and unity, and too much one can hold on to.' Both have the same meaning: because there is nothing one can hold on to, because blind nature rules, there is too much to hold on to and too much law and order; they spring from the same source. Thus, either Mahagonny must fall or the big cities, which are referred to at one of the work's brightest moments: 'We are still inside, we did not enjoy anything. We are quickly expiring, and slowly they are expiring too.'

The representation of capitalism is more precisely that of its downfall through the dialectic of anarchy contained within it. This dialectic does not blankly follow an idealistic schema, but has intermittent elements that cannot be resolved in the process—just as the entire opera eludes rational resolution; the images of the prevailing mischief it presents are moved according to their own formula, and only at the end do they fully collapse into the social reality whose origin they hold. The intermittent elements are of two kinds: firstly nature, the amorphous being underneath society, intervenes, crosses the social process and forces it further. Then comes the hurricane, a natural event noted on the map as a bugbear, and in the fear of death the hero, Jim, discovers 'the laws of human bliss'—to which he then falls victim. Then comes a splendid turn of the story that grotesquely snatches the historical dialectic away from the compulsion of nature, which had still influenced events a moment ago: the hurricane bypasses the city, continuing along its path as history continues along its own after a single encounter between them. But what happens in the night of the hurricane, what explodes and, in the confused entanglement of anarchy, points beyond it, is improvisation; the unruly songs in which the freedom of humans expresses itself; 'We don't need a hurricane, we don't need a typhoon', the antinomist theology of the saying 'You've made your bed, now lie in it.' Thus intentions of freedom appear from unexpected angles and under cover in capitalism and its crises, and it is only in them that one can see the signs of a future condition. Their form is that of intoxication. And indeed the opera *Mahagonny* has its positive centre in the intoxication scene, where Jimmy builds himself and his friends a sailing ship out of a pool cue and a curtain rail, then sails at night across the South Sea to an Alaska that borders on the South Pacific. They accompany this by singing the song of the mariner's lot, that immortal piece of catastrophe kitsch, the polar light of their wobbly seasickness, and steer their dream ship towards the sunny, polar bear paradise. The interlocking of events at the end is placed just right in the conception of this scene; anarchy is foiled by improvisation, which comes out of it and exceeds it. Jim is pardoned for murder and seduction, which can be paid for through justice and money—but not for the curtain rail and the three glasses of whisky, which he cannot pay for and which cannot in fact be paid for here, because the dream function they gained through him can no longer be expressed by any exchange value. This Jimmy Mahoney is a subject devoid of subjectivity: a dialectical Chaplin. Just as orderly anarchy bores him, he wants to eat his hat like Chaplin his shoes; he follows the law of human bliss, the law that one should be allowed to do everything, to the letter, until he becomes entangled in the confused net woven from anarchy and order, and to which the city of Mahagonny in fact owed its name as the city of nets. He fears death, and forbids the sun to rise so that he might not die; but when, beyond all childlike images of the Wild West, he encounters the electric chair as a stark emblem of this culture, he sings 'Don't Be Seduced' as an open protest of the oppressed class to which, being unable to pay, he belongs. He bought his woman, and had her dispense with underwear for the sake of convenience, but as he dies he begs her to forgive him: 'Don't hold it against me'; and her disdainful 'Why should I?' has more radiant reconciliation in it than all novelists of noble resignation put together could ever muster. He is no hero, any more than *Mahagonny* is a tragedy; he is a bundle of overlapping stirrings and meanings, a human being in the scattered jumble of his characteristics. Certainly not a revolutionary, but not a law-abiding citizen or Wild West figure either; rather, a shred of productive power who realizes and uncovers anarchy, and must die for it. Perhaps a being that can never be fully integrated into social relations but manages to shake all of them up. His death means the death of Mahagonny, and there is little hope left; the hurricane has passed, but the rescue has come too late.

The aesthetic form of the opera is that of its construction, and nothing would be more mistaken than an attempt to find a contradiction between its political, realistic intention and a method in which that same reality is not mirrored in a naturalistic fashion; for the change undergone by reality here is demanded by the political will to decipher existing conditions. Merely pointing out that *Mahagonny* is epic theatre does not take us very far. It serves the purpose of positing not the closed bourgeois totality but, rather, the fragmented accumulation of its ruins, taking possession of the immanent fairy tale in the cavities between them, to destroy it at close quarters and even by means of the infantile gold-digger's passion. The form used to capture a decayed reality, without a better one having transpired, must not itself take on the semblance of totality. Furthermore: the element of intermittence that has a profound influence on the dialectic of *Mahagonny* can only be established in an intermittent form—for example, in the morality of the second act, where, after the rescue from the hurricane, the dark happiness of anarchy is proved with four allegorical images: food, love, boxing and drinking; a happiness that must always be paid for with unreconciled death. But the intermittent form is not that of reportage, as in the morally didactic plays of the new naturalists, but that of montage; the ruins of the crumbled organic totality are constructively stitched together. The beginning and end of the construction lie in empirical reality; between the two it is autonomous, wrapped tightly around the archetypes of capitalism. Only at the end does it transpire that these archetypes are fully present, and that the aesthetic continuum has thus been ruptured once and for all. There is that well-known moment in Wagner when the Dutchman seems to emerge simultaneously from under his portrait and from within it; the *Mahagonny* finale follows the same logic. When the earth trembles beneath the newspaper readers in the 'Benares Song', everything is over after Jimmy's death, and God appears in Mahagonny—an ambiguous demiurge whom they obey until the final 'No!' that comes resounding from hell, the hell into which he placed them by creating them, and which now sets the limit for his demiurgic powers. The woman banished furthest into the hell of the nature context finally utters this 'no', followed by the processions of demonstrators away from the burning Mahagonny that conclude the scene. Bourgeois immanence is threatened less profoundly by any montage or *Songspiel* intermittence, however, than by the language and fantasy form in its individual elements, which forces the work's skewed and terrible childish aspect. *Mahagonny* is the first surrealist opera. The bourgeois world is presented as having already died out at the moment of horror and as having been demolished in the scandal in which its past expresses itself. The natural occurrence of the hurricane, beginning and ending without reason, is one such moment of shock, as is the blurred magnification of Jacob Schmidt's gluttony scene, whose real name is Jack O'Brien—like Captain Marryat's character—and who eats two calves, which kills him; a soldiers' association then sings the burial song. The photographic whitewash effect of this scene comes from wedding portraits by Henri Rousseau; in its magnesium light, the astral bodies of the citizens' underworld pre-existence grow visibly towards them. Or the scene in the 'Do it' tavern: 'under a great sky', fixed above it like a glass roof, on which the cloud of gentle madness that the wild men of Mahagonny follow with their dreaming gaze drifts back and forth—an image that arises with the fearful certainty of memory. That nature appears only in the form of a disaster—the hurricane, the newspaper earthquake—is because the nature-bound, blind bourgeois world, of which the typhoons form as incalculable a part as the crises, is only illuminated and made open to change in the shock of catastrophe. The surrealist intentions of *Mahagonny* are carried by the music, which, from the first note to the last, aims for the shock created by abruptly bringing to mind the decayed bourgeois world. Only with its help will the gloriously misunderstood *Threepenny Opera*, which lies between the first *Mahagonny-Songspiel* and the final work, take its rightful place, and show just how little its clear melodies have to do with successful entertainment or rousing vitality—that these qualities, which are undoubtedly to be found in Weill's music, are only means to convey to listeners the horror of the demonology once it is recognized. This music, except for a few quasi-polyphonic moments such as the introduction and a few ensemble passages, uses the most primitive of means—or rather, it drags the worn-out, scratched-up household items of the bourgeois parlour to a children's playground, where the other sides of the old items spread terror as totem figures; this music, cobbled together from triads and wrong notes, the nails hammered down with the strong beats of old music-hall songs that are not known but remembered as parts of the genetic makeup, and glued with the stinking adhesive of softened opera potpourris—this music, made from the ruins of past music, is entirely contemporary. Its surrealism is radically different from all new objectivity and classicism. It does not seek to reinstate the music of the destroyed bourgeois tradition, to 'revive' its forms, as one says nowadays, or to refresh the preterite by resorting to the pluperfect; rather, its construction, its montage of dead material, makes its dead and illusory nature evident, and from the attendant terror draws the power for a manifesto. This power stems from its improvisatory, wandering, homeless vigour. In a manner matched only by the most advanced music of material-immanent dialectic—that of Schönberg—this collection of shards that have already been seen through exceeds the bourgeois musical realm, and whoever expects to find communal experiences like those of the youth movement in it will reach a dead end, even if they remember all the songs ten times over. Hence, it is allowed to use triads because it does not believe the triads itself, instead destroying each one through the manner of its employment. This is evident within the music in the use of metre, which bends and eliminates the symmetrical relationships contained in tonal chords, as the triads have lost their power and can no longer create a form, which is now, rather, put together from outside using them; this is mirrored by the nature of the harmony itself, which hardly has anything to do with the principle of development, of leading-note tension or cadential functions any longer, instead omitting those smallest of communications between chords that characterize late chromaticism, so that the results of chromaticism are now simply left standing, devoid of any functions. In all these aspects, *Mahagonny* goes far beyond the incidental music for *The Threepenny Opera*; the music no longer serves, but rules in this through-composed opera, unfolding according to its own infernal standards. At the same time, it also has its digressions into the unassuming and realistic. Especially in the expressionless, mysterious duet of Jimmy and Jenny, with its *Carmen*-like sense of imprisonment; in the pool table ensemble; in the grandly conceived passage at the end, where the 'Alabama Song' appears as a quiet cantus firmus with the line 'We've lost our good old mamma' and, striving for the utmost scenic effect, becomes transparent as the creature's lament about its abandonment. The 'Alabama Song' is in fact one of the strangest pieces in *Mahagonny*; nowhere does the music display the archaic power of remembering long-gone, lost songs recognized in pitiful melodic phrases more potently than in this song, whose mindless repetitions in the introduction give it the air of a homecoming from the realm of dementia. When nineteenth-century Satanic kitsch, the song of the mariner's lot and the prayer of a virgin are consciously quoted and paraphrased, this does not indicate the daring of a literary joke but the threshold condition of a music that struggles through that region, even without mentioning it, only uttering at caesuras the name of that which no longer holds sway over it. One hears a peculiar strain of Mahler throughout the opera, in its marches, its ostinato, its dulled major and minor chords. Like Mahler, it uses the explosive force of 'low' elements to break through the middle and partake of the highest. It smashes all the images present within it—not to be left with nothing but, rather, to salvage those it has looted as flags of its own endeavour.

1930

Except for a short appendix, Schönberg's *Theory of Harmony* deals only with conventional harmonic means. In his lessons he evidently also restricted himself to this, only working with advanced students on free compositions that exceeded the tonal reservoir. Such self-restraint was undoubtedly due first of all to the teacher's sense of responsibility, which tells him that only someone who has thoroughly studied the traditional craft can create something truly productive and new: only a reliable knowledge of everything it demands leads to the necessity of breaking through its barriers. He also realized the questionable nature of teaching new techniques such as the twelve-note method: it does not permit that generality of rules whose application to each individual case simply happens to form the core of musical pedagogy. His concern that some may have been turning his technique into the opposite of what it had meant to him when he discovered it relates to the same matter. But there was also something deeper. Perhaps he was hesitant to give the new method, which is extremely fragile, and not a collection of rules that threaten to become taboos, an overly fixed form by teaching it. Perhaps he was thinking of those of his students who did not take the step of using the new compositional material, and also of his own experiences. The more he immersed himself in questions of the right and wrong ways of composing, the clearer it became to him that the true substance of his innovations concerned not so much the material itself, those stylistic peculiarities that everyone associates with the name Schönberg. It is rather a matter of what happens to them, what their use is: in other words, the actual result of composition. The compositional procedures unquestionably developed from the discoveries of new resources, above all the abolition of the notions of consonance and dissonance, but subsequently became independent of them. In his mature works, Schönberg increasingly moved away from the mere sensual surface of the music, making composition ever more spiritualized through its standardization, and also published numerous tonal compositions, justifying his inclination to do so in the essay 'On revient toujours' (1948). These were by no means merely secondary or occasional works but pieces of considerable weight, such as the Second Chamber Symphony. In its finale, he seamlessly transferred some of the achievements of the twelve-note technique, namely the emancipation of polyphony and its entwinement with the form, back to the older material of what we call extended tonality, as he had used it almost a lifetime earlier in such works as the F-sharp minor quartet. Ultimately, that tendency in Schönberg conceals an element of being out of step with himself which can also be observed in other composers of his generation, such as Bartók and Stravinsky. Their primary musical reactions were not quite identical to the radical development of compositional means which the progress of their compositional methods had forced them to undertake. It was more than pure irony on Schönberg's part when he said of some of his more extreme pieces, for example the Wind Quintet, that he had not yet fully understood them himself. He was unabashed enough not to deny this aspect, instead dragging it into the vicinity of the progress he had gone through in the compositional material and many of its dimensions, yet without ever falling back on the stale excuse that he was too honest to pursue modernism at all costs. In most cases, that assertion is simply used to disguise the anger of those left behind as moral superiority.

Such considerations lead us to the phenomenon of Winfried Zillig. He worked with Schönberg, and thinks of himself emphatically as his pupil; Schönberg, for his part, considered him the most gifted of those who came to him after Berg and Webern. Among these younger students he would, together with Hanns Eisler, have been the first to adopt the twelve-note technique. The wind serenade, which uses it, had an uncommonly aggressive character when performed before the Hitler era; the First String Quartet no less so. In his artistic attitude he only ever felt at home in what one refers to with a word that is overused, but also mockingly reviled today, as the avant-garde. What Zillig achieved for New Music as a conductor, especially in the case of Schönberg's *Moses and Aaron*, cannot be esteemed highly enough. With a courage that can no longer be taken for granted today, he took a stand against musical obscurantism. But his extremely large œuvre, which I can by no means say that I know comprehensively, is largely tonal: not only works with particular uses, but also autonomous ones such as his numerous songs, including the Verlaine cycle. Not that his music rejects the possibilities of new, expanded harmonies; one finds them repeatedly. The basic harmonic-melodic structure remains tonal, however, sprinkled with chromaticism like that of the young Schönberg, though also with the tendency of taking the added notes that are foreign to the key as independent harmonic steps. And this in turn shapes all other elements, especially the form. It spreads itself out in an unrestrained fashion generally inconceivable among the composers associated with Schönberg's school; entire complexes are repeated and shifted around. The fate of his music did not remain unaffected by this. In 1933, it was considered self-evident that his music should fall under the barbaric ban on so-called 'degenerate' music; after the war, however, he was neglected by many of those with whom he felt kinship because he was not sufficiently radical. Only recently, now that a substantial number of his works have been published, has Zillig, who became famous as a conductor, also been receiving some of the attention he deserves as a composer.

Zillig's taste for expansive pieces that do not eschew repetition points to a peculiar aspect of his compositional temperament. It makes one think about what a cliché like that of the 'born composer' actually means. For as degraded as such catchphrases may be; as suited as they, like everything related to the sphere of supposedly minstrel-like music-making, may be to the persecution of that 'intellectualism' in music which is the favourite term of those who are not content to speak of musicality—something of this is also in such notions as the aforementioned one, which must therefore be preserved from ideological misuse. A born composer: this is certainly not the natural quality suggested by the word 'born'. Music is culturally mediated to its core, and no one is seriously able to pinpoint where absolute predisposition or culturally acquired traits begin. It seems likely, however, that the instinctive feeling—in a form of an 'aha' experience—that someone is a born composer is triggered precisely by that composer's relationship with culture as a second nature. To such musicians, the language of music is natural and self-evident as a language; rather than resisting the musical idiom through the principle of individuation, they are deeply saturated with it and in agreement with it. In Germany, where—as has often been noted—musicality is concentrated in the individual, rather than pervading the collective like some ethereal quality, and where social development has long since overtaken the folk elements of the musical, which can only be reinstated forcefully and untruthfully, this kind of musicality is extremely rare. It is familiar from Bohemians such as Dvořák and Smetana. Zillig, a South German, a child of the Würzburg cultural environment, has an element of this. It is almost anachronistic in his case how strongly the compulsion and consolation of the inherited musical language are stronger than the individual will, which rebels against it, and the critical awareness, which knows that the dominant musical language is no longer secure in its legitimacy. To his credit, however, he never draws on folklore, nor does he consciously invoke the collective language or pander to it. The moral smugness of referring to cultural ties for validation would be unbearable to his sensibility. But the collective undercurrent pulls his development and his aesthetic intention along with it. His most individual quality, a lyrically passive devotion in the act of composition that is at times suddenly reminiscent of Alban Berg, with whom Zillig otherwise has nothing in common, is almost certainly of the same nature as that idiomatic element.

As if instinctively acting against the danger this element involves, he exposed it to the work and effort that Schönberg's teaching demanded of him. The results of this tension made his music what it is. What stands out is not so much the technical mastery, which someone as talented as Zillig gained effortlessly during his studies; nor is it the distinctive hand he developed through decades of practical experience. It is rather the way in which he infused that idiom, from which he was unable to emancipate himself, with all the differentiation and richness of structure that Schönberg taught as the legacy of Brahms and Viennese Classicism. And, though Zillig's lyricism has certain external traits in common with Romanticism, his time with Schönberg also led him to engage, in his own way, with the objectivity his teacher shared with Loos, as well as the critique of set phrases in language practised by Kraus. In a certain sense, Zillig's method could also be called one of reduction. Not in the manner of Webern, whose *moments musicaux* are the complete opposite of Zillig's expansive structures. Zillig's economy, not least in his orchestral writing, does not lie—like Webern's—in compositional self-reflection and contraction as much as in his treatment of the orchestra and dramaturgically applied music. He internalized the skill of achieving the most vivid effect with the most sparing of means. He also had a peculiar way of working with only the bare necessities. One can still sense a Romantic opulence, a sumptuous quality, but as if it has been boiled down to a sketch. Compositional events in his music very often draw their intensity from the things they leave out, but which still tremble within them. The vocabulary of Romanticism, which is his own, seems to have been reduced to its naked archetypes—yet without turning into archaism. The modern aspect of Zillig's music lies in a highly selective economy amidst differentiation, presumably increased by his intellectual and spiritual engagement with France and Italy. It is not the means themselves that are advanced but, rather, a peculiar process of filtration to which they are subjected and which changes them, purging them of everything ornamental. Bombast is counteracted by lightness and naturalness. They harmonize precisely with the passive nature of the expressive content, which does not especially insist on its autonomy. The closest parallel would be the late music of Hugo Wolf. His *Spanisches Liederbuch* shows traces of similar reduction, as well as something of the yearning tone of Zillig's lyricism. This tone relates to the sorrow of sensual happiness, which, according to the poem on which Nietzsche founded the figure of eternal return, longs for eternity, yet, in so far as it is happiness, is transience; sometimes it staggers exaltedly, as if the expression of erotic addiction were attempting to intensify until it finally drowns its own frailty.

There could not be any more perfect literary counterpart to this expressive core than Paul Verlaine. The six songs bear the title *Ariettes oubliées*, in George's translation *Vergessene Weisen*; the text of the final song, admittedly, is from *Sagesse*.

Of all the works that I know by Zillig, these strike me as the most specific, and the most successful. They were composed during the war, at the time of the collapse of France, out of passion for the country; the comparison of the beloved to the country in 'Birds in the Night' becomes cryptic, a testimony both to the resistance among Germans and the necessity of declaring it in a non-political fashion during the years of terror. The poems belong to the period of Verlaine's work in which the demand for nuance as the highest principle of poetry is realized in complete simplicity—without, to quote George, any Parnassian pomp. The combination of a traditional tone that manages to avoid becoming a folk tone and a sensitive nervousness is the perfect match for Zillig. George's translation is not only one of the very rare examples of a foreign poem being mirrored faithfully, with no meaning wasted; it belongs to the body of great German poetry in its own right. Three of the poems were also set by Debussy, though Zillig's compositions remain unaffected by this; they neither resemble the older songs in the slightest nor seek any contrast with them, simply following their impulse freely and ingenuously—impressionism from afar.

The *first* song, 'Dies ist die müde Verzückung', is the famous 'C'est l'extase', with a two-part piano accompaniment that, although completely transparent, holds within itself the possibility of flickering much as Verlaine's muted pastel contains all hues of light. The end of the song, which joins the final two lines as a single breath, gives the clearest idea of Zillig's special tone; it is difficult to describe in words, but unmistakable in its painful tenderness.

The *second* song, whose text was not set by Debussy, is the most beautiful of the cycle; it uses the incomparable poem 'Je devine, à travers un murmure, / Le contour subtil des voix anciens' [I divine, through a murmur, / The subtle outline of ancient voices]. Its chord sequences show the strongest presence of Schönbergian artistry, both through the constantly varying harmonic interpretation of the basic motives and through its unobtrusively irregular metre. One could believe that the first verse was not composed, but was simply already there—like the children in the stork's pond, except written down, as it were; a feeling that New Music had to sacrifice in taking autonomous control of its material, and which, delayed, rises with the melancholy of the last time. Only someone who knows how used up the conventional formation of cadences has become, and then witnesses the utterly compelling and fresh character of the verse's ending, can understand the extraordinary nature of Zillig's achievement, presented in so unassuming a fashion. He makes something possible that is no longer possible. For a moment, the inexorable consistency of music's historical progress is softened. For in art, necessities are not literal; the logic of development has a level of aesthetic authority above it that delays their execution. Schönberg's school of morphological richness and Zillig's sensitivity, his avoidance of all stark contrasts, are both evident in the song's continuation. It is unmistakably like a second subject that does not stray very far from the first, and remains merged with it through the accompanying motive. The contrast is achieved primarily through a frequently repeated, shadily dissonant chord. Such recurring chords were also employed by Schönberg in his first songs. In Zillig's case, they are placed into the tonal context as scribal abbreviations. The third verse, a reprise of the first, varies this using the results of metric augmentation. At the end, the voice enters a tone higher than at the corresponding point in the first verse, with the interjection 'O', hinting extremely discreetly at eruption and climax. For the entire song, the tonic of B minor or major is either absent or only circumscribed. Even in the final chords, until its resolution in the very last, it is undermined by the retaining—in the manner of Wolf—of one of the accompanying motives. Nonetheless, there is no doubt as to the key.

The *third* song heightens the basic character of yearning into an affective allegro, but remains disciplined through the slim piano writing.

'Green' is the *fourth* poem, 'Voici des fruits, des fleurs' [Here are fruits, flowers], set by Debussy. Zillig makes an adagietto in 5/8 out of it. Its irregularity, in contrast to the prosody, which is otherwise very simple once again, imitates the halting beat of the heart that is offering itself to the beloved; it holds the possibility of the rushing moment. The halting is felt on the fourth beat; the entire song crystallizes around this rhythmic conception. Within it, the smallest seeds develop, following the principle of diminution and rejuvenation, into ever richer rhythmic shapes; finally the 5/8 structure also comes to affect the smallest note values in the accompaniment.

The *fifth*, the song of France in the tempo of a funeral march, has a certain stylized echo of the marching bands that play 'Le régiment de Sambre et Meuse'. Some of Rimbaud's poems have this tone. One could see the influence of Weill in the unstable harmony, the crooked cadences and also the inclusion of elements from popular music. But the modulations are precisely harmonized and shaded, as in Schönberg's earlier works. Despite the abrupt changes of perspective, the continuity of the composition is never lost.

The *final* song is Pauvre Lelian's[1] plea for forgiveness, with bizarrely simple chordal writing—but of such a nature that the sparse reservoir of motives and harmonies constantly gives rise to new constellations. With the same strophic form as the others, it is structured according to the principle of constant deviation; as with Mahler—by whom Zillig was profoundly influenced, but without taking on Mahlerian traits—the music always continues in a different way to that expected by

1 An anagram of Paul Verlaine. [Trans.]

the ear upon the return of the same elements. This gives the song's character a distraught quality, as if a vow were constantly being made and broken. On the ominous path of good intentions, it vainly stretches out its hand in reconciliation. The self- exaggerating simplicity of the end, with the turn, then comes as a complete shock. The cadential convention of consonance is in sharp conflict with the dissonance of the emotion: intimacy in an ambiguous guise.

The decisive factor in the quality of these songs, namely that their simplicity is not primitive but, rather, the result of reduction, can be shown technically using the orchestral version. Zillig did not, as the inane phrase goes, cloak his songs in a robe of instrumental colours. Rather, the instrumentation has an appropriate purpose: to call back into sensual manifestation what was sacrificed by the process of reduction. Nowhere does this alter the substance of the songs. The piano version is like a sketch; it longs for the orchestra, but the orchestra must neither leave it in its bare state nor bloat it. The instrumentation of the first song is the most imaginative. After the piano version, one is amazed by the complexity of the score at first glance. And yet there are no additions; only orchestration, realization of the hidden structure, in a similar fashion to Berg's Seven Early Songs. If one examines the piano accompaniment more closely, one becomes aware of its ambiguity. On the one hand, it is conceived in harmonic and chordal terms, often changing on the first and fourth beats. On the other hand, the harmonic figurations are rhythmicized in so distinctive a fashion that they take on a melodic profile related to that of the voice, yet also differing from it in their shorter note values. Zillig realized this ambiguity by means of the orchestra, technically grasping and defining the floating, indefinite element itself. The latent accompanying melody is given to the flute, and in short sections—where it pushes its way into the foreground in steps of a second—to the oboe and cor anglais. The chordal interpretation, on the other hand, takes place in the *divisi* first and second violins, celesta, harp and piano, the latter merging highly inconspicuously with the rest of the orchestra. The chord entries are used to mark the characteristic syncopation hidden in the original accompaniment; *divisi* violas and cellos add the basic harmonies in pianissimo harmonics, while the horns supply the piano pedal. The overall sound does not opalesce or ornamentally upgrade the music to a pretty tinkling: it is derived from its own structure. While the basic colour is retained, the slightest changes— such as the pizzicato entry of the low strings together with the contrabassoon, playing without the violins and high winds for a few bars—are sufficient to achieve a contrast, yet one that does not depart from the work's quiet sonorities.

I shall name only a few more of the many examples of instrumentational finesse. In the piano version, the march 'Birds in the Night' imitates the sound of the snare drum. Zillig's judicious ear refrains from crudely employing any actual percussion effects in the orchestration. Just as the reference to France in the poem is purely metaphorical, the same is true of the marching sound. The percussion effect is kept virtual and left to the piano, occasionally in conjunction with the harp. It is unmistakable, however, that Zillig prevents the piano sound from standing out for the entire song. The final song holds a dangerous temptation for the instrumentation: a trombone chorale. Zillig circumvents it by transferring the chorale-like chords to the strings and turning the wind sound—which is simply demanding to be used—into something far more implied by doubling with the horns. The trombone, playing *dolce*, is relegated to an inconspicuous inner voice. Later on, the wind doublings are passed on to the woodwind in several cases; the transparent passage '*von geistiger Begleitschaft*' [of spiritual companionship] is accompanied by the organ-like sound of only the flute and clarinet, then by the oboe and cor anglais with the bass clarinet as the lowest voice. There is one unmistakable sign of the instrumentation's success: the fact that one does not sense even in a single bar the act of orchestrating, of remodelling the black-and-white of the piano version in colour. The orchestra sounds as if it had been a primary part of the original idea, because the colours have themselves been elicited from that supposed black-and-white.

1961

Whoever speaks in a decidedly polemical fashion of reaction in music today is already suspected in advance of believing in the possibility of progress in the very area where the great works of art, in their incomparability, are supposed to be protected from any such standards. It will not be possible, however, to speak productively of progress and reaction in relation to the qualities of individual works written at different times, as if the quality increased or decreased with time from work to work. Speaking of progress does not amount to claiming that one can compose better, or produce better works through the mercy of history today than in Beethoven's time—any more than one would argue that social conditions had become 'better' in the last century, despite the predictions of increasing impoverishment having proved untrue. Progress in art is not located in the individual works but, rather, in their material. For the material, unlike the twelve semitones with their physically dictated overtone relationships, is not naturally unchanging and identically given in every period. Rather, the figures in which the composer encounters it bear the marks of history; and the composer never finds the material devoid of those figures. The same overtone relationship, for example, that made the diminished seventh chord—as has often been noted—the strongest possible instance of musical tension in relation to the general state of the material in Beethoven's time was demoted, in a later state of the material, to a harmless consonance, and even in Reger's day became an unqualified means of modulation. Progress means nothing more or less than always grasping the material at the most advanced stage of its historical dialectic. This dialectic should not, however, be thought of as a historically closed one taking place in the head of the composer while he, powerless, merely had to run after the unbound material as if chasing a balloon and seek to meet the 'demands of the time' as promptly as possible, or, as even serious musicians are still best at claiming, to 'do justice to the requirements of the contemporary formal style'. Nothing could be more wrong and deceptive than attempting to meet a demand of the time that, viewed from the outside, is abstract and empty, and can at most seduce artists into the bandwagon-jumping that allows those left behind to pass judgement by cheaply pointing it out. It is equally unhelpful to ignore the demand of the time and rely instead on creative ingenuity to reveal, through some pre-stabilized harmony, what is required at that moment. Rather, the dialectic of the material incorporates the freedom of the composer, and the communication between the two takes place in a strict fashion in the concrete work, measurable by its inner coherence; it is this, as incomparable as the work may be alongside another, that determines progress and reaction within its smallest cells without consideration for the other work. For only in its immanent coherence does a work prove itself advanced. In every work the material makes concrete demands, and the movement that brings each new one to light in it is the only binding manifestation of history for the author. But a work is coherent if it completely fulfils this requirement. The author becomes aware of history in the windowless, tightly woven work—in what the work calls for him to do and he legitimates himself as advanced by realizing the coherence of the work, whose possibility is objectively contained within the work itself.

All opposition to the aesthetic reaction must therefore take place primarily in the immanent analysis of works, not in a vague evaluation of their 'style'. This provokes objections of the kind common among all reactionary music today, and the more serious the intention of the reactionaries, the more they like to employ them. That dialectic, they claim first of all, forgets the freedom of the composer, who appears not as a mere executor of material dictates but, rather, as an autonomous moulder. Furthermore, they argue with reference to him, the dialectic of material reaches its own limits when it comes up against the 'primal meaning' of the material, which, despite being distorted and almost lost in history, can be seized upon once more and reinstated by the creative artist. Both objections can only be responded to in a truly appropriate fashion by referring to the works themselves, stringently showing that the composer does not act independently of the material, any more than the material can be restored in its primal meaning. Berg's polemic against Pfitzner, carried out using the strictest technical categories, supplies the model for such material-based critique. In so far as reaction does not only produce works but also seeks to evade historical constellations in the field of theory, a number of general responses are possible. First of all, a view that ties progress and coherence of the work to each other does not deny the freedom of the composer. Rather, it points out that the locus of that freedom does not lie beyond the objectivity of the work in the psychological acts through which he approaches it: a work can be entirely constrained in its material constitution despite complete psychological freedom, the blind execution of a historical dictum. The closer an author's contact with his material, the freer he is. It is precisely the one who disposes over it freely from without, as if it did not demand anything, that falls prey to it by accepting it at the level of historicity that the new demands of the material, which he opposes in the name of his supposed freedom, point beyond. But the one who subordinates himself to the work, and seemingly does nothing except follow it wherever it calls upon him to go, responds to the historical constitution of the work contained in its questions and demands with answers and fulfilment, and thus adds something new that does not follow purely from the historical manifestation of the work; and it is in the power to sublate the strict question of the work through a strict answer that the true freedom of the composer lies. A sovereign control over the material only glides over the work without penetrating to its core, and bounces off its centres, which remain mere unchallenged sites of faded history. It is only in the subordination to the work's technical dictates that the author, by allowing himself to be dominated by it, learns to dominate it himself.

The same applies to the reinstatement of 'primal meaning'. The wider surroundings of the current means amid which the author moves in relation to the narrow range of possibilities he quotes from the past, as if within a horizon opened up through history, influence those means; their meaning—not only their affective but, above all, their formally constructive meaning—has changed. Assuming, then, that an author wanted to re-establish the 'primal meaning' of certain harmonic phenomena of the kind one encounters in Schubert—changes from major to minor, the small shifts of key at formally analogous points, or altered chords—with the intention of wresting all these elements, which are genuinely meaningful in Schubert, from the 'chaos of an all-purpose chromaticism' into which, compared to their original meaning, they seem to have declined in the nineteenth century. Then there are two possibilities. First: the author believes he is enforcing the 'primal meaning' of those past materials amid those that have meanwhile been uncovered by history and have already moved away from that 'primal meaning'. The 'primal meaning' of the old means, however, would not be able to assert itself amid the new ones. Either the triadic effects, shifts to the minor, brief modulations or altered chords would be powerless when faced with the stronger dissonant tension and the much greater range of chord types. Then, as elements among others, they would be lost in the composition and none of the intended primal meaning would be apparent—to say nothing of how the older aspects would fit into the new totality. Or second: as this primal meaning cannot become perceptible through the harmonic disposition alone, it would be consciously brought out and emphasized through the formal construction. Then it would be wilful and ideological, not coming from the formal disposition itself but introduced deliberately in an act of historical reminiscence, at best a literary effect. In any such case, the formal immanence of the overall structure, whose eradication is certainly not the business of an author, who means what he produces literally, would crumble in the face of such a harmonic event. The recognition of this fact supplies the most profound justification for the musical style which, in analogy to tendencies in literature and painting—and no more than analogy—I have termed the surrealist style; this style is probably only espoused in its extreme form by Weill, but is also evident in certain tendencies in the best works by Stravinsky, who is no more of a musical surrealist than Cocteau is a literary one, yet whose subcutaneous connections to surrealism are nonetheless as strong as those of the latter or Picasso. Offering 'resentment' as the psychological explanation, as Krenek did in his Milhaud essay, does not suffice to deal with the phenomenon. Rather, it is based on a recognition of the unrestorable nature of that 'primal meaning' which Krenek's current approach strives to reach. By using obsolete means, surrealist composition uses them *as* obsolete and derives its form from the 'scandal' of the dead suddenly jumping to their feet among the living. The surrealist composer knows that formal immanence breaks apart if based on old elements—but seeks the demise of that formal immanence itself, which is being effected over its head, as it were, in restorative music. Admittedly, even surrealism cannot maintain organic formal immanence; it is generally doubtful whether it can still be justified, considering that the material-immanent dialectic in the twelve-note technique also takes control of the organic-herbaceous nature of music through construction. But the surrealist technique can certainly provide constructive unity, coherent precisely in its illuminated, harshly exposed incoherence: a montage made of the ruins of things past. The true 'meaning' of phenomena, their historically current contemporary expression in the here and now, would not contradict it.

The other possible restorative approach, which is used less because of the suspicion of mere artisanship that accompanies it, but is nonetheless prefigured in certain products of German Neoclassicism, is that of stylistic pastiche: an approach that abstains entirely from a confrontation with current means, invoking the material in its 'purity'. The question is not one of originality or unoriginality but, rather, of possibility per se. All pastiches identify themselves as such, however, and their style is recognized as 'stylization'. Every pastiche is accompanied by the aura of the means from whose wider context it has been arbitrarily isolated. Even if philological acumen produces a completely successful pastiche here and there—though even this is doubtful—its means are so dead in themselves that not even the most accomplished copy could bring them back to life. The 'primal sense' of all musical finds is inseparable from their presence. When Schönberg says that Ortrud's call 'Elsa!' or a passage from the *Well-Tempered Clavier* feel as fresh to him today as they did the first time he heard them, one must remember that they only have this freshness through the power of coming first with which, like transparent writing, they suddenly became legible and were notated. Whatever part of that beginning is nature, it only receives its seal of authenticity from history. History enters the constellations of truth: whoever wants to partake of them ahistorically is struck with confusion by the stars through the deathly sight of their speechless eternity.

Snatching the musical archetypes away from speechless eternity is the true intention of musical progress. Just as the process of society cannot be interpreted on the basis of all its individual facts, or as progress in the sense of consistent 'development', but as progressive demythologization, the same applies to the genesis of music in time. Though a work with the dignity of Beethoven, let alone Bach, is radically out of the question in the current state of society, though an individual cannot achieve anything in comparison with them today— even though he can achieve more in the greatest works of the time than is generally acknowledged—the material has grown brighter and freer, and has been wrested for all time from the mythical numerical bonds that dominate the harmonic series and tonal harmony. The image of a liberated music, once envisaged as precisely as we have done, can probably be suppressed in the current society whose mythical foundations it opposes; but it cannot be forgotten or destroyed. The path to the 'primal meaning' does not lead to the realm of archaic images but to the realm of images that appear to us as fresh: this supplies the best justification for the notion of the avant-garde, currently unpopular in Germany. Whoever fears that the demythologization of music, the growing empowerment of consciousness in the musical domain, is only to be had at the expense of qualitative differences and ultimately nature itself, and that it ends in a mere empty game, must be given an adequate response. Qualitative differences in music had diminished precisely under the dominion of its final and most violent natural principle: the leading note and the dominant. Once their power was broken, 'all-purpose chromaticism' was also lost. The different levels of internally constructed twelve-note music are qualitatively different and have differing significance, without this significance being blindly dictated by overtone relationships. Finally, as far as the anxiety about nature is concerned, it reminds one distantly of the efforts to preserve endangered forms of traditional dress. Whatever aspects of nature are unchanging can look after themselves; our task is to change it. But a nature that insists dully and heavily on its position, and has to shy away from the light of an illuminating and warming consciousness, should certainly be treated with suspicion. In an art of real humanism, there will no longer be any place for it.

1930

Until now, Schönberg's Wind Quintet has only been examined in terms of the twelve-note technique. And rightly so, for it was the first of Schönberg's major works to crystallize the new technique in its pure form, and proves the capacity of its principles for the constitution of symphonic form after a complete abandonment of tonality. There is indeed not one note in the score whose position is not governed by that technique, and it is understandable that an examination which has revealed the work's twelve-note structure in its entirety could easily make one believe that the quintet, at least as a musical organism, has thereby been deduced. Such faith in the deducibility of the piece from its twelve-note rows, however, can quickly become a hostile argument: if every note in the piece is deducible, then the whole piece is equally so. The favourable conclusions are clear enough, and have already been drawn in so extensive and subaltern a fashion that they will not be detailed here.

Instead, we must ask: is the quintet truly deducible? Is there no more to it than its dodecaphony? What would remain if all its twelve-tone aspects were subtracted?

To begin with, one can say that the construction of the twelve-note rows in the first place, the formation of themes using them, their vertical application and the selection of complementary notes are already acts of the imagination, derived from nothing else in their origin and subject only to musical criteria, never mathematical ones.

This alone is not enough. Leaving aside the genetic problem of whether twelve-note events are inspired as such or not: the arrangement of pitch material conditioned by the twelve-note technique only encompasses a fraction of the musical relationships that make a piece of music. Everything that can be considered rhythm in the broadest sense—from the formation of the individual motive to the architecture of the total form—cannot be constructed from twelve-note rows. All thematic work, in so far as rhythm is part of it, and in so far as decisions are made about which elements to repeat and which ones to change—and thus equally any kind of variation—is governed by other principles than the twelve-note relationships. That is not to say that those layers of compositional technique remain untouched by dodecaphony; Schönberg does not use several independent techniques—someone who merely has techniques is incapable of anything—only a single one in which no procedure stands by itself. Hence, he certainly knows how to achieve all manner of effects concerning periodicization and architecture as well as thematic work and variation through dodecaphony, just as, while he was still dealing with tonality, he always employed its means tectonically and with a view to thematic variation—for example in the Chamber Symphony. And one should not forget that Schönberg's twelve-note technique stems precisely from his mastery of variation. It is not acceptable, however, to regard the musical entelechy displayed by every one of his works as the sum of twelve-note events, informed by no other relationship than their dodecaphony. Even if one concedes that an examination of the dodecaphonic structure, as a method of heuristic analysis, can provide insight into the thematic construction and form of the most recent works, one can only do so legitimately if one bears a contrasting fact in mind: that the analysis can, conversely, begin just as readily by tracing formal-thematic connections without taking their dodecaphony into account, which may ultimately lead to a description of the latter.

We are proposing, then, that for an understanding of the Wind Quintet in its musical nature it suffices to understand its thematic and formal structures, without consideration for the assumption of dodecaphonic relationships. And furthermore: that this thematic and formal understanding uncovers the same wealth of purely intra-musically determined connections, relationships not derived from any scheme, that can be found in any of Schönberg's earlier works, even the Chamber Symphony.

The Wind Quintet is a sonata; it was no coincidence that he chose that name for a transcription. This return to the sonata, though anticipated in some respects by the Serenade, could leave a sour taste; after all, what Schönberg's harmonic-melodic revolution did was precisely to break apart the sonata as a prescribed scheme, and the destruction of all symmetrical harmony that resulted from his formal critique seems conversely to prevent a form based on symmetrical harmonic relationships. He does not, however, attempt wilfully to restore the lost symmetry of the tonal frame of reference, nor are the twelve-note rows that occasionally stand within the formal architecture as elements of symmetry intended as a replacement for something like the tonal scheme of modulations. This is already clear from the fact that the rows are never made explicit to the ear in the same way as clarity of key was striven for through the use of cadences. In the quintet, then, the sonata is divested of its harmonic component: hence the completely linear textures, which—more than in any previous work by Schönberg—make the harmony purely the result, never the origin, of the thematically constructive fabric. This simultaneously supplies the completely altered meaning of sonata form in the quintet. The sonata structure follows from the thematic relations, the arrangement of themes with contrasting or corresponding characters, the manner of mediation between them and their combinatorial development, and their heterogeneity, not only in terms of the melodic (row) material but also the architecture of the themes themselves. It is representative of the quintet's style, for example, that the first subject in the first movement enters as a long, widely spun melody, motivically bound yet free in terms of its overall rhythmic disposition, whereas the second subject comprises a short, rhythmically striking, frequently repeated motive. Now, Schönberg had admittedly worked in a similar fashion when determining the divisions of expository complexes in the D-minor quartet, and all of the quintet's tectonic-thematic peculiarities may originate from the tonal sonata. But their formal meaning has been radically transformed, and it is this transformation that substantially justifies the return to the sonata in the quintet. For whereas those tectonic aspects were formerly tools for creating a unity between a movement's harmonic-modulatory tendencies and the form that is imposed upon it, the disappearance of those—expressive—tendencies has made them the central focus of the sonata. Like its harmonic intentions, the sonata's predetermined scheme has also been eliminated. Once ruptured, the sonata is created—for the second time, as it were—with the technique of a complete thematic economy; thus it is transformed to its very core. It has turned from a formal space that holds thematic elements to a principle of construction that is directly identical to the thematic structure. While it could be said of Schönberg's earlier works that the difference between the individual idea and the work applied to it had disappeared, the indifference between theme and form was guaranteed primarily through modifications of the form, which was torn away from its prescribed objectivity and adapted to the needs of the individual

thematic element in such a way that it merged into it. In the
quintet, the sonata itself is contained by the thematically constructive will, and an indifference between sonata form and
sonata theme has been reached. This does not mean that this
is the first example of an adequation of the two; it is also found
in Beethoven. In Schönberg's most recent works, however, the
sonata has ceased to exist as a steadfast form to which the
themes correspond. Or, rather, it has been lost in the thematic
construction, and is restored by it. When Schönberg began his
critique of the sonata under the compulsion of his harmonic-
contrapuntal emancipation, the form was still so powerful
that the transformation of means called for by his intention
could not be carried out; hence sonata form was abandoned.
With the idea of development, however, it had itself provided
a decisive impulse for the abandonment of the tonal frame of
reference. This made it possible, after the harmonically symmetrical barriers of the sonata had fallen once and for all, for
the critique of the sonata to return to it and fulfil itself in it.
The force of the exploding monad is sufficient to spawn the
sonata, which it had shattered, anew. Schönberg's path traced
a spiral that led back to the sonata.

Only once this has been understood does the formal character of the quintet become entirely clear. It is not a sonata per
se, something adapted after the fact to an objectively lost ontological postulate; it is rather, one could say, a sonata about the
sonata, which became completely transparent and whose vanishing formal essence has been recreated here in vitreous
purity; and it is this commanding, definite level of knowledge
in the quintet, far removed from the fortuity of an individuation taking place within the frame of an existing form, and
directed solely at the manifest formal nature, that makes it difficult—not the twelve-note selection. In the quintet, the
sonata has become evident to itself; hence, it makes the listener
fear for the life of the sonata. It no longer exists in isolation as

an objective determining principle placed above the individual musical events; it is, rather, drawn into them. At the same time, however, it has also ceased to cling to those individual events and to specify itself according to their particular meaning. Its generality has itself become an individual musical event; there is now no room for any other. It is, to use an allegory from the language of philosophy, as if the transcendental scheme of the sonata, the condition of its very possibility, were no longer filled with content as in the past but presented as its own immediate content in the quintet. The sonata has been snatched away from its dark emotional foundation and illuminated in positive rationality. Just as dodecaphony rationally dissolves instinctively natural harmony, the tonality operating with leading notes and cadences, the form of the quintet dissolves the instinctive, natural origin of the sonata, which is assigned to tonal harmony, at the true moment. And thus we find the identity of dodecaphonic and thematic construction asserted at the outset without referring specifically to the twelve-note technique.

1928

ALIENATED MAGNUM OPUS
THE *MISSA SOLEMNIS*

Neutralization of culture—the phrase has the ring of a philosophical concept. It indicates a more or less general reflection on the fact that intellectual constructs have lost their binding nature because they have given up any possible connection to social practice and become what aesthetics retrospectively terms them: objects of pure observation, mere contemplation. As such, they ultimately lose their own aesthetic weight; the disappearance of their friction with reality is accompanied by that of their artistic truth content. They become cultural artefacts, exhibited in a worldly pantheon in which conflicting forces, works that would like to kill each other, coexist in false détente: Kant and Nietzsche, Bismarck and Marx, Clemens Brentano and Büchner. This wax museum of great men then ultimately confesses its dreariness in the countless unviewed pictures every museum has, and in the editions of classics locked away tight-fistedly in bookcases. As widely as the knowledge of all this may have spread by now, however, it is still difficult—if one leaves aside the fashion of biographies, which reserves a niche for every queen and microbe hunter— to define the phenomenon conclusively. For there is no surplus Rubens that would not be admired by the connoisseur for its skin tone, no house poet of Cotta by whom some anachronistically compelling verses are not lying in wait for resurrection.

From time to time, however, one finds a work that aptly demonstrates the neutralization of culture; even one that achieves the greatest of renown, that has an uncontested place in the repertoire, yet remains enigmatic and incomprehensible, and—whatever its hidden treasures might be—does nothing to support the popular admiration it is afforded. One such work is none other than Beethoven's *Missa Solemnis*. To speak seriously about it can only mean, in Brecht's sense, alienating it; breaking the aura of unconnected veneration that encloses and protects it, and thus perhaps contributing something to an authentic experience of the work beyond the paralysing respect of the educated sphere. The attempt to do so requires, as its medium, critique; qualities the conventional consciousness indiscriminately ascribes to the *Missa Solemnis* must be examined in preparation for an understanding of its substance—which is still only a task that lies ahead, certainly nothing that has already been achieved. This effort is not intended as a 'debunking',[1] a tearing down of approved greatness merely for the sake of tearing it down. The posture of disillusionment that feeds off the eminence of its object is obedient precisely to that eminence. Rather, with regard to a work of such weight and in the face of Beethoven's entire œuvre, critique can only be a means to assist the unfolding of the work; the fulfilment of a duty to the matter itself, not the spiteful satisfaction that there is now one less thing to respect in the world. It is necessary to point this out, for neutralized culture itself ensures that, although the constructs are no longer perceived first-hand, only consumed as socially endorsed artefacts, the names of their authors remain taboo. Anger automatically flares up as soon as a reflection on the matter threatens to undermine the authority of the person.

This can be pre-empted by saying a few heretical things about a composer of the highest authority, comparable in his

1 English in the original. [Trans.]

force only to the philosophy of Hegel and no less great in a time during which his historical preconditions were irretrievably lost. But Beethoven's power, one of humanity and demythologization, demands the destruction of mythical taboos by its very nature. Furthermore, there is a lively underground tradition of critical reflection on the *Missa* among musicians. Just as they always knew that Handel was no Bach, or that Gluck's genuine compositional qualities were questionable, and only remained silent because they feared confrontation with established opinion, they also know that the *Missa Solemnis* is a peculiar case. And, indeed, little of insight has been written about the *Missa*. Most of what there is contents itself with general expressions of veneration for an immortal *chef d'œuvre*, and one can sense that their authors cannot really say what makes it so great; the neutralization of the *Missa* into a cultural artefact is mirrored, not undone. Hermann Kretzschmar, a member of a generation of music historians who were not yet repressing the experiences of the nineteenth century, has come closest to permitting himself to marvel at the *Missa*. By his account, earlier performances of the work, before its admission into the official Valhalla, did not make any lasting impression. He sees the difficulties primarily in the Gloria and the Credo, explaining them with the wealth of brief musical images that need the listener in order to be unified. Here, Kretzschmar has pinpointed at least one of the disconcerting symptoms displayed by the *Missa*; at the same time, admittedly, overlooking how this is connected to the essential aspects of the composition, and thus believing that framing the piece with powerful main themes in the two long movements is sufficient to overcome its difficulties. But this is no more the case than a listener can come to terms with the *Missa* simply by calling to mind at each moment what preceded it, as one can in the long movements of Beethoven's symphonies, and thus following the development of unity from diversity. Its unity is itself of an entirely different kind to the unity of the productive imagination found in the *Eroica* and the Ninth Symphony. It is hardly a crime to doubt that this unity can even be readily understood.

The historical fate of the work is indeed peculiar. It seems to have been performed only twice in Beethoven's lifetime: once in Vienna in 1824, together with the Ninth Symphony but incomplete, then complete in St Petersburg that same year. Until the start of the 1860s, there were no more than a handful of performances; it was only more than thirty years after the composer's death that it attained its present standing. The interpretative difficulties—posed primarily by the vocal writing, not by any particular musical complexity for the most part—are barely sufficient to explain this; contrary to legend, the last quartets, which are far more exposed and demanding in several respects, were received favourably from the start. And yet Beethoven, deviating conspicuously from his usual practice, used his authority directly on behalf of the *Missa*. When he offered it for subscription he referred to it as '*l'œuvre le plus accompli*', his most accomplished work, and above the Kyrie he wrote the words: 'From the heart—may it reach the heart', a declaration of a kind one would seek in vain among the printed editions of Beethoven's works. One should neither belittle his attitude to his own work nor blindly accept it. The tone of those statements is that of an invocation: as if Beethoven had sensed something of the *Missa*'s intangible, inaccessible and enigmatic nature and attempted, by force of the will that normally governs the manner of the music itself, to impose it from without upon those who were not as compelled by the work itself. This would not, admittedly, be conceivable if the piece did not truly hold a secret for whose sake he believed it justified thus to intervene in the history of his work. But once it actually established itself, as one would say, it was presumably assisted by the meanwhile uncontested prestige of its composer. Following the model of the Emperor's New Clothes, his chief sacred work was acknowledged as the sister piece to the Ninth Symphony, without anyone daring to pose questions that would only have incurred charges of a lack of depth.

The *Missa* would hardly have been able to integrate itself into the concert repertoire if, like *Tristan*, it had been drastically shocking in its difficulty. But this is not the case. Leaving aside the occasionally unaccustomed demands on the singers, which it shares with the Ninth Symphony, it contains little that would have exceeded the resources of the established musical language. Large parts are homophonic, and the fugues and fugati consistently follow the scheme of figured bass. The progressions of chord degrees, and thus the surface relationships, are barely ever problematic; the *Missa Solemnis* goes against the grain far less than the final quartets or the *Diabelli Variations*. It does not fit into the same stylistic category as his late works, such as those quartets and variations, the five late sonatas and the late Bagatelle cycles. The *Missa* is characterized more by certain archaic harmonic elements, a hint of church modality, than by the bold complexity of the *Grand Fugue*. Throughout his work, Beethoven not only kept compositional genres apart far more strictly than generally supposed; they also embody, as it were, different temporal phases of his œuvre. Just as the symphonies, despite—or precisely because of—the richer resources of the orchestra, are simpler than the great chamber works in many respects, the Ninth Symphony stands out from his late style, rather turning retrospectively towards the Classical symphonic Beethoven and eschewing the sharp edges and cracks of the final quartets. He did not, as one might think, blindly follow the command of his inner ear in the late period, by necessity growing more and more estranged from the sensual aspect of his work but, rather, had firm control of all the possibilities that had developed in the course of his compositional history; desensualization was only one of these. The *Missa* shares moments of abruptness, absences of transitions, with the late quartets; but little else. On the whole, it shows a sensual aspect that is the exact opposite of the spiritualized late style, an inclination towards pomp and monumental sounds, that is normally absent from his works. In compositional terms, this is exemplified by the technique, reserved in the Ninth Symphony for moments of ecstasy, of doubling vocal melodies with the brass—especially trombones, but also horns. A related phenomenon is the frequent succinct use of octaves, coupled with effects of harmonic depth, in the manner of the well-known song 'Die Himmel rühmen des Ewigen Ehre'[2] or in the decisive passage 'Ihr stürzt nieder' in the Ninth Symphony; this later became an important feature of Bruckner's music. Certainly, these moments of sensual brilliance, displaying a penchant for the sonically overwhelming, were central factors in the ultimate authority of the *Missa*, and helped listeners to overcome their own incomprehension.

The difficulty is of a higher order; it lies in the work's substance, its meaning. One can perhaps understand the issue best by imagining whether, if one did not know it, one would even recognize the *Missa* (aside from certain parts) as a work by Beethoven. If one were to play it to an audience that had never heard it and have them guess the composer, one would be in for a number of surprises. Though a composer's 'signature' does not constitute a central criterion, the absence of such points to the fact that something is amiss. If one pursues the matter by looking at Beethoven's other sacred works, one encounters this absence of the Beethovenian signature once again. The difficulty of even finding *Christus am Ölberg* or the Mass in C Major—by no means an early work—demonstrates how far they have sunk into obscurity. The latter, unlike the *Missa*, could barely even be attributed to Beethoven in isolated passages or progressions. Its indescribably tame Kyrie would

2 This is the fourth of Beethoven's Six Songs Op. 48 for voice and piano, on poems by Christian Fürchtegott Gellert. The title translates as 'The Heavens Extol the Glory of God'. [Trans.]

at most suggest a weaker Mendelssohn piece. Throughout the work, however, one finds characteristics that return in the far more substantial, crafted and larger-scale *Missa*: dissolution into passages that are often short and by no means symphonically integrated, a lack of the powerful individual 'ideas' normally present in every Beethoven piece, and equally of expansive dynamic developments. The Mass in C Major reads as if Beethoven had made the difficult decision to understand a genre essentially alien to him; as if his humanism had resisted the heteronomy of the handed-down liturgical text and turned over its composition to a routine that lacked his genius. In order even to approach the riddle of the *Missa*, one would probably have to recall this aspect of his earlier church music. Here, admittedly, it became a problem for his powers to tackle; but it can help to pinpoint something of the work's invocatory character. It is inseparable from the paradoxical circumstance that Beethoven composed a mass in the first place; if one fully understood why he did so, one would probably also understand the *Missa*.

It is customary to state that it goes far beyond the traditional mass form, introducing the entire wealth of secular composition into it; even in the recently published music volume of the Fischer encyclopaedia edited by Rudolf Stephan, which confronts a number of conventional assumptions, the piece is praised for its 'extraordinarily artful thematic work'. In so far as one can speak of such work in the *Missa*, it uses a method of kaleidoscopic shaking up and subsequent combination not found anywhere else in Beethoven. The motives do not change with the dynamic flow of the composition—for it has none—rather appearing time and again in a changing light, yet still identical. The idea of an exploded form would apply at most to the work's external dimensions, and Beethoven is likely to have had this in mind when he considered having a concert performance. By no means, however, does the *Missa* break out of the predetermined objectivity of the scheme through subjective dynamism, let alone create a totality from within itself in the symphonic spirit—which is that of thematic work. Rather, the consistent eschewal of all this severs any immediate connection between the *Missa* and Beethoven's remaining output, except for his earlier sacred works. The inner constitution of this music, its fibre, is radically different from everything that characterizes Beethoven's style. It is itself archaic. The form is not derived from motivic cells through developing variation, but through an addition of sections that are mostly internally imitative; the only other examples of such an approach would perhaps be found in certain mid-fifteenth-century Dutch music, though we do not know to what extent Beethoven was familiar with this. The formal organization of the whole is not that of a process carried by its own strength, it is not dialectical but, rather, meant to come about through a balance between the individual sections of each movement, and then finally through a contrapuntal interweaving. This is the source of all its peculiar characteristics. The fact that Beethoven avoids Beethovenian themes in the *Missa*—for who could sing one of its melodies in the same way as one from his symphonies or *Fidelio*?—is due to the exclusion of the developmental principle: only when a theme is presented and developed, and therefore needs to be recognizable in its changes, does it require a vivid shape; this idea is as foreign to the *Missa* as it is to mediaeval music. One need only compare Beethoven's Kyrie with Bach's: in Bach's fugue, one hears an incomparably memorable melody that suggests the image of humanity as a trudging procession, bent under the heaviest of loads. The Beethoven, on the other hand, consists of complexes with barely any melodic profile that follow the outlines of the harmony and, by adopting the air of the monumental, avoid expression. This comparison points to a veritable paradox. According to the widespread, albeit questionable view of Bach, which sees him as summarizing the closed, objective musical world of the Middle Ages one last time, he was perhaps not the originator of the fugue but certainly the one who developed its pure, authentic form. It was as much his product as he was a product of its spirit; the two were immediately connected. This is why his fugal themes, except perhaps for the speculative late works, have a freshness and spontaneity that was later found only in the lyrical melodies of the subjective composers. By the time of Beethoven's historical moment, the musical order whose reflection had still supplied Bach's compositional aporiai, thus enabling an agreement between the musical subject and musical forms, something like a naïveté in Schiller's sense, was gone. For Beethoven, the objectivity of the musical forms with which he operates in the *Missa* is problematic, an object of reflection. The first part of his Kyrie takes his own subjective-harmonic point of view; through being shifted to the horizon of sacred objectivity, however, it too takes on a mediated character separated from compositional spontaneity: it becomes stylized. Hence, the *Missa*'s simple harmonic opening section is actually more remote and less eloquent than the learned contrapuntal style of Bach. This applies all the more to the genuine fugal and fugato themes in the *Missa*. They have something strangely citatory about them, an air of being built after models; one could, in analogy to a widespread literary custom of antiquity, speak of compositional topoi, a treatment of the musical moment according to latent patterns intended to reinforce its claim to objectivity. This is probably the cause of the strangely intangible quality, that remoteness from direct consummation, that characterizes these fugal themes, and subsequently informs their development. The first fugal part of the *Missa*, the Christe Eleison in B minor, already offers an example of this, and also of the work's archaic tone.

The work not only distances itself from all subjective dynamism, but even from expression per se. The Credo seems to rush over the Crucifixus—one of the expressive centrepieces in the Bach—albeit not without marking it through a highly conspicuous rhythm. Only at the words '*et sepultus est*', that is to say after the actual suffering has ended, does the music reach an expressive focus, as if thinking of the frailty of human life rather than the passion of Christ, without assigning the contrast of the subsequent '*Et resurrexit*' that pathos which reaches for the highest in Bach's treatment of the same passage. Beethoven only makes an exception in one section, which indeed became the most famous of the work: the Benedictus, whose main melody suspends the stylization, so to speak. Its prelude is a piece of such cryptic harmonic proportions as are found only in the twentieth Diabelli variation; the Benedictus melody itself, however, which has not been termed inspired without reason, is reminiscent of the variation theme from the E-flat major quartet Op. 127. The entire Benedictus recalls the alleged practice among late mediaeval artists of placing a picture of themselves somewhere in their tabernacle so as not to be forgotten. Nonetheless, even the Benedictus remains loyal to the character of the whole. Like the other pieces, it is divided into sections according to 'intonations', and the polyphony only ever circumscribes—as a form of pseudo-polyphony—the chords. This in turn relates to the deliberately non-committal method of thematic composition: it allows Beethoven to treat the themes imitatively while conceiving them in primarily harmonic terms, in keeping with the basic consciousness of Beethoven and his age, which was homophonic. The archaisms still wish to respect the limits of the musical experience available to Beethoven. The great exception to this is the '*et vitam venturi*' in the Credo, in which Paul Bekker rightly saw the core of the whole, a polyphonically fully elaborated fugue related in certain details, especially the harmonic progressions in the finale, to the *Hammerklavier* sonata and concerned with large-scale development. This is why it is also very melodically explicit, and why it is taken to the extreme of intensity and power; the piece is probably the only one that deserves the epithet 'explosive'. In terms of complexity and demands on the performers, it is the most difficult in the *Missa* but, through its immediacy of effect, it is, along with the Benedictus, the easiest to understand.

It is no coincidence that the transcendent moment in the *Missa Solemnis* relates not to the mystical essence of transubstantiation but to the hope of eternal life for humanity. The riddle of the *Missa Solemnis* is the balance between an archaist approach that mercilessly sacrificed Beethoven's past achievements and a human quality that seems to mock those same archaic means. That riddle, the combination of the idea of the human with a dark fear of expression, can perhaps be deciphered through the assumption that the *Missa* itself already contains a palpable taboo which subsequently characterized its reception: one concerning the negativity of existence, which one could only deduce from Beethoven's desperate will to salvation. The *Missa* is expressive where it addresses salvation, literally invokes it; it usually cuts off all expression at those points where evil and death appear in the text of the mass, and it is precisely this silence that testifies to the emerging dominance of the negative: despair through the fear of its becoming audible. The Dona Nobis Pacem takes up the burden of the Crucifixus, so to speak. Accordingly, the carriers of expression are held back. It is not dissonance that carries expression, except in very rare cases—as in the Sanctus, before the allegro entry of '*pleni sunt coeli*'; rather, expression clings to the archaic, to church-modal chord progressions, to the shuddering of what has passed, as if to transfer suffering into the ephemeral realm. It is not the modern that is expressive in the *Missa* but the ancient. In a similar fashion to Goethe's late works, the idea of the human asserts itself only through a frantic, mythical denial of the mythical abyss. It calls upon positive religion for help, as if the lonely subject had lost faith in itself to calm the imminent chaos of control over nature—and rebellious nature—on its own strength, purely as a human being. Referring to Beethoven's subjective religiousness is as insufficient for an explanation of why, despite being emancipated in the extreme and autonomous in his spirit, he tended towards a traditional form as, conversely, the educated platitude that in this work, which adapts to the liturgical purpose with zealous discipline, his religiousness expanded beyond a specific dogma into a form of general religiousness, and that his mass is a Unitarian one. The work, however, suppresses any declarations of subjective piety in relation to Christology. Steuermann made the remarkable observation that, at the point where the liturgy proclaims unwaveringly 'I believe', Beethoven betrayed the opposite of such certainty by repeating the word 'credo' in the fugal theme, as if the lonely composer had to convince himself and others through repeated invocation that he really does believe. The religiosity of the *Missa*, if one can speak so readily about it, is neither that of the believer who is secure in his faith nor a world religion of such an idealistic nature that believing in it makes no demands on the subject. Beethoven is concerned, to express it in the language of later times, with the question of whether ontology, the objective spiritual order of being, is still possible at all, with its musical retrieval in the condition of subjectivism; and the resort to the liturgy is intended to achieve this in a manner known only from Kant the critic's appeal to the ideas of God, freedom and immortality. In its aesthetic manifestation the work asks what, and how, one could sing about the absolute without deception; this leads to that shrinking which estranges it and moves it towards incomprehensibility—not least because the question it poses resists any conclusive answer, including a musical one. The subject in its finitude remains banished; the objective cosmos can no longer be imagined as a binding one. Thus the *Missa* balances on a point of indifference approaching nothingness.

Its humanist aspect is defined through the chordal opulence of the Kyrie, and extends to the construction of the final piece, the Agnus Dei, which is designed with a view to the Dona Nobis Pacem, the plea for inner and outer peace whose words Beethoven wrote above the music; it sees a final expressive eruption following the threat of war presented allegorically by the timpani and trumpets. The music already warms up at the words '*Et homo factus est*', as if touched by a breath. But these are exceptions: most of the time, for all its stylization, it withdraws in its style and tone to something unspoken and undefined. This aspect, a result of its mutually contradictory forces, is probably the greatest obstacle to comprehension. Conceived non-dynamically and in expansive, relatively static, textures, the *Missa* nonetheless eschews pre-classical 'terraced' gradations in favour of blurred contours; often, brief inserts neither lead into the whole nor stand alone and, instead, rely on their proportions to other parts. The style is contrary to the spirit of the sonata, yet is not so much of a traditional ecclesiastical character as rather secular, but in a rudimentary church language summoned from memory. Beethoven's relationship with this language is as ambiguous as his relationship with his own style, in distant analogy to the position of the Eighth Symphony in relation to Haydn and Mozart. And except for the '*Et vitam venturi*' fugue, the fugal sections are not genuinely polyphonic; yet neither is there a single melodic-homophonic bar in the manner of the nineteenth century. Whereas the category of totality, which certainly takes priority in Beethoven, normally results from the independent movements of the individual aspects, it is only preserved in the *Missa* at the cost of a form of levelling-out: the omnipresent principle of stylization no longer tolerates anything truly particular any more; instead, it wears down the characters to the point of didacticism; these motives and themes are devoid of the power of the name. At times, the lack of dialectical contrasts, which are replaced by the mere contrasting of self-enclosed sections, weakens the totality—particularly evident at the ends of movements. Because no path was trodden, no individual resistance overcome, the mark of arbitrariness is transferred to the whole itself; and the movements, which no longer terminate by reaching a goal dictated to them by the force of the particular, end without the guarantee of a conclusion. All this does not simply create—despite an external unfolding of forces—a feeling of something mediated, as distant from liturgical commitment as it is from the compositional imagination; what results is, rather, that enigmatic quality which, as in the short allegro and presto sections of the Agnus Dei, touches on the absurd.

One could think after all these reflections that, having characterized the *Missa* in all its peculiarities, we had now recognized its essence. But what is dark does not become light as soon as we perceive its darkness; understanding that one does not understand something is the first step to understanding, but is not itself understanding. The characteristics touched upon may be confirmed upon listening, and the attention that is focused on them may prevent the listener's disorientation; but by no means do these alone permit the ear to perceive spontaneously a musical sense in the *Missa*, which—if at all—lies precisely in a resistance to such spontaneity. At the very least, one can say that its strangeness does not disappear if one applies the convenient formula that the composer chose a heteronomous form beyond the reach of his will and his imagination, and that his music was prevented from unfolding in a truly specific manner by this. For it is clear that in the *Missa*, Beethoven was not—as is certainly sometimes the case in music history—attempting to prove himself, in addition to his 'real' works, in a genre remote from his artistic personality that would also not be overly strained by the undertaking. On the contrary: every bar of the work, as well as its compositional process, which was unusually long for Beethoven, reveals the most insistent effort. But this effort is not, as is usually the case with him, expended on the assertion of the subjective intention but, rather, its reduction. The *Missa Solemnis* is a work of omission, of constant abstinence; it can already be counted among those efforts of the later bourgeois spirit that were no longer intended to conceive and shape the generally human in the concretion of particular humans and circumstances but, rather, through abstraction, by cutting away everything fortuitous, so to speak, by clinging to a generality driven to insanity by the attempt to reconcile itself with the particular. In this work, metaphysical truth becomes a residuum— like the purity, devoid of any content, of the mere *cogito* in Kant's philosophy. This residual character of truth, the abstention from a penetration to the particular, not only condemns the *Missa Solemnis* to an enigmatic existence, but also leaves, in the highest sense, the indelible mark of powerlessness upon it; not so much the powerlessness of the most powerful composer as that of a historical state of the spirit that can no longer or not yet say what it is attempting to say here.

But what induced Beethoven, that unfathomably rich artist in whom the power of subjective production reached the level of the hubris of man as a creator, to the opposite—to self-limitation? Certainly not the psychology of the person who was exploring the opposing possibility to its outermost limits at the same time as the *Missa* and continued to do so after it but, rather, a necessity in the matter itself that he, reluctantly enough and yet with the utmost effort, obeyed. Here, one encounters something the *Missa* shares with the last quartets after all, pertaining to spiritual constitution: they all avoid the same thing. The unity of subjectivity and objectivity, the well-roundedness of successful symphonic composition, the totality resulting from the movements of all individual elements—in short, all those things that give the middle works their authenticity must have become suspicious for the musical experience of the late Beethoven. He sees through the Classical period as Classicism. He rebels against the positive, against all uncritical affirmation of being in the idea of Classical symphonism— that aspect referred to by Georgiades in his study on the finale as 'festive'. He must have felt the untruthful element in classicist music's claim to the highest: that the epitome of divergent movement among all individual components, which is submerged in that epitome, is positivity itself. At this point, he rose above the bourgeois spirit of which his own œuvre forms the highest musical manifestation. Some part of his genius, probably the deepest, refused to present a reconciled image of something unreconciled. This would have become musically concrete in a gradually emerging aversion to thematic fragmentation and the developmental principle. It is connected to the reluctance that quickly took hold of the most developed poetic sensoria as a result of dramatic entanglement and intrigue, especially in Germany; a sublimely plebeian reluctance, hostile to all things courtly, that entered German music for the first time with Beethoven. Intrigue in the theatre always has an element of the ridiculous. Its busyness gives the impression of being instigated from above, by the author and his idea, yet never entirely motivated from below, from the dramatic persons themselves. To Beethoven's mature composer's ear, the busyness of thematic work may have been reminiscent of the machinations of courtiers in Schiller plays, costumed wives, broken caskets and purloined letters. There is something realistic in him, in the true sense of the word, that does not content itself with the far-fetched conflicts or manipulated antitheses used in all forms of classicism to create a totality that is supposed to take priority over the individual elements, but is really forced upon them like a decree. Scars of this wilfulness can be found in the resolute turns of musical phrase in the development sections, even in the Ninth Symphony. The truth-claim of Beethoven's final works discards that semblance of equivalence of the subjective and the objective that is almost one with the classicist idea. What follows is a polarization: unity transcends into the fragmentary. In the final quartets this occurs through the abrupt, unmediated juxtaposition of bare, speechlike motives and polyphonic complexes. The rift between them, which admits to itself, turns the impossibility of aesthetic harmony into the music's aesthetic content, and failure—in the highest sense—becomes a measure of success. The *Missa* also sacrifices the idea of synthesis in its own way, but now by imperiously denying the subject—which is no longer secure in the objectivity of the form, yet also cannot bring forth the latter intact from within itself—entry to the music. For the sake of its human generality, it is willing to pay the price that the individual soul must be silent; and perhaps even subordinate itself. This, not the concession to church tradition or the desire to please his pupil Archduke Rudolf, may point towards an explanation for the *Missa Solemnis*. The autonomous subject, which knows of no other way to remain in control of objectivity, concedes to heteronomy out of freedom. Pseudomorphosis towards the estranged form, identical to the expression of estrangement itself, is meant to achieve what could no longer be achieved otherwise. Beethoven experiments with the rigidly bound style because formal bourgeois freedom is not sufficient as a principle of stylization. The composition tirelessly checks how far this principle, dictated from without, can be fulfilled by the subject—what it is capable of. Rigorous critique is applied not only to any impulse that would contest the principle but also any further manifestation of objectivity itself that would degrade it to a Romantic fiction when it is meant, rather, to become real, stable and free of illusions, even as a skeleton.

This double critique, a form of constant selection, forces upon the *Missa* its distanced, merely outlined, character: despite its fullness of sound, it brings it into conflict with the sensual appearance no less rigorously than in the ascetic last quartets. The aesthetic brittleness of the *Missa*, the abstention from vivid crafting in favour of asking, with an almost Kantian stringency, what is still possible at all, corresponds—despite the deceptively closed surface—to the gaping cracks displayed by the fabric of the final quartets. The *Missa*, however, shares its tendency towards an archaism, still restrained here, with the late styles of almost all great composers from Bach to Schönberg. All of them, exponents of the bourgeois spirit, reached its limits without ever being able to exceed them within the bourgeois world on their own strength; all of them were forced by their suffering under the present to fall back on the past as a sacrifice to the future. One cannot judge whether this sacrifice bore fruit for Beethoven, whether the epitome of omission is indeed the cipher for a fulfilled cosmos, or whether, like the subsequent attempts to reconstruct objectivity, the *Missa* was already a failure, until historico-philosophical reflection has penetrated the structure of the work and reached its innermost compositional cells. But the fact that today, now that the developmental principle has been driven to its historical conclusion and transformed into something else, composers are pursuing the layering of sections, the articulation of 'fields', without any consideration for the procedures of the *Missa*, encourages us to see more in Beethoven's invocatory reference to his greatest work than an invocation alone.

1959

II

THEORY OF NEW MUSIC

NINETEEN ENCYCLOPAEDIA ARTICLES
ON NEW MUSIC

Atonality: originally a polemical journalistic term directed
against the sonic language of New Music, but later used positively. For music to be atonal, it is by no means sufficient for
it simply not to be tied to a particular key. The works from
Reger's middle period, for example, are characterized by a state
of such incessant modulation that any choice of starting or
final key seems entirely arbitrary. Yet, it has never occurred to
anyone to call Reger atonal. The predominance of dissonance
is also inadequate as a criterion. Stravinsky's harmonic language is often very dissonant, but hardly ever atonal: either
the notes that form his chords, consonant and dissonant alike,
all belong to a scale in a particular key that need not actually
appear as such, or the dissonances are deliberately 'wrong'
notes, substitutes for 'right' ones that continue to be felt.
Lastly, it is also insufficient to define atonality as a form of
harmony that cannot be represented in terms of Riemann's
chord functions. The harmonies of impressionist music often
lack functions; but they are never atonal. It would be most
accurate to apply the term to music predominated by multi-
note chords that cannot be viewed as comprising scalar pitches
of a particular key, and remain fundamentally 'unresolved'. It
is even questionable to refer to the concept of dissonance, as
it presupposes the counter-concept of consonance which does

not apply here. The sonic language of atonality is essentially that of the expressionist works of Schönberg's middle period. The multi-note complexes of *Die glückliche Hand* are perhaps the most explicit example. As the 'tonal' principle of the smallest step, the leading note, is still present even in the works of free atonality—to say nothing of the equally 'tonal' equivalence of octaves, these works did not crystallize a style of truly 'pure' atonality. This came about only through the twelve-note technique, which abandons all chromatic and leading-note tendencies in favour of the intervallic sequences contained in the row. It follows the principle of atonality to its conclusion. Because of the similarity—albeit only formal—between the connection to a main row and the connection to a main key, however, twelve-note music is hardly referred to as atonal.— Aside from Schönberg's school, the best examples of atonal music would probably be the early works of Krenek, much by Varèse, and some Bartók (the first movement of the First Violin Sonata). In the case of Hindemith, the diatonic design of his melodies, as with Stravinsky, was already enough to separate him from genuine atonality.

Linear counterpoint: a term coined by Ernst Kurth that exercised considerable influence as a New Music catchphrase, but also caused much confusion. It originally referred to Bach; it was meant to indicate that in his music the simultaneous voices do not merely serve as a decorative exterior for a chordal scheme but, rather, are conceived as independent, and that the harmonic relationships result from the momentum of such independent voices. As the poly-phony in the New Music movement came about in explicit contrast to the ornamental, 'harmonic' polyphony of the Wagner Strauss period, and followed the aim of replacing the polyphonic embellishments of late Romanticism with a real multiplicity of parts, the motto of linear counterpoint encountered a genuinely related tendency long before so many composers were seeking refuge in the imitation of Bach and so-called pre-classicism. The misunderstanding lay in the fact that the primacy of true polyphony was mistaken for an indifference towards the simultaneity of sounds and harmonic logic. This misunderstanding was admittedly more on the part of the critics and theorists than that of the composers. No responsible composer threw himself headlong into counterpoint, and it was precisely those who went furthest in their use of dissonance, namely the members of Schönberg's school, that subjected their polyphony to the most stringent regulation through an awareness of harmonic progression—albeit one that no longer had anything in common with tonal chords. The 'lack of consideration' for the vertical dimension in modern music is a myth, and the dissonances are not chance results but themselves stem from harmonic tendencies. The misguided belief in the harmonic fortuity of New Music has contributed more than any other factor to its defamation. In reality, the problems faced by counterpoint today are, as always, actually problems of simultaneity. Without a simultaneous connection to a given voice, all counterpoint is senseless.

Quartal harmony: harmonies produced by layering fourths. This was already hinted at by Chopin in certain suspensions (Ballade in A-flat Major), and actual chords in fourths were introduced by Debussy in his opera *Pelléas et Mélisande* and in Schönberg's tone poem of the same name. Fourths play an important part in the construction of Schönberg's First Chamber Symphony, both harmonically and melodically. Here, the fourth chords are always resolved into triads in different ways. Quartal harmony originally served to curb the dominance of chromatic leading-note harmony, rather like the whole-tone scale, which began to appear around the same time. It displays a certain rigidity that predestines it to be used for special effects, but scarcely permits the establishment of a harmonic system comparable to the tertial one based on it.

Composers soon moved on to the alteration of fourth chords, and ultimately to the merging of such chords with free multi-note complexes.

Klangfarbenmelodie: timbral melody, a term introduced by Schönberg in his *Theory of Harmony* to show how mere changes of timbre take on an almost melodic function, that shifts of colour are intended to become musical events in their own right. An example of this principle is the orchestral piece 'Farben' from Schönberg's Op. 16, where the musical context is created through the constantly shifting instrumentation of a particular chord-complex. This principle is taken to the extreme in one passage from Alban Berg's *Wozzeck*, after the murder scene in Act III, where a sustained note, the B below middle C, takes on a life of its own in a crescendo produced through an extremely artful changing of colours, without any actual melodic activity. Since the introduction of the twelve-note technique, the idea of *Klangfarbenmelodie* has not been pursued further. It is extremely significant, however, because it constitutes an extreme formulation of the idea of treating instrumentation as an integral, constructive factor of composition itself, rather than adding it externally as a contingent aspect of the work.

Musical expressionism: As music has always, especially since the early operas and the age of figured bass, been associated with the idea of expressing emotions, one cannot define the pithy stylistic category of expressionism simply as expressive music. It should rather be taken to refer to that music which, in its impulses and its technique, was connected to the simultaneous movements of visual and literary expressionism. It essentially spanned the decade between 1910 and 1920, and is represented most clearly by the works of Schönberg and his school from that period. But the most advanced works of other authors from the same years, for example Stravinsky's Japanese songs and the last sonatas by Scriabin, display somewhat related tendencies, while after 1920 the youthful works of Krenek (Second Symphony) and Hindemith (*The Young Maid*) still show clear traces of the expressionist phase. The expressive ideal of expressionism is generally one of expressive *immediacy*. This means two things: first, expressionist music seeks to eliminate all of traditional music's conventional elements, everything formulaically rigid, indeed all generality of musical language that supersedes the unique moment and its character—in analogy to the literary ideal of the 'scream'. Second, the term 'expressionism' concerns the *content* of the music. To find this, it seeks the truthfulness of subjective feeling without illusions, disguises or euphemisms. Expressionist music, as Alfred Einstein astutely noted, attempts to provide psychograms: documentary, unstylized records of the soul's activity; in this respect it shows a proximity to psychoanalysis. The realm of expressionist content is that of the unconscious: the depiction of fear lies at the centre, and Schönberg's monodrama *Erwartung*, one of the most thorough products of musical expressionism, offers an entire phenomenology of fear. The harmonious, affirmative element of art is banished: this is decisive for the choice of means in musical expressionism, its 'torn' quality, and the predominance of dissonance. The very concept of the 'work' as a rounded, conciliatory totality becomes suspicious; all products of musical expressionism share a shrinking tendency, an inclination towards merciless brevity. Webern took this the furthest.

The determinate negation of traditional musical means results in principles of selection that, paradoxically enough, turn expressionism into a style. These include such implicit rules as the avoidance of consonance and consonant intervallic sequences in melodies; of homogeneous sounds; of uniform rhythmic development; of sequences; of 'thematic work' in the conventional sense; of formal symmetry—essentially, the avoidance of any repetition at all. This leads to a 'compositional approach based on extremes'. The imperative of immediacy is realized in the compositional technique itself: extremes of dynamics, texture, agogics and expression are juxtaposed without mediation or placation, and musical continuity is polarized. The organizational formal principle is that of contrast; the medium of musical expressionism, however, is free atonality. This musical language, constituted by expressionist prohibitions, already latently contains the grammar of the constructivist language, while the musical vocabulary was expanded indefinitely through the expressionist revolt. The most serious and radical forces in music drove it towards expressionism, and one can hardly imagine great music today in which expressionist elements do not play a decisive part. Looking back, however, one can say that the innovations of expressionism were not introduced in external adaptation to the spirit of the times but, rather, developed from the inner tendencies of the musical material itself, and that expressionist anarchy was the only stylistic idea in contemporary music to contain the entire wealth of the very tradition of musical shaping that expressionism seemed to negate.

The number of pieces that are expressionist in the strict sense is limited. Schönberg crystallized the procedure in engaging with the poetry—itself very much pre-expressionist—of Stefan George (in the vocal movements of the Second String Quartet Op. 10 and the Op. 15 songs). The first fully expressionist work was Schönberg's *Three Piano Pieces* Op. 11 (1909), the third of which contains a veritable canon of expressionist prohibitions. Other expressionist works are the Op. 16 orchestral pieces, the monodrama *Erwartung* and *Die glückliche Hand*. Some of the most authentic and thorough expressionist creations are the *Six Little Piano Pieces* Op. 19, the song *Herzgewächse* Op. 20, and finally the four orchestral songs of Op. 22. In *Pierrot Lunaire,* one already finds, alongside thoroughly expressionist pieces like 'Madonna' or 'Die Kreuze', constructivist ones such as 'Nacht', 'Parodie' or 'Der Mondfleck'. In its substance, Webern's entire œuvre belongs to expressionism. He took this furthest in pieces for violin and piano, cello and piano, the Bagatelles for string quartet and the chamber orchestra pieces Op. 10. The Trakl songs with chamber ensemble are among the most perfect and musically rich examples of Webern's expressionism. Of Alban Berg's works, the pieces for clarinet and piano and the orchestral songs on texts by Altenberg can be considered expressionist works.

Musical New Objectivity: a collective term for all anti-Romantic, but to a certain extent also anti-expressionist, tendencies in New Music. This applies to music from the most contrasting schools and with the most divergent of intentions: the majority of works by Stravinsky and Hindemith, the song style of Weill, a number of Krenek's works, but in a certain sense also twelve-note music. The impulse of New Objectivity is a twofold one: first, to divest music of all superfluous ingredients and develop it purely from the necessity of the concrete musical idea. This principle was formulated by, of all people, the expressionist Schönberg: 'Music should not be decorative, but rather true.' Secondly, however, New Objectivity has been understood as an elimination of all music's expressive elements, its reduction to a mere game with reference to Hanslick's anti-Wagnerian doctrine of 'sounding forms in motion'. Though both tendencies are unquestionably deeply related, flatly equating the two has caused a great deal of damage by associating the ideal of a materially suited, technically responsible and illusionless compositional approach with a spiteful enjoyment of the base, the mechanical and the repressive. The problem of the New Objectivity mirrors a social one: the revolt against the element of untruth in the individualism of the nineteenth century, which threatens to

turn into fascist collectivism. The works that are most 'objective'—in the sense of inner coherence—are probably those
that devoted themselves least to musical baseness.

The wide divergence between the phenomena united
under the name of New Objectivity makes it advisable to qual-
ify the term, and in particular to exclude neoclassicism and
twelve-note music. In the stricter sense, it applies to a number
of works of an aggressively anti-Romantic character that
negate not only expression but even any elevated 'style' at all.
The most authentic example of this is perhaps Stravinsky's
Concertino for string quartet, which the composer allegedly
compared to the whirring of a sewing machine. This stance of
mechanistic disillusion was very quickly taken up by conformist attempts to 'deepen' it.

Twelve-note technique: compositional procedure developed by
Schönberg for the organization of the musical context. The
procedure consists in the assignment to every piece of a 'row'
or prime form containing all twelve notes of the chromatic
scale in a respectively specific and fixed order. This order of
the twelve notes is maintained throughout the piece, excluding
any free notes, so that every note in the composition has its
position in the row or one of the derivations formed according
to certain rules. For it is not the case that the row is simply
played over and over again in the form of its first appearance
for the entire piece. Rather, the row is subjected to extensive,
albeit strictly defined modifications that prevent any merely
mechanical repetition. The most common of these modifications are the inversion of the row, such that each of its original
intervals is turned in the opposite direction (as in an inversion
fugue), the retrograde, i.e. the prime form beginning with the
last note and ending with the first, and finally the inversion
of this retrograde. As the four main forms of the row can be
transposed to all twelve degrees of the chromatic scale, these
few methods already provide every twelve-note composition

with forty-eight available forms of the row. A further possibility for modification arises from the fact that the choice of octave is free for each individual note. After all, the row does not simply constitute a melodic principle but, equally, a harmonic one, that is to say the notes sounding simultaneously at a given point are also subject to the principle of the row. In simple cases, this means that the row is 'collapsed'—for example, if notes 1–3 appear simultaneously and the upper voice, which began on note 1, continues with note 4. In general, however, richer forms of application predominate—it could be that the row is divided into two and the notes of the first half are accompanied by those of the second, or that several forms and transpositions of the row are used simultaneously (the Variations Op. 31 take the latter principle especially far). Instead of having a single prime row and its derivations, a piece could also be based on several prime rows (Third String Quartet). In more extended compositions, complicated arithmetical procedures are sometimes used to develop new prime rows from the original one (Berg's *Lulu*). The construction of the row is a substantial factor in the wealth of relationships created by the twelve-note technique. It can be divided into groups that are in turn related to one another in the manner of variations (Webern).

Schönberg himself referred to it not as the twelve-note technique but as 'composition with twelve notes'. The suggestion in this phrase characterizes the approach. The twelve-note structure of a piece of music is not the same as its actual composition. It constitutes a preformation of material, and the real compositional work occurs only on the basis of this preformed material. The most widespread misconception is found among laypersons and composers with twelve-note aspirations alike, namely that the twelve-note structure amounts to the compositional act, whereas the twelve-note technique is in fact only justified where the concern is to organize a music of such density and complexity that the highly developed twelve-note procedure corresponds to the highly developed musical substance itself. If twelve-note rows are used to create primitive structures, the method loses its entire purpose and turns into an over-definition of musical events that could easily be held together by far simpler means. The truth is that the twelve-note technique is only legitimate if the musical material is accompanied by quite specific historical experiences: it is never a mathematical formula for composition, and never a 'substitute' for the disintegrating binding agent of tonality, as the twelve-note row can never become transparent as a frame of reference in the same way the key of a tonal piece was in the past. The historical tendencies in question are in particular those of complete motivic-thematic economy and constant variation as developed by Schönberg in the wake of Brahms. The ideal of permitting no note that was not derived from the motivic-thematic workings of a piece was foreshadowed by classical music. The twelve-note technique crystallized through an application of the principle of compositional economy to the material of chromaticism: broadly speaking, through a synthesis of Wagner and Brahms. Through their total application, however, the motivic-thematic relationships cease to form the main musical event and are, to a degree, shifted back into the predisposition of the material. Twelve-note music is one in which the universality of technical relationships prevails independently of the manifest course of the composition—indeed before any 'theme' is formulated at all, just as the themes of twelve-note works do not necessarily coincide directly with the row. A further historical motif that led to the twelve-note technique is the growing sensitivity towards note repetitions, which was then formulated in the twelve-note technique in the manner of a law. Finally, the twelve-note technique does justice to the tendency of every freely atonal chord to turn into one that contains the notes it lacks.

Schönberg already used row-like material on occasion in his expressionist phase (1st orchestral piece from Op. 16, passacaglia from *Pierrot*), without consciously accounting for it to himself. Following his long compositional hiatus, he developed the technique of prime forms in the Op. 23 piano pieces and the Serenade Op. 24. The last of the piano pieces and the vocal movement of the Serenade were his first published twelve-note compositions; the Suite Op. 25 and the Wind Quintet Op. 26 were the first major works that, each relying on a single row for all movements, were composed with the new technique. At first, he applied the twelve-note technique to more or less traditional musical forms (sonata, variation). Starting with the first movement of the Third String Quartet, he then developed increasingly free twelve-note forms more remote from traditional formal schemata (Fourth String Quartet, Violin Concerto). The opera *Von Heute auf Morgen* is also a twelve-note composition. Schönberg's pupils Webern and Berg were the first to adopt the twelve-note technique. Webern initially applied it to his expressionism-based approach (String Trio) before reaching a curious simplification of his style in which relationships within and between rows become the main musical event (Variations for piano, String Quartet). Berg used the twelve-note technique from the *Lyric Suite* for string quartet onward, but absorbed it as inconspicuously as possible into his chromatically infused style; in addition, he introduced extensive tonal complexes into his twelve-note structures through his choice of note-rows (Violin Concerto). Among younger composers Krenek, Eisler and Steuermann have sought to develop individual approaches to constructing twelve-note forms.

Communal music: endeavours, particularly common in Germany but also noticeable in other countries, to overcome the alienation between New Music and the audience resulting from the technical development of the music itself, by deliberately adapting to the receptive capacity of the audience, especially the 'youth'. The primary intention was to stop the reification of music as an object exhibited in concerts, instead basing musical forms on the playing abilities of amateur performers. The aim was to overcome not only the separation between the music and the audience but also that between performers and listeners. As the ideal of such an immediate position for art in today's society conflicts with the realities of the latter, however, the project of communal music failed. Musically speaking, it is essentially a simplification, thus regressing behind the current state of musical resources; the results are usually nothing more than watered-down versions of neo-objective and neoclassical works whose primitiveness stands in constant conflict with the modern sonic language which remains implicit throughout. In Germany, the music was augmented with a sectarian, fanatical hatred of the individual and all supposedly individualistic musical elements which the protagonists believed to have overcome by suppressing them. The spirit and interpretation of the music were intended to be 'collective'; nonetheless, this collectivistically planned music was never able to compete with the light-music industry for the attention of the masses. Ultimately, communal music was swallowed by political music in Germany. The only attempts at collectivist music that truly presented something new, and offered something more than empty claims of fellowship, were the works of Eisler.

Forms in New Music: with regard to large-scale forms, it is very difficult to point to any uniform tendencies in the New Music movement. Neoclassicism manipulates past formal types as quotations, without asking too much how they might contradict its own material; in fact, the contradiction is one of the forces responsible for the music's effect. The music of Schönberg's school sprang directly from a critical engagement with the great 'dynamic' forms of 'classical' music, especially the sonata and the variation. While Schönberg's earlier works up to his expressionist phase use the actual forms, but contracting them through motivic work and polyphony, his later works since the invention of the twelve-note technique take up the problems of these traditional forms once again as problems of construction. It was only expressionism that dispensed entirely with existing forms. Characteristically, however, it either restricted itself to very brief pieces, thus preventing the problem of form as an engagement with musical time from arising in the first place, or drew on the poetic word for the organization of forms. The only exception to this would be something like the last of the Op. 16 orchestral pieces, 'The Obligatory Recitative', which strives for a prose-like, completely free yet nonetheless logical formal development. The approaches tending in this direction, which were taken furthest in the monodrama *Erwartung*, have hardly been taken up since then, except in the 'athematic style' of Alois Hába and his school. One example that comes quite close to a large-scale expressionist prose form, though it is admittedly still of a rondo-like nature, is the second movement of Berg's String Quartet Op. 3. In the sphere of the twelve-note technique, the extensive use of the retrograde row also suggested complete reversal and circular closure as a principle of formal shaping. Even before the development of the twelve-note technique, this was demonstrated in the double retrograde canon in *Pierrot Lunaire*. Berg made particular use of such forms: his œuvre contains many palindromic forms, whether literally or hinted at, for example the Adagio of the Chamber Concerto, the Allegro misterioso of the *Lyric Suite* and the large orchestral interlude in *Lulu*. Krenek adopted a similar approach. Berg, for whom the division into the smallest musical atoms is accompanied by larger-scale plans and the will to great architecture, took on the problem of large forms time and again. One of the most peculiar results of his formal methods is the first movement of the *Lyric Suite*, a sonata form without a development section, and 'Monoritmica' from *Lulu*, a large palindromic movement whose internal coherence is achieved through an artfully employed underlying rhythm.

In Schönberg's case, formal questions return to the foreground with the first movement of the Third String Quartet, which dispenses with sonata-like divisions and, instead, maintains ostinato elements for long stretches and contrasts large thematic complexes with one another without relying on the schema of development and recapitulation. Intentions of this kind are fundamental to the Fourth String Quartet and the Violin Concerto, works that are certainly in the spirit of the sonata, are built dialectically and have themes that are formulated, developed and preserved—yet without resorting to any given schemata. The first movement of the Violin Concerto is a combination of sonata and scherzo character.

If it is at all possible to speak of an 'idea' of formal shaping in New Music, it would be that of the static form: a form in which each individual event is equally close to the centre, in which such notions as development and progression—albeit for very different reasons in the different schools—increasingly lose their meaning and in which, in a certain sense, the music behaves indifferently towards time. Stravinsky underlines the 'standing' character of his music through the wilfully undynamic nature of his works; in twelve-tone music, stasis results, almost against the composers' will, from the weight of the material. Strangely enough, this very idea creates a profound connection between New Music and impressionism, to which it is antithetical in every other respect. One can view Schönberg's most recent works as attempts to break out of this stasis, whereas Stravinsky is seeking to make it the immutable and binding law of the new musical language.

Motor rhythms: a particularly widespread compositional feature in the early days of the New Music movement that attempts to connect individual musical events through a uniform, incessantly stamping activity. The principle is related to the *perpetuum mobile* of the nineteenth century, as well as to certain varieties of eighteenth-century music. It differs from them, however, in that here, with the disappearance of traditional harmonic binding agents, this continuous movement *alone* is burdened with a formally constitutive function, and further influenced by the notion of the mechanical, which makes—as in jazz—the beats entirely rigid while simultaneously attempting to create diversity through fitful, irregular counter-accents. Simple examples of motor rhythms can be found in certain works by Bartók (Allegro barbaro, second movement of the Second String Quartet) and Hindemith (Finale of the String Quartet Op. 16). The primitiveness and monotony of the approach was quickly felt. One way in which composers sought to tackle this problem was, while maintaining the basic movement, to develop the counter-accents into irregular rhythmic groups so that there would simultaneously be a rigid identity of beats and the greatest multiplicity of metres. By establishing this principle early on, Stravinsky exercised the strongest influence, especially on the younger generations in Western countries. The characteristic model for this variety of the motoric style is the dance of the sacrificial victim from *Le Sacre du Printemps*. Other composers, in particular Hindemith (First Piano Concerto), have attempted to develop the motoric style further through the inclusion of contrapuntal imitation.

Jazz: the style of dance music originating in America directly after the First World War, and meanwhile common throughout the world, played by a larger or smaller ensemble known as the 'band'. This style is first and foremost one of *representation*. It originally revolved around the paraphrasing, especially rhythmic improvisations of individual players or the entire ensemble within the framework of specified, usually very basic compositions. The commercial form of jazz increasingly reduced the element of improvisation. It was replaced by the jazz arrangement, the treatment—in some cases highly skilled—of the original compositions by specialists, either standard versions for general use or special ones for particular bands. With few exceptions, however, the starting material of these arrangements is either established, older popular melodies or current ones promoted by a small group of publishers, which very often have little to do with the jazz style as such and can be modified in the most varied ways. The only exception is that of the 'rhythm numbers', which are designed for jazz arrangement from the outset.

The most conspicuous characteristic of the jazz style is the predominance of syncopation and extended syncopated formations that join to form new symmetries—'false metres'. The basic cakewalk rhythm can already be understood in terms of the false metres $3/16 + 3/16 + 2/16$ within a $2/4$ time signature. But it is not the syncopations as such, which correspond to the original improvisatory element, that are decisive but, rather, their connection to a mechanical, rigidly maintained basic beat either marked by crotchet strokes or at least tacitly respected and imagined. The attraction and understanding of jazz are tied to the simultaneity of an immovable regularity and the tendency to stumble out of this, so to speak, yet always land on a secure rhythmic foundation again. Jazz, one could say, subjects the play and the listener to a constant test: how far his musical consciousness is able to play a trick with the norm while never seriously deviating from it. This dual character is particular to jazz in all its elements. Its sound too, which 'vocalizes' the instruments, adding a subjective veneer to something mechanical, reflects the same intention.

Historically, the jazz style evolved partly from the folk music of the American Negroes (spirituals and blues) and partly from the syncopated American popular song (ditty), which can be traced back to the 1830s. Since Winthrop Sargeant's meticulous and learned book *Jazz, Hot and Hybrid* (1938) the Negro origins have been clarified and identified in all technical details, but the faith in the primitive spontaneity of current jazz has simultaneously been sharply refuted. An extremely significant factor in the development of the style would have been the introduction of step dancing, which defines the basic rhythm as march-like. The disposition of the jazz orchestra is indeed inconceivable without that of the military band. The expressive elements come from salon music; the exotic harmonic elements from impressionism. The idea of jazz is most closely related to that of the eccentric clown and American film grotesques. All these latter aspects, however, have been emphasized far less by researchers than the folk-musical ones. In its basic melodic, harmonic and metric structure, however, jazz is very much grounded in conventional dance music, which it may have ornamented but did not substantially change. The innovations lie primarily in the area of rhythmic and instrumental tricks. Instrumental techniques, especially those of the clarinet, trumpet, saxophone, trombone and percussion, owe a great deal to jazz.

The jazz style was already largely developed before the First World War in ragtime. This, however, was restricted to the piano. The first jazz 'fad' came with the appearance of the first bands; it was also then that the name 'jazz' came into use. As the basic idea and rules of play have been fixed since then, one can hardly speak of history in the true sense of the word; the situation could, rather, be compared to trends in the world of fashion. Behind this lies the will to ensure the sale of the same product by constantly presenting it in new ways, and to make the respective presentation as authoritative as possible through rigorous 'stylization'. With the increasing technical and economical concentration of the popular-music industry and the accompanying standardization of products, the stylistic changes of jazz ultimately take on the character of mere manipulation for advertising purposes.

In so far as one can speak of genuine developments in jazz, they are connected precisely to the tendency towards concentration and standardization as well as the will to escape from it. Jazz, originally a phenomenon on the fringes of society that came from the underclass, was increasingly smoothed by the communication industry, divested of its modestly shocking aspects and completely consumed. The tendency has two extremes: on the one hand, the smoothing of all edges, the rejection of all 'rawness' in favour of a rounded, full, often over-sweetened sound; and on the other, the ideal of using syncopations and false metres in a well-craftedly elegant, virtuosic system of tricks that combines rhythmic finesse with harmlessness. The advertising terms 'sweet' and 'swing' refer to these two extremes. Swing was initially a reaction on the part of the best ensembles against standardization and smoothing out in favour of bolder, more spontaneous music-making, but was immediately taken over by the industry.

From Debussy onwards, the influence of jazz on the art music of both continents was considerable. While many serious composers undoubtedly hoped to escape their isolation and establish a connection to the market by pandering to the smart, technically advanced dance music, it must be conceded that, even in the more autonomous areas of composition, one can scarcely name any figure in whom jazz did not stimulate some reaction. The purely musical reason for this, aside from the supposedly modern character of jazz, is that the emancipation from the symmetrical relationships inherent in tonality, especially the accent on the strong beat, was very much in keeping with jazz. We shall mention only Milhaud (*Le Bœuf sur le toit*), Hindemith (*Kammermusik* Op. 24, No. 1; *Suite 1922*), Krenek (*Jonny spielt auf*) and Weill (whose *Threepenny Opera* was played in jazz arrangements from the start). The most important result of this encounter would be Stravinsky's *Ragtime* and *Piano Rag Music*, but especially *L'histoire du soldat*. In the latter work, he turns the whole range of jazz techniques, especially in the percussion, to the purpose of a compositional intention through which he in turn interprets them, so to speak.

Dissonance in New Music: All new harmonic tendencies are crystallized in the aspect of dissonance, which moves to the foreground in almost all compositional schools, and to which the new structures of harmonic cohesion can ultimately also be traced. The independence of dissonance came about during Romanticism. Dissonance is the most substantial carrier of expression, a symbol of pain and suffering. At the same time, it has a purely musical purpose, namely to free itself as far as possible from the dominion of the musical formula, the tonal system of triadic harmony, and to realize the singularity of the musical moment through a singular, concrete, non-clichéd element. Both tendencies of dissonance were finally released completely in New Music. As early as the mid-nineteenth century, however, Wagner (*Die Walküre*, Act II, one bar before Wotan's great outburst 'O heilige Schmach' [O holy shame]) ventured to form a chord containing six different notes (C–F–A flat–D flat–C flat–E double flat) in which, separated by their respective registers, the four notes C flat, C, D flat and E double flat, highly dissonant through the repeated interval of a minor second, appear simultaneously; a chord, then, of a type that played an especially important part during a particular phase of free atonality. Naturally, such dissonances can all be explained with reference to traditional harmonic theory as 'non-harmonic' notes (a combination of pedal tone and suspension), but they take on such a prominent position through their heightened expressivity and pointedness that they assume a certain independence and are largely perceived as 'chords' *sui generis*, independently of their genesis in the harmonic scheme.

This tendency towards the independence of dissonance became so strong in Wagner's late works that certain chords, such as that of E–C sharp–G–B flat–F in *Götterdämmerung* (the Rhine Maidens' warning) and in *Parsifal* (the Kundry motive, especially upon Parsifal's outburst '*Amfortas*! *Die Wunde!*' [Amfortas! The wound!]) function virtually as leading chords. The aspect of dissonance was expanded ever more by all Wagner's successors. The recognition chord in the Orestes scene of Richard Strauss's *Electra*, which contains seven different notes, was also something of a turning point. It is no longer an expression of despair but, rather, of the contradictory emotions, the fluctuations of the sentiment in the ecstatic moment: one could almost speak of an internally animated and internally articulated chord. From then on, dissonance develops the capacity to hold all expressive possibilities; the opposition consonance = enjoyment/ dissonance = pain becomes obsolete, the concept of consonance loses its validity, and hence that of dissonance also loses its universality. Now there is only dissonance—and therefore none at all. At the end of this development, the universal dissonance ceases to have any real expressive function at all and simply becomes harmonic material, entirely free of the bonds of the tonal schema, fully articulated and 'polyphonic' within itself: the medium of a constructive approach. This development was no longer reflected in Strauss's own music, however, in which even the boldest harmonies always remained momentary effects and were revoked by the tonal schema. The totality of dissonance was forced beforehand by Schönberg, in whose music the expressive development of dissonance was simultaneously elaborated purely musically from the construction which it in turn affected. His theoretical critique of the concept of the non-harmonic note, his introduction of previously forbidden inversions of dissonant chords (as early as *Verklärte Nacht*), the incorporation of quartal harmony, the increasing employment of the major seventh and the minor second for the internal articulation of chords, the polyphonic superimposition of entire harmonic complexes in *Die glückliche Hand*—all these aspects point in the same direction: the establishment of the principle of dissonance as the binding principle of harmonic selection. Other composers were also involved in the expansion of the principle of dissonance, however. Ravel in particular developed the harmonic language of impressionism towards an attainment of independence on the part of dissonance. One finds similar elements in early Schreker. Stravinsky made dissonance, in contrast to its psychological function in Romanticism, a representation of extreme physical pain (*Le Sacre du Printemps*), used it to break up musical 'culture' through a dissociation of harmony in 'wrong notes', and, finally, in his neoclassical works, as a way of hardening harmonic cells. The highly extensive use of dissonance in Bartók results partly from the sharpening of the impressionist comma to the minor second, and partly from the desire to find an equivalent in art music for the folk-musical interval of the neutral third by combining major and minor thirds (as shown by Edwin van der Nüll). One of the aforementioned ways of treating dissonance always becomes palpable when dissonances appear in New Music. The tendency towards movement in dissonant harmony thus seems given through the fact that each multi-note sound virtually pushes towards one containing those notes of the chromatic scale absent from it (complementary harmony). This tendency, noticeable since *Tristan*, is clearest in some of expressionism's more homophonically conceived moments, for example in *Erwartung*, and in twelve-note music. The conformist version of New Music largely corresponds to a softening of dissonance by relating it to the tonal schema.

Chamber orchestra: a form of ensemble that has existed for thirty-five years and is highly characteristic of the New Music movement in all its variety. The first work for chamber orchestra is Schönberg's First Chamber Symphony (1906). Coming very much from the other side, Richard Strauss approached the chamber orchestra in *Ariadne*. The two exemplary chamber orchestral works, followed by countless others, were Schönberg's *Pierrot Lunaire* and Stravinsky's *L'histoire du soldat*. The idea of the chamber orchestra is not limited to a particular combination of instruments. The resources employed range from those of the small classical orchestra to very small chamber groups. Strauss's *Ariadne* and Schönberg's Second Chamber Symphony belong to the former category, the quintet of *Pierrot* to the latter. What is decisive is rather that the full range of colours, extending far beyond the traditional chamber music sound determined by the string quartet, is made amenable to the ideal of soloistic effects. Here, the woodwind play a special part, while the infinite string perspective of the neo-Romantic orchestra and the 'pedal effects' of the horns are both negated. The basic principle of the chamber orchestra is to dissolve the compact, floating tutti sound in a transparency that is fully articulated internally. While the chamber orchestra strives towards an extraordinary refinement of instrumental colours and effects, it is simultaneously defined by the intention to represent the musical construction as such in the most appropriate possible way, without additional ornaments, doublings or parts serving as harmonic filler. The demands of the real polyphony of New Music play the decisive part here: the fifteen instruments of Schönberg's First Chamber Symphony were selected to make the contrapuntal events, some of them very intricate, as clear as possible. Hence, the idea of the chamber orchestra is closely connected to that of 'objectivity'. Among the younger composers, it is Hindemith's œuvre in particular that is characterized by the technique of the chamber orchestra.

New polyphony: the tendency towards genuinely multi-layered formations that is characteristic of New Music, though by no means universal, cannot be understood simply as a reaction against the dominance of chordal-homophonic thinking in the entire figured bass period and especially Romanticism. It has far more specific technical reasons, and is a function of the new compositional idea itself. The quest, dating back to Brahms and ultimately also Beethoven, for complete economy, an exclusion of anything fortuitous or not stemming from the thematic substance itself, necessarily leads to a thorough internal shaping of everything that was formerly mere harmonic filler. What was previously accidental is now connected to the main thematic event, resulting in an increasing profile and independence of the secondary voice. It is highly characteristic of this approach that most of the accompanying voices in early Schönberg are based on 'leftovers' from the principal voices, and remain constant while the main activity has already moved on. Furthermore, the increasing density and concentration of thematic relationships made the laborious succession of thematic expositions and developments seem diluted and weak. The tautening of diachronic relationships equally demands a tautening of synchronous events if the horizontal and vertical dimensions of composition are not to point in different directions. Hence, the tendency to superimpose, as it were, developments that would previously have been presented in succession, and to treat them contrapuntally and combinatorially. This step is particularly clear between Schönberg's First String Quartet and the substantially shorter First Chamber Symphony, whose long development section and later passages consist largely of complex canonic textures and thematic combinations. The harmonic tendency towards dissonance is highly amenable to this—first, because it makes harmonies that had previously been excluded available for polyphonic treatment and, second, because every chord is already virtually polyphonic through its real multiplicity of voices. The polyphonic techniques of imitation and canon, after all, were initially the clearest means of holding together a musical context after the abandonment of the tonal frame of reference, though that same clarity can easily take on a mechanical character, and Schönberg has always taken the utmost care in employing them.

The primacy of polyphony only really applies in Schönberg's school. The twelve-note technique leads to a form of 'pure' polyphonic composition. One can observe original, highly polyphonic tendencies in Krenek. Hindemith's polyphony comes partly from resorting to its historical form, and partly from the way he envisages instrumental activity: in his music, the problem of polyphony's harmonic sense is clearly secondary to the establishment of connections through movement. On the whole, it is the significance of polyphony that distinguishes the style of New Music in the German-speaking countries—before Hitler—from that of both the Western and the Slavic ones, which, for all their harmonic differentiation and instrumentally vivid treatment of the individual voice, hardly ever acknowledge the principle of real polyphony.

Musical impressionism: In popular usage, musical impressionism includes all music that somehow seeks to capture subjective reflexes in connection with features of the visible world. As a stylistic term, however, impressionism must be characterized rather more precisely if it is to remain distinct from descriptive programme music on the one hand and late-Romantic mood music on the other. Impressionism would then have to be defined in terms not of its connection to the outside world, which is always problematic in any case, but, rather, of its actual technical procedures. These, however, would most likely include those learned from the French impressionist painters, without necessarily having the reproduction of 'impressions' in mind. In this adoption, the correlate to the

idea of atmosphere among impressionist painters is the
floating sound, unrestricted by fixed contours, that originally
resulted from pedal effects on the piano—especially in Liszt's
works—and the orchestral techniques derived from them.
This sonic ideal involves the dissolution of all compact textures. The 'commas' of the painters are mirrored in the music
by the employment of the smallest dabs of sound, which blur
into an opalescent, extraordinarily differentiated whole that
eschews any cruder means of articulation. This is not achieved
only through the instrumental treatment—for example, the
laisser vibrer of the piano—but also and especially through the
choice of harmonic material. One could say that through the
inclusion of more distant overtones in chords, the irrational
'vibration' of every sound, which normally only appears as a
function of subjective perception, is now subjected to actual
compositional treatment. The most common harmonic formula for achieving this is the dominant ninth chord, while
simultaneous seconds, which in turn refer back to the ninth
chord, are used as 'commas'. The sound complexes resulting
from such methods are shifted about rather than developed:
thinking in harmonic degrees is abandoned in favour of the
parallel movement of chords, which greatly reduces harmonic
tension. The 'floating' sound, which knows no real harmonic
progression, often results in a form of withheld, suspended
stimulus that is simultaneously pleasing and tantalizing. Such
effects are also assisted by the use of the augmented triad and
the whole-tone scale derived from it. One could describe the
tendency towards a suspension of musical progression as the
central principle of impressionism. One could almost define
impression as a music that enters into a symbiotic relationship
with painting—not in the sense that it depicts external objects
but, rather, through the fact that it eschews any real temporal
shaping, and remains hanging in time as a picture hangs in a
room. Hence, the peculiarly static, often almost prelude-like,

character of so much impressionist music. The dissolution into tiny units in impressionism never has the intention of 'motivic work', but simply that of dividing up the overall sound in such a way that it can be kept in a state of floating temporal stasis. The difficulty of listening to such music therefore lies in refraining from waiting for 'melodies', motivic-thematic developments or escalations—generally in listening not in categories of temporal progression but, rather, almost spatially, simultaneously. As all music proceeds in time, this impressionist idea is paradoxical in itself and is never realized literally, only symbolized through artful constellations. It does, however, explain why impressionism consistently relies on shorter forms, that it dispenses with both polyphony and melodic shaping in the traditional sense, and that it consists almost entirely in the exhibition of harmonic and colouristic complexes whose melodic-motivic core is so reduced that it too only really demands a harmonic and sonic interpretation. The insistence of impressionism on what are referred to as natural overtone relationships means that there is no undermining of music's triadic foundation or the actual preconditions for tonality. Its dependence on tonality, however, simultaneously places tight restrictions on the impressionist idiom's quality of dissolution. This is what distinguishes impressionism from other 'dissolved' compositional approaches, especially that of expressionism.

The definition of impressionism developed here describes its idea. It is an extreme characterization, and by no means does justice to the full range of 'impressionist' compositions. It is most applicable to Debussy's middle period. While his early works, even innovative ones such as *Prélude à l'après-midi d'un faune* and the String Quartet, contain all elements of the impressionist language, but apply them to a more traditional understanding of musical progression, Debussy's late works attempt to set up contoured musical constructions from the sounds themselves. Their relationship with orthodox musical impressionism is akin to that between Cézanne and visual impressionism. Ravel belongs to impressionism more in his vocabulary than his formal approach; only his earlier piano works can be considered impressionist in any stricter sense. In the case of Dukas, who was mentioned in the same breath as Debussy for a while, the impressionist ideal was diluted to the point of sweetness from the outset. Neither the rigour of Debussy's principles of selection nor the subtlety of his methods have been matched by any other impressionist. One could, in a broader sense, speak of something like German expressionism in the case of Strauss on account of a certain lightness of brushwork, though he never adopted the impressionist vocabulary. The idea of that floating impressionist stasis is closely connected to Scriabin. Finally, the impressionist way of thinking in harmonic-colouristic complexes provided the point of departure for Stravinsky's development.

New Music: collective term for all musical developments roughly since impressionism that have a certain character of modernity, in the sense that they begin by breaking out of the continuity of music's development, abruptly alienating the musical language and declaring war on the audience's taste for contemplative enjoyment. It makes little difference here whether or to what extent some of the divergent movements in New Music later made their peace with the audience, or even joined in directly with collectivist tendencies. What is decisive is the experience of the breach itself, from which even the New Music that later submitted was unable to disassociate itself. The category of breach and abrupt estrangement does deeper justice to the phenomenon than that of 'anti-Romanticism', a term commonly used by academics to group most representatives of New Music together, even though the concept of the anti-Romantic offers the most generous leeway for epigones and fellow travellers. The clearest sign of the breach is dissonance's attainment of independence, which could originally be observed in all schools of New Music and continues to have an effect wherever the motto is *l'ordre après le désordre*. Impressionism is located at the threshold of New Music; it already displays the character of technological modernity quite clearly, but proceeds more or less smoothly from the traditional language of music. The following are treated as schools of New Music: expressionism, New Objectivity, communal music, neoclassicism and twelve-note constructivism. One could also include the radical folkloristic tendencies found in Bartók, early Stravinsky and in a certain sense also Janáček, through which they sought to break with the major–minor tonality of Western music and all the structures musically connected to it by resorting to an older, pre-tonal language or to musical idioms that were not completely absorbed by Western musical culture. Radical folklorism, especially in its early days, brought forth innovations that had nothing in common with the blood-and-soil Romanticism of the fascist era, and overlap in many respects with the most advanced intentions of expressionism. One can generally speak of an analogy to the visual arts here.

It is clear, then, that the notion of New Music is by no means equivalent to that of contemporary music. Hence, the entire œuvre of Richard Strauss, for example, lies before the threshold of New Music—though *Salome* and *Electra* are very close to the edge. The same is true of Reger, who took chromaticism to its limits, and of Mahler, whose last works constitute the true mediation between Schönberg and the Viennese tradition. Finally, it should be noted carefully that traditionalist modes of composition continue everywhere in parallel with New Music, especially the offshoots of the New German (Wagnerian) School, impressionism and earlier academic directions such as those of Brahms and César Franck.

Construction in New Music: If it is at all possible to identify a point at which the various currents in New Music converge, it is the ideal of construction. The different attempts to emancipate the language of music from the shackles of its traditional ties, and subsequently to reorganize it, come together in the desire for the composer to dominate the natural musical material in all its dimensions of conscious and calculating control. One can observe the emergence of the notion of an integral musical work of art in which every aspect owes its existence purely to its function within the whole, and in which the weight of the individual material elements is absorbed in favour of the thoroughly organized unity of the whole. A defining characteristic of such music is the principle of complete economy: nothing superfluous is tolerated. The principle of total determination continues to apply: each detail fulfils its entire purpose in the service of the preordained whole. All blind, irrational, 'aimless' elements are liquidated: hence, the music's virtual stasis, and its critical, albeit not entirely clear, stance concerning the aspect of expression. The work of art approaches the image of absolute technical functionality. Technically speaking, this amounts to an attempt to eliminate the disproportionalities between the different compositional dimensions. There is a tendency to do away with the tensions between melodic and chordal elements, between harmonic and contrapuntal thinking or between fugal and sonata character. In twelve-note music, vertical and horizontal structures are essentially equal. The dissonant chords are polyphonic 'within themselves', while the contrapuntal lines are harmonically complementary. Webern's last works achieve a complete equivalence of imitative and sonata form. Timbre takes on equal significance in the construction—but, through the imperative of clarity, is determined entirely by it. Whereas neoclassicism develops the image of such total construction playfully, out of its own taste and with a particular gesturality, the purpose of the twelve-note technique is to fully realize the integral work purely from the conditions of the material. Certainly, it is questionable whether the impulses of New Music fulfil themselves in the idea of constructivism, or whether the explosive force of its earlier phases will not return and push aside the total economy of the construct. Schönberg's most recent works at least suggest that the complete dominion of the whole over the parts will not have the last musical word.

Polytonality: style of composition consisting in the simultaneous use of musical shapes in different keys, either with entire structures appearing in different keys or, at the very least, chords from different, remote keys being combined. One of the earliest examples of polytonality can probably be found in Bartók's Bagatelles Op. 6 (1908). Polytonality then became especially significant in France during the first post-war years in the school known as 'Les Six' (in particular Milhaud). Stravinsky's harmonic language (especially in *Le Sacre du Printemps*) is close to polytonality in certain respects, and among German composers it was Schreker and, later on, occasionally also Krenek (*Durch die Nacht*) who worked with polytonal elements. The origin of polytonality is a twofold one. First, it suggested itself through the incorporation of more distant overtones into harmony, and one can accordingly observe polytonal tendencies in Debussy and Ravel (Violin Sonata). Second, polytonality results from the literary notion of the simultaneous sound of music coming from different points in space, which one finds in impressionism and which was also encouraged by some of Stravinsky's scenic ideas (*Petrushka*). After the collapse of tonality, the polytonal approach, along with the related techniques of the ostinato, motor rhythms and parallel movement, became one of the most convenient and palpable means of organizing complex multi-note harmonies that still profit from the logic of traditional music through the noticeable tendencies of the two combined keys.

The superficiality of the organizational means and lack of connections between the different polytonal components, however, soon made the charm wear off and exhausted the possibilities of polytonality.

Musical neoclassicism: the most common style in modern music since *c.*1920. Here 'style' is the operative word; for if it is at all possible to define neoclassicism in a deeper sense within the 'New Objectivity', it is that it constitutes an attempt to elevate those anti-Romantic tendencies which initially go against the stylization principle in music, and present it as an undistanced image of senseless, mechanical life, to a style, as it were, through a conscious decision. It aims to re-establish the binding character of music, to turn the senselessness of yesterday into the positive meaning of tomorrow. The means to this end is the recourse to 'pre-classical' musical models: Bach, Handel, Pergolesi, Scarlatti and many others. The decisive factor here is the pre-individualistic and pre-bourgeois character of the models invoked, which leave as little room for subjective dynamics, psychology or functional transitions as for the 'moist' sound of leading-note harmony and any transcendence of musical shaping. The character of music as play is emphasized; the idea of the concerto in the older sense is the most cherished role model for neoclassical composers, and, indeed, the neoclassical movement has produced innumerable concerti. The musical language into which those models are incorporated, however, essentially consists of the vocabulary left to neoclassicism by modern music history. One can identify the ubiquitous effects of elements that resulted from the emancipation from tonality, dissonant harmony and in some cases impressionism. The elements, however, are almost shut down or frozen: they are no longer connected to others in the sense of the principle of transition but, rather, atomized and juxtaposed through an architectural plan in an emphatically harsh, cold state. Neoclassicism in its thoroughgoing form—which was admittedly softened by most of its disciples, whether due to misunderstanding or conformity—constitutes a reconstruction of pre-bourgeois and pre-dynamic musical forms through the dictate of a musical engineer, who produces them by setting up a montage consisting of unrelated fragments of the modern musical language. The effectiveness of genuine neoclassicism lies precisely in the opposition between the given form and the atomistic, often shock-like estrangement of elements from one another. This explains why neoclassicism must be viewed in the present situation, not simply as an artisanal rehashing of vanished objectivity but, rather, as a highly precise, up-to-date and advanced expression of the most fatal and threatening but very real social tendencies. The truth of neoclassicism lies in the ruthlessness with which it admits to that threat.

The extreme idea of neoclassicism developed here is represented in its strict form only by Stravinsky; most of his works are neoclassical. When his piano concerto was published, one could observe a radical departure from the supposedly radical tendencies of his earlier periods. Looking back, it is apparent that the gestural character of the works may have changed, but the actual musical substance is much the same. The harmonic language of the Octet and *Les Noces*, for example, or even *L'histoire du soldat*, is not so far removed from the shifted, dissonantly displaced harmonies of his neoclassical period. The only real change was that a musical language originally intended to express negativity and disintegration was suddenly, with hardly any alterations, presented in such a way that the forms which had only recently been debunked were suddenly portrayed as positive, as binding structures capable of holding together the dissolved material that had previously served to denounce them. It is very revealing that one finds almost exactly the same reinterpretation of negativity as a s upposed law in the work of two other famous exponents of neoclassicism: Hindemith, after works such as *Das Nusch-Nuschi* and *Kammermusik* Op. 24, No. 1, in *Das Marienleben*; and Weill, following *The Threepenny Opera* and *Mahagonny*, in *The Affirmer* and *The Pledge*. Admittedly, a dependence on Stravinsky as a role model may also be a factor in these two cases.

An in-depth technical analysis of the neoclassical approach to composition has yet to be carried out. A substantial aspect is the treatment of tonality in such a way that all 'organicist', mediating tendencies are excluded. The harmony is clouded by dissonances normally formed from 'non-harmonic' notes whose 'resolution' is deflected or omitted entirely. Cadences are plucked apart, as it were. The formation of melodies is often restricted to small note-groups that are not developed, only repeated. This shows a clear effect of impressionism, as does the non-developmental stringing-together of complexes —except that these no longer have a floating, vague sound but are, rather, figurations set apart with exaggerated clarity. Neoclassical counterpoint remained undeveloped for a conspicuously long time in Stravinsky; Hindemith's contrapuntal inclinations point back to other contexts (Reger). In the construction of larger forms, the pre-classical models are clearest, though in Stravinsky these are almost always shifted around and artfully defamiliarized. The style of instrumentation aims for clarity and sobriety, without an expression of the actual compositional differentiation such as one finds in late Schönberg. Instead, neoclassical instrumentation—related in this respect to its counterpart, impressionism—strives to be as instrumentally specific as possible, adapting to each instrument's particular mode of playing rather than exploring new effects and mixtures stemming from the sonic imagination.

Neoclassicism was anticipated in literary terms by Nietzsche's battle against Wagner and the writings of Busoni and Cocteau (*Le Coq et l'arlequin*, 1919). The ballets of

Diaghilev also exerted a great influence, as did the late painting style of Picasso, though it never submitted to conformism in the same way as neoclassical music. Unlike Picasso, Stravinsky clung to neoclassicism without permitting himself the slightest anarchic deviation from it. Neoclassicist doctrine—with its connections to Dada—was taken to its ultimate extreme by Satie, whose *Socrate* (1918) is still considered by many to be the purest paradigm of neoclassicism. Stravinsky transferred neoclassicism to the realm of masterful composition, with complete control over its technical means. But even within the framework of the style, once established, his neoclassical works are extremely uneven: there are very weak, insubstantial ones such as the Serenade for piano, *Apollon Musagète* and the Duo Concertante, but also very rich and highly articulated creations such as the Capriccio for piano and orchestra, the Concerto for Two Pianos or the extremely enigmatic Tchaikovskyan phantasmagoria *Le Baiser de la fée*. In so far as one can identify a development in Stravinsky's neoclassical works, it unquestionably tends in the direction of augmenting the stark, at times almost tedious, approach with richer and more diverse compositional means. Hindemith assimilated the neoclassicism of the German compositional tradition and freed it from its rigidity, but in doing so diluted the idea to a 'minstrel-like' style and expunged its provocative traits entirely. Masters like Bartók (in the First Piano Concerto) and Ravel (in his last works) showed a neoclassical influence. Young composers in almost all countries have devoted themselves to this direction; since Debussy, no composer has been imitated as much as Stravinsky. The dangerous attraction of neoclassicism lies in the fact that it offers a convenient way to compose in a harmlessly traditionalist fashion while creating the semblance of modernity. Thus, the current neoclassicism poses an indisputable threat to the compositional hygiene of an entire generation.

1942

ATONAL INTERMEZZO?

Contrary to expectations, the essay 'Scarlattiana' by Alfredo Casella, published by the journal *Anbruch*[1] in order to present his extremely drastic thesis for discussion, did not succeed in provoking such a debate. It is understandable enough: the one camp, whose members are certainly numerous, agreed so wholeheartedly with Casella's manifesto that they saw no need to add any thoughts of their own; no one, after all, expands a manifesto whose tenor they already follow. The other camp is so opposed to his position that its members cannot even engage dialectically with it; they lack the possibility of critical involvement because of their complete remoteness, and, though they might feel compelled to act, they would rather refrain than enter the realm from which Casella's arguments originate. If, despite Schönberg's response,[2] which displays precisely this attitude and almost rules out any further discussion because the very person most entitled to respond refuses to do so—if, despite such a resoundingly laconic answer, the matter is taken up again, it will not be to effect a cheap fulfilment of the promise of a debate after the said debate fails to occur. Rather, Casella's opinion is so representative of the current mood, and concerns most musicians today so directly, even in

1 See *Anbruch* 11(1) (January 1929): 26ff.
2 See Arnold Schönberg in Arnold Schönberg, Ernst Krenek and Gian Francesco Malipiero, 'Zu Casellas Aufsatz "Scarlattiana"' ['On Casella's Essay "Scarlattiana"'], *Anbruch* 11(2) (February 1929): 79.

their material existence, that it must be examined more closely despite the difficulty of confronting it polemically. Casella's essay is an example of a thoroughgoing decision; I shall attempt to formulate some thoughts on that decision. Schönberg was able to dispense with a reply because his entire œuvre stands as a reply, and indeed the only conclusive one. My intention is simply to point to certain aspects of that reply which were already active in the works long before the attack came. It will not, admittedly, be possible to stay within the realm of pure musical immanence—any more than music itself does. The problem is, rather, one of sociological insight, one that presents itself above all as a sociological problem today.

Casella's programme is one of deliberate, declared *reaction*. He acts more consistently than reactionary artistes who know not what they do; for him, reaction is not an object of free aesthetic choice but, rather, something that he traces back to its real social preconditions. He unambiguously uses fascism to justify neoclassicism. This connection was admittedly not discovered by Casella; I already asserted it in 1927 in the September issue of *Musik*, in a critical review of the Frankfurt concert held by the International Society for New Music, speaking of a stabilization of music that rushes to keep up with the stabilization of the economy.[3] At the time, I attempted to assign neoclassicism to the advanced industrial nations and folklorism to the more backward agrarian ones, and concluded by attributing the special situation of the fascist states, Italy and Spain, to the acceptance of a costumed, fake folklorism that no longer has anything to do with the actual tradition of its people but, rather, creates a surrogate thereof for ideological purposes. It is this form of *a posteriori* tradition and deliberately cultivated folk art that Casella's essay serves. For once, the ideological construct was actually preceded by its

3 See Theodor W. Adorno, *Gesammelte Schriften*, VOL. 19: *Musikalische Schriften VI* (Frankfurt a. M.: Suhrkamp, 1984), pp. 100ff.

sociological destruction: the theory of practical mystification. It was certainly to be expected that the new European nationalism would demand nationalist art; that it would play the earthy off against the rationally enlightened and disunited, the collectively commodifiable against the anarchically individual that now poses a threat once again; the traditional surface structure against the freedom of the irruptive imagination. The only surprise in Casella's essay is that he does not presuppose the sacred autonomy of intellectual history but admits of his own accord to the dependence of his artistic programme on the political developments. Otherwise, his like-minded colleagues would certainly be ready to attack the exposure of this dependence as sceptical disruption; in the rapture of the New Objectivity he demystifies his own ideology. He utters what is generally carefully disguised: he makes it clear that the current stabilization of music adapts itself to whatever the dominant politics might be. This connection through adaptation, however, is of a transparently ideological nature: there is not some dark purpose of being common to these two, politics and music; rather, stabilized music blankly follows the interests and dictates of the ruling class. He who pays the piper calls the tune: Casella's argumentation supplies the most pointed objection to any artistic practice seeking to preserve the claim to truth. His manifesto makes a clarifying and destructive impression. It provides confirmation—presented by an all-but-dubious authority—of what is really meant by the new communal art, the return to nature and clear *serenitas*. They are conjured up by the spirit of fascism, not by the historical state of music.

Casella's *argumentation* has already been commented on incisively by Krenek.[4] Nonetheless, it merits further consider-

---

4 See Ernst Krenek in Arnold Schönberg, Ernst Krenek and Gian Francesco Malipiero, 'Zu Casellas Aufsatz "Scarlattiana"' ['On Casella's Essay "Scarlattiana"'], *Anbruch* 11(2) (February 1929): 79.

ation. Krenek assumes a stance that rejects any fundamental statements about music in favour of individual empirical findings. This is certainly understandable after the decades of concealment of concrete aesthetic problems through the hollow *a priori* approach of abstract-idealist artistic doctrine; but it can hardly be pursued in the light of the force of genuine historical insight, which does not simply produce theory but, rather, if it is to become in any way concrete, already presupposes a body of theoretical ideas. For example, Krenek criticizes—quite rightly—Casella's notion of *order*, which he desires to exclude entirely from the discussion on account of its ambiguity. It is quite clear what kind of order Casella means, however, and the discussion about it is hence already sufficiently concrete. Casella's order is the natural order, a form of musical class system, in which the secondary degrees submit as willingly to the tonic and dominant as workers and private businessmen yield to authoritarian state syndicates in the fascist state. Romanticism, on the other hand, is not simply constructed here as the sphere of musical-expressive individualism—whose crisis no one will deny—but refers instead to any musical intentions that might destroy this supposedly natural, static and ahistorical order in music. Casella makes very clever use of the ambiguity inherent in the word 'order': he means something quite particular, namely that natural and static order, and then proceeds to attack all artistic attitudes that do not conform to his understanding of the word. That understanding by no means corresponds to the universal meaning of order, however, merely to the order of a particular period: one in which there was no subjective dynamism to undermine the structure of the simplest natural givens in music, specifically—in keeping with his nationalist ideology, which music had already outgrown by the time of Verdi's dramatic subjectivity—the golden age of Italian instrumental music, that is to say the late seventeenth and early eighteenth centuries. The order advocated by Casella is a *predefined* one, one in which, to refer once again to Krenek, the individual is indeed 'more strongly confined in relation to the material'—because the material of music had not been infiltrated by the liberated individual to remotely the same extent as in later times. That old order, however, is dead. What it contained has long since expired in intra-musical terms; attempts at restitution are the business of ideological, backward petty-bourgeois, and are taken care of immediately. The social preconditions for such music are in the past: not even fascism can reinstate feudalism within today's thoroughly rationalized capitalist economy, so, even if one marches to the master's tune, anyone who takes the seventeenth century as a model is following an aestheticist fiction. For it is then no longer the master's tune; at best, having such a tune is one of his fantasies and, accordingly, remains unreal. The order of the feudal collective in music has long since been replaced by others: the order of Romanticism was dominated by the bourgeois notion of unity of person, known as personality. It passed, but constituted no less of an order than that of the eighteenth century and was no less valid a representation of social reality. Today, perhaps, rationally illuminated construction is finally beginning to overcome the mere natural determination of the material: a completely new form of order that cannot be culled from any previous version. It is possible without the fiction of a collective consciousness, which in reality no longer exists. 'Order is necessary in all art,' Casella claims, without surprising anyone with this formal assessment. But order, as questionable as the word may have become, is as present as ever in today's art: simply not a collectively binding one—for lack of any suitable collective—only one that follows its own criteria and justifies itself through the state of knowledge it realizes within itself. Nor would the order Casella means be dictated by the collective, not, as the members of that class like to say, 'organically grown'—it would be formed abstractly on the model of a past collective in order to serve the fictional collective constructs of Romantic fascism as ideology. The anti-Romanticist Castella is far more Romantic than any elements of Romanticism one still finds in music today: he wants to flee from the current musical reality into the dream-world of an epoch full of meaning that is unattainable and never existed.

The ambiguity of the concept of order becomes apparent in the fact that Casella equates order with *tonal* order. One of the great achievements of Schönberg's *Theory of Harmony* lies in showing that tonality is not the nature-given, eternal order of things but, rather, a transient, limited and clearly demarcated period. One should not have to explain to Casella, that former advocate of *Pierrot lunaire*, how much order—or, to replace that police state term, how much form—it was possible to realize beyond obsolete tonal bonds. 'Classical' construction was certainly negated—but in favour of a brighter, more rational and more powerful construction that cannot be labelled with any past cultural titles, but is objectively evident in Schönberg's most recent works even if it is not yet evident to listeners. One must reject the gesture with which Casella declares: 'I do not need to polemicize against a musical direction that has meanwhile been overcome to almost the same extent as Cubism in painting.' No, he does need to; for the fact that a considerable number of composers adapted, were forced to adapt to, the stabilization of the economy in order to live, because the new bourgeoisie wanted to ensure it had helped to forget the war and the threatening change of consciousness that accompanied it—this does not prove anything about whether some determined composers were right to draw consistent conclusions from their own situation. It is clear to anyone who has investigated the matter that one cannot speak of an invalidation of thematic work through atonality.

Nonetheless, one must once again contest Casella's claim that thematic work is an eternally valid law of musical shaping: the score of Schönberg's *Erwartung* is sufficient on its own to show that one can still compose not only meaningfully, but also with the utmost vividness and clarity while dispensing with all conventional thematic work. The fact that atonal music did not find a home in Italy simply confirms that a large-scale change of musical consciousness failed to occur as much there as everywhere else—in addition to which Italy, especially with regard to harmony, still has to catch up on a nineteenth century of its own; it should therefore not be surprising if atonality is considered more alien there than in other countries, as the process of chromaticization has not yet been pushed far enough. And the best works of Casella and Malipiero are certainly those in which they departed most radically from tonality. The fact that today's reactionary could be in tomorrow's avant-garde does not mean that he is not a genuine reactionary; it only demonstrates the low reliability of snobbist avant-gardes. When Casella suspects even the prince of avant-garde reaction—namely Stravinsky, who is clearly the target of the passage about Paris—of being a snob, he seems to be denying the origin of his own efforts: it is a sign of the demonic greatness of Stravinsky, whose classicism in *Oedipus Rex* seems insincere even to fascists after the diabolically elegant irony with which he presented that same classicism in *Pulcinella*. Compared with the serene blood-and-soil art espoused by Casella, at any rate, the threateningly hollow masks of Parisian snobbery merit some defence. At the same time, one should note that in his manifesto of musical fascism, Casella is forced to recall the illusorily playful origin of what he wishes to promote as the simple, serious credo of a new collectivity. He senses that what he is offering is far more like a tonal intermezzo than the suitable art for a humanity that 'longs for clarity and joyful optimism', but evidently—because it longs for them—does not possess those valuable qualities.

It remains to observe what the reference to an atonal inter-mezzo is intended to mean: it does not simply reflect the opin-ion of the fascist Casella but is, rather, symptomatic of a mentality that is currently quite widespread.

People have become accustomed to discrediting the con-cept of atonality by first of all attacking the *word*—the bour-geois reactionary knows that there is no such thing as music without tones, atonal music; more informed persons say that everyone means something else by the term, hence it is of little use. One cannot escape the impression that so many people wish to battle against the word 'atonal' because they think they can do away with the matter through terminological discus-sions. The expression is not as bad as some make out: it dis-tances itself emphatically from what has been and from any confusion with what has been. The most useful definition—that is to say, the one best supported by a historical under-standing of what is relevant today—is Westphal's, who uses the word to refer to 'functionless' harmony. According to his interpretation, it is reasonable to call a music atonal in which neither individual chords nor the connections between them can be identified in terms of Riemann's functions. One could object that some music contains individual chords that are tonal—for example, ones composed of notes from the scale of a particular key—but would nonetheless be atonal by Westphal's definition. This shows that the connections between chords are a more important criterion for determining tonality or atonality than the chords themselves; much of Stravinsky's music, for example, must be considered atonal even though most of the harmonies are based on scales, because the placing of chords in relation to one another occurs without any function-tonal connections. For tonality is not defined simply by the use of scalar relationships but also by those of modulation—just as Reger, conversely, whose music contains barely a single chord that can be unequivocally assigned to *one* particular key, is nonetheless a tonal composer because of the purely functional structure of his modulations. A further objection to the distinction between tonal and atonal music would be that all possible harmonic events can ultimately somehow be expressed with the coordinate system of Riemann's—expanded—functional theory. Admittedly, one can exclude those cases in which such a representation would require such complicated alterations that functional relationships are no longer recognizable as such. In addition, the ear can generally discern—excepting such difficult borderline cases as Scriabin's last works—instinctively whether it is dealing with functional or functionless, tonal or atonal music. Certainly, the boundary between them is a blurred one; but the distinction between two spheres of artistic method that are, after all, formed in history, not according to definitions, cannot take place according to mathematical criteria, only by determining conceptual extremes in relation to which the material between them is interpreted. Notwithstanding the problematic nature of these concepts, the distinction between tonal and atonal is one that should be maintained.

Let us repeat: the abandonment of functional harmony was inaugurated by necessity through the collapse of tonal unities themselves, through the independence of secondary scale degrees, and the claims of contrapuntal lines to an autonomous status. Atonality is not the chance product of an experimenting will but, rather, a step called for by a contemporary understanding of the historical state of music and musical material. The more fully such insight proves itself, the more 'purely' atonal a work of New Music is, the more one can trust it; it is no coincidence that the works in which atonality crystallizes most completely are those with the highest degree of technically immanent consistency. It is not the works of the fellow travellers—who are the first to apply that description to others—not the technically indiscriminate and uncontrolled works but the most tightly constructed and rigorous works, and those most distant from any fashions, that deal seriously with atonality. Atonal music is still the most advanced of our time; that other kind, by contrast, which also employs functionless sounds but clings to tonal chords at the crucial points in order to avoid falling apart, is backward and mediating—a genuine intermezzo between the past and present phases of music. No œuvre of the musical present displays its intention and technical criteria as bindingly as Schönberg's, whose twelve-note method provides a summing-up of atonality: it seems likely that strict, developed atonality will enjoy greater longevity than the music of those composers who seek to make a pact with a past after the fact, now that mediation is not even required any longer. Nor those who use new elements, but simultaneously rob them of their new formal sense, lumping them together with the old to form an artisanal stew. Atonality is not some undisciplined stimulus that must first be made consumable by honest or dishonest brokers if it is not to remain an isolated curiosity. It is, rather, in atonality that we find the internally consistent, self-aware music of our time, and all those who dilute it with elements from the past are falsifying it.

And so we finally see through the motive for presenting atonality as an intermezzo. First of all, there is the bitterness of those who were left behind, who—as they would say—were stimulated by it but could not muster the strength to follow the loosening of tonality through to its conclusion. The decisive motives are ones relating to *content*. Atonality is not a phenomenon within an airtight space of music history, avoiding all contact with the outside world; rather, the breaking of tonal boundaries has a *real* significance: tonality is forgone by a consciousness that will no longer content itself with the nature-like stasis of its existential conditions and, instead, recognizes its own inflammatory productive power. It no longer simply aims to change music's natural preconditions but seeks to take control of the natural material and, paying the closest attention to the character of that material yet immune to its demonic compulsion, infuse it with intention. Such a will is not exclusively musical, however, but simultaneously—whether consciously or not—political. As long as the immutable existence of nature as an eternal force forms the basis of all ideology and reaction, reactionaries of all kinds will detest music that demystifies this same eternal nature in whose preservation they have so great an interest. It is no coincidence that the polemic against the theory of overtones as a method to get 'back to nature' occupies a central position in Schönberg's *Theory of Harmony*. His opposing motto 'onwards to nature' already resembles a declaration of war on the lethargic continuation of natural being, a political maxim. This is why atonality is so hateful to both dull-witted minstrels and fascists. Because they cannot simply pretend it does not exist, they pass it off as obsolete and act as if they were already a step ahead—when all they have done is once again to stabilize the ruins of what collapsed under the onslaught of the finally liberated consciousness. They sense the explosive power of that music; hence, they want to assign it to the past. There is hope, however, that the intermezzo will break down the walls of past formal approaches with which they seek to obstruct it. At present, it is still as self-enclosed as a conspiracy. What is more favourable than an acceptance of slothful progress, however, is that the forces of extreme reaction now sense the danger threatening them. They will not be able to ward off this danger; the intermezzo is the future of music.

1929

AGAINST THE NEW TONALITY

In his essay 'Man trägt wieder Dur',[1] Hanns Gutman describes
the trend of new tonality. He identifies it within the general
reactionary thinking evident in the public consciousness,
rightly combining it with the images of false resurrection one
finds everywhere: long dresses and military comedies, images
of naïve neutrality and prejudiced censorship. The phrase 'new
tonality' refers to a section on the broad front—or at least
secure behind the lines—of the movement that began with
stabilization and was accelerated through the economic crisis,
especially in its character as a crisis of rationalization: the
march into the nineteenth century. While Gutman sees the
social origin of the new tonality clearly, he is, however, not
able to draw material conclusions from this general insight
and formulate concretely in an elaborated aesthetic critique
what such a social analysis can only touch on: that this new
tonality has an ideological function—it conceals the social
reality, conveying the illusion of self-sufficiency. Gutman stops
halfway. He sees the social-reactionary origin of the new
tonality, or at least its connection to phenomena of general
cultural reaction, but shies away from its intra-aesthetic being,
falling back on the convenient distinction between those

1 See Hanns Gutman, 'Man trägt wieder Dur' ['Major Keys Are Back in
Fashion'], *Der Scheinwerfer. Blätter der Städtischen Bühnen Essen* 4(14)
(March 1931): 9ff.

authentically and inauthentically neo-tonal composers. This distinction tells us as little about the truth or untruth of art as any psychological one. For if the origin of the new tonality is ideological, if it serves the purpose of concealment, then the bona-fide old fogies are as much swindlers as the honest profiteers among them; if one can seriously differentiate between authentic and inauthentic works in the new tonality, however, the criteria must lie in the actual works and the nature of their material, not in a mentality that evades any critical standards and can only be explored on the basis of material insight.

This is where Gutman commits his decisive logical error. He views general reaction with intellectual-historical vagueness, without understanding that its true location is the technical constitution of works of art. He calls it 'nonsense' that 'atonality as such is revolutionary, while tonality is *a priori* regressive.' Certainly, atonal music can also be arch-reactionary: if it dresses up an outmoded formal construction or Romantic expressive complexes in multi-note chords that have no compositional consequences. This can only be judged, however, by the coherence or incoherence of the respective compositional *technique*. Gutman believes that 'the synchronous fabric of a music, after all, is simply a composition-technical aspect; and it is highly questionable whether or to what extent technical findings permit conclusions about artistic mindset.' The only aspect of a particular music that is given with any certainty, however, is the nature of its material; nothing that does not ultimately fall into the categories of 'technique'. Only if one operates with an outdated notion of compositional technique, as something that can be learned at will and separated from the material constitution of a work, can extra-technical aspects of the sonic phenomenon be emphasized—namely, those that do not conform to the pre-defined, traditional canon of techniques. If one defines technique simply as the internal laws of a construct, however, there is nothing unconnected to it. To replace it with the 'mindset' as the defining criterion would not only remove the work from the reach of any conclusive examination, but also constitute a regression to the ideas of expression and creator status from which New Music is beginning to free itself—though not those of its apologists who consider not the matter itself and its binding nature but, rather, the psychological constitution of the authors. This psychological constitution is only of art-critical interest in so far as it can be ascertained from each actual construct and its coherence—i.e. from its 'technique'. If someone 'is a Sinding,[2] at heart, yet sets the boldest disharmonies down on paper', one cannot ascertain this by looking directly into his heart but through the fact that the disharmonies are disharmonies—introduced arbitrarily and unconnected into a music whose immanent structure is of such a different nature, so fundamentally based on conventional symmetrical relationships, that multi-note chords appear within it as disharmonies. Disharmonies do not exist as such, only relative to the total structure of a given music, and it is the business of technical analysis to show what the context is. The secret Sinding will, in the cases referred to by Gutman, be found not in anyone's heart, but first of all in their compositions: unimpaired, 'closed' melodies will be found accompanied by 'dissolved' sounds; eight-bar periods with perfect and imperfect cadences will frame harmonic progressions that are by their nature incompatible with such symmetries; chords whose inner tension demands particular voice-leading solutions will instead be subjected to parallel motion—all these methods work to achieve a clarity that, disregarding the music's own laws and imitating tonal structures instead, conceals the requirements of the material. Those who operate in such ways are swindlers; not simply in relation to tonality,

2 A reference to Norwegian composer Christian Sinding (1856–1941). [Trans.]

which they veil without breaking it, but also precisely in relation to atonality, which they feign without meeting its standards. A critique that draws on a rigorous understanding of
atonality can expose it better and more strictly than conventional tonal critique, whose criteria cannot be applied when
the demands of such new chords do not even come into the
equation.

As well as the atonal swindlers, there are also—according
to Gutman and in reality—the neo-tonal ones. He now
assumes that there is a legitimate and an illegitimate return to
tonality, but without offering any technical criteria, as the
technical findings do not permit him to draw any conclusions
about the 'mindset'. Instead, he distinguishes between 'pio-
neers' and 'fellow travellers'—words whose sound alone should
arouse suspicion, as it is all too reminiscent of a stale ideal of
personality opposed most loudly by the spokesmen of musical
neoclassicism, which—according to Gutman—is concerned
first of all with 'binding' contexts. There is little use in trusting
in our great men in a situation where Stravinsky is unsure
whether he should dedicate his *Symphony of Psalms* to God or
to the Boston Symphony Orchestra, and in which Hindemith
has been writing the same chamber concerto again and again
for years, simply with different instrumentation, the only variation being that he returns more energetically to the genre
each time; a petty bourgeois, the kind that does not otherwise
appeal to Gutman. The authority of personality no longer
deserves any credit. It is apparently supported with the polemical notion of 'snobbery', which is supposed to take care of the
fellow travellers. But even its democratic claim should not be
too readily accepted. For reactionaries have always invoked the
idea of snobbery to discredit new, foreign ideas by passing off
their own habitual and generally comprehensible position as
the one that is in the communal interest. Conversely, the intellectual radicalization of the bourgeoisie is largely determined

by that 'snobbery', the will to march forward and not let oneself be fooled, and it is very uncertain whether there is any
other intellectual access to Marxism, for example, than the
'snobbery' of the most advanced insight. The work of Stravinsky or Picasso—to say nothing of Proust—is inconceivable
without that snobbery, which, in a different order of things,
will appear in an entirely different light than within the bourgeois order: namely as the dialectical anticipation of the latter's
demise. Gutman is not concerned with this, and refers in any
case not to the true, prominent form of snobbery, but more
of a middle-class variety; he hangs the little snobs while letting
the big ones go. Only an engagement with the big ones, however, would be fruitful. Nothing is more agreeable to them
than seeing the little ones dangle—to their greater glory.

Such nuances are not even necessary for a critique of the
new tonality, however. For it is the compositions that determine which is the only legitimate way to use tonality today.
Tonal chords cannot simply be attributed to natural conditions, but have developed historically and bear the marks of
their historicity in all aspects: once Romanticism had discovered their expressive values, these could no longer be removed,
any more than the psychological character of all leading-note
dissonances from which tonal music always takes its impulse.
If New Music makes use of these resources, they necessarily
are bound to clash with everything that points beyond the
trappings of tonality in New Music: a principle of construction
that can no longer be guided by psychological, expressive tension or organic leading-note relationships; but also a social
condition that no longer offers a homogeneity of the kind
always presupposed by the binding nature of tonality's claim
to validity. The situation of the new tonality is characterized
by composition-immanent contradictions and a generally
illusory stance. It would, admittedly, be too easy to prohibit
the use of tonal means categorically because of this, and only

suitable if one considers 'snobbery' the greatest sin and the direct adequacy of artistic means to the needs of art and the social situation its only proof of legitimacy. One can certainly demand, however, that the immanent contradictions of the new tonality are made fruitful, that their full illusory nature is productively employed and revealed, instead of serving the purpose of concealment. The new tonality is justified only as a *dialectical corrosion of the old*. Thus one finds in Stravinsky's *L'histoire du soldat* or Weill's *Mahagonny* a compositional manifestation of the falsity that stale triads, the 'music of back then', show today; the wrong notes mixed into the triads were derived, so to speak, from the historical deterioration of pure triads. Hence, the dislocation of harmonic joints, the shifting of harmonic emphases, serves to depict the stale and fallacious nature of the chromatic expressive language; and hence, at the climax of Stravinsky's *Le Baiser de la fée*, the splendour of the Romantic orchestra is exaggerated to the point of ghostliness: not through the creation of a vague mood but, rather, through an exact composition and instrumentation of that splendour's falsity. Those who always speak of 'destruction' in the cases of Weill and Stravinsky in particular are therefore right in their instinct; they only fail to recognize that such an approach is the only one that draws the necessary conclusions from the current state of compositional resources, whereas an unbroken, serious neo-tonality promoted as 'communally minded' precisely disguises the decayed state of its resources—but pays the price, as the composition's very claim to authenticity, and immediacy does not stand up to thorough technical analysis. In the avant-garde too, one cannot shake off the feeling that a knowing, critical use of tonality could pave the way for a primitive and ahistorical one—just as people began ironically delighting in pre-war films as soon as long dresses came back into fashion. It is precisely here, on the other hand, that something decisive is happening to the engagement with the generation of our fathers, something that perhaps only desires that danger of ambiguity in which the two generations are intertwined with both love and hatred. Just as the latter is accompanied by the risk of insanity, the atmosphere of this engagement is exposed to the danger of ideological appeasement. Stravinsky and Weill have largely explored and mastered both possibilities. The 'unliterary', naïve security of the other neo-tonal composers stems purely from the fact that they never even penetrated this atmosphere, that their endeavour has thus already failed before it begins and their obstinacy should not be mistaken for richness of nature. It is uncertain how long the dialectical—or, as I have called it, the 'surrealist' —variety of new tonality will remain usable. It cannot be denied, however, that its prolongation would be accompanied by the danger of consolidating the illusory, forgetting the true intention and ultimately arriving at a questionable stabilization.

This stabilization, however, is what Gutman ends up propagating after all. He places social analysis above the material-technical; but he precisely neglects to frame the phenomenon of neo-tonality in sociological terms. Here he suddenly ascribes a technical autonomy to the music that he had disqualified as a part of the critique of neo-tonality in favour of the idea of coherence. He unexpectedly argues:

> There are very substantial reasons for the reinstatement of tonality in its position of dominance. They all stem from the understandable desire among musicians to leave the chaotically unconnected state of atonality and establish new ties. And the fact that the new law is essentially only a comprehensive revision of the old one is not necessarily a shortcoming.

These 'ties', however, are synonymous with those that characterize the state of society, which, after being exposed as a lie, is to be sold to people once again in order to make them believe they are a community, because they get on so well in the natural realm—when they should instead be shown that they are no longer a community, and that nothing tears them apart more demonically than the blind natural force to which they cling musically in the shape of triads, whose natural primacy is questionable to begin with. The normative character of a positive new tonality can be contested both sociologically and technically. Sociologically, because it feigns ties that are no longer present in society, and, in so far as they might still exist, are subject to radical critique; and technically, because precisely the notion of coherence—which Gutman rejects—demands *pure* atonality once the pre-eminence of tonality has been undone. Gutman at least acknowledges this to the extent that he credits Schönberg with being 'the only one to follow the atonal problem through to its conclusion'. It is precisely in intra-technical terms that atonality is characterized not by any 'chaotically unconnected state' but by the most rigorous dialectic of question and answer. Here, however, Gutman hypostatizes the concept of social rather than technical bindingness. His argumentation is characterized by a quid pro quo between sociology and immanent compositional critique that prevents any clear statement. It is only resolved once the final sociological thesis is clarified: that of the exclusion of atonality, or at least the consistent kind, on account of its 'incomprehensibility'. For this incomprehensibility is not itself a fundamental attribute of the music, but only a function of the social condition which was forced to rely on a preservation of the glue holding the status quo together in all intellectual and artistic matters after the economic power structures became too problematic to justify the state of society any longer. If the political agitation music of the radical Left therefore uses tonal means, it may at first sight be acting legitimately—though any popular song would have more power and immediacy than pretentious, elevated neo-tonal pieces attempting to reach a 'standard' they could never achieve in any reliable material terms. But beyond this momentary effect, one should ask whether neo-tonal composition is not fundamentally opposed to the aims of Marxism, the perpetuation of a blind natural state whose timelessness stems purely from bourgeois ideology. One could easily imagine that, if a more rational form of labour division enabled the countless people who are remote from the most advanced art of today to approach music in something other than a tired state, if they had the time to understand music in technical terms as only experts can at present, if the inhibiting factor of education as privilege were to be eliminated—that such a situation would break down the barriers that separate people from atonality today; that they would recognize not only the exhausted but also the limited nature of tonal resources, and reach the same judgement that Brecht formulated about the current state of technology: 'It is not yet natural, but rather primitive.' Only an undialectical mode of thinking that acknowledges musical production as historical, but views its consumption in rigid terms, can rule out such a possibility. The divide between the production and consumption of music existing today, however, is one of the contradictions of the bourgeois order. Seeking to overcome it by following the consumer demands within the current order means declaring this state sacrosanct: yet musical production points beyond it, perhaps at the very points where the current order is not adequate to accepting it.

Gutman ends by attacking the concept of musical means being 'progressive' as I use it. 'In art, it is not only the technical aspects that are evidential. The stalest backwardness can be draped in new methods.' Such a conclusion can be reached only if one uncritically adopts the separation into form and content found in conventional aesthetics and judges complacently by its standards. In reality, the 'stale backwardness' of artistic content will only be revealed through the realization that the 'form' is mere drapery: not purely and fully developed, but itself backward. Gutman's reference to literary expressionism makes little difference. For the ephemerality of expressionism stems not from its radicalism but from a lack of radicalism, its murky mixture of atmospheric, psychological and constructive elements—and, above all, from the fact that, unlike atonality, expressionism was never able to develop an articulated and clear language, instead remaining trapped in the fortuity of the single utterance. It seems beyond doubt to me that expressionism, for all its flaws, is more suitable as a genuine starting point than the neo-objectivist industry of today, which simply acts as if nothing had happened. Certainly, expressionism remained undialectical, and did not progress beyond the subjective arbitrariness of the ego. But the basic experience that nonetheless informed it, the disintegration of all linguistic conventions, all predefined forms of language that Gutman's and my generation witnessed: it must, I believe, still form the basis of any language if it is to have a binding character. The prose of Kafka, in France even that of such authors as Green, Jouhandeau or the surrealist Aragon, as well as the poetry of Brecht cannot deny that origin: Brecht, who adopts a formal dialectic and never accepts the mere form of an utterance as an art form. Abandoning the content that had disintegrated, he developed the construction of precisely the formally constitutive elements of expressionism further, achieving a bindingness that the conventional reportage form of the New Objectivity fails to reach just as the stammers of expressionism failed before it. Its constructions are built from the ruins of language, from solitary, unconnected words, just as our atonal music—which does not mind calling itself 'atonal', a term that is ambiguous but at least gives it its polemical place—starts from the ruins of musical language and the solitary note, unconstrained by any syntax other than that which results from the here and now of its appearance between other notes.

Therefore any authentic form of artistic language today is on the level of musical atonality. A book such as Mottram's, in which—despite the idea of repeating the report three times—the formal law does not occupy a central position, instead lending the account a reality that is immediately and undialectically presupposed in the construct as genuine. Despite its qualities, this book, a factual account, is located beneath the question of form and shaping and is therefore as powerless to refute atonality as Flake's *Stadt des Hirns* proves it (though the latter did strive more loyally for the construction of being than the majority of post-war novels, which, the more naïvely they accept its power, fall short of it all the more thoroughly).

The question of atonality, as Schönberg formulated it, is not a question of mindset but, rather, one of insight. But this insight holds the moral aspect: namely, whether art is to change human consciousness or rather to affirm it in its torpid, persistent thusness.

1931

EXCURSUSES ON AN EXCURSUS

I shall take the liberty of making a few remarks on Hans Georg Fellmann's article 'Exkurs über das Thema "Moderne Musik"'.[1] The excursus touches on problems that I have treated in my own writings, recently also in *Der Scheinwerfer*: in the essay 'Against the New Tonality'[2] and the radio lecture 'Why is the New Art so Hard to Understand?'[3] Fellmann's view is opposed to mine in every respect; so thoroughly opposed, in fact, that I might take his article as a polemic against me and defend myself immediately, if only the thoroughness of Fellmann's opposition were lent clear contours through the thoroughness of his argumentation. But Fellmann forces me to attack while making it difficult for me to defend myself; for he does not actually attack me at all but insistently repeats formulations I thought I had long since exposed. Polemic is undoubtedly easier if one ignores the opponent's objections and remains fixated upon their initial theses— especially when, as is the case here, those claims are very commonplace ones. Such an approach, however, is not especially

1 See Hans Georg Fellmann, 'Exkurs über das Thema "Moderne Musik"' ['Excursus on the Subject of "New Music"'], *Der Scheinwerfer. Blätter der Städtischen Bühnen Essen* 5(6) (October 1931): 12ff.

2 See Adorno, 'Against the New Tonality' in this volume, pp. 226–36. [Trans.]

3 See Adorno, *Essays on Music*, pp. 127–61. [Trans.]

fruitful: it stops with the thesis, instead of using the polemic to develop it further in a positive fashion. All I can do is to remind Fellmann of a few ideas he prefers to ignore. As this response is not addressed privately to Herr Fellmann, however, but to an audience, namely the readership of *Der Scheinwerfer*, Fellmann will have to permit me to treat him not only as a polemical subject but also as an example of an intellectual approach that I consider it an objective necessity to point out. I cannot react to a position that is none, only add further excursuses to certain sentences and words of the 'excursus' in the hope of making them transparent. It should not be held against me if I repeat myself—least of all by Fellmann, who repeats statements not only made but also already refuted.

'Respect and admiration for the unflinching consistency of an intellectually valuable body of work are not the only criterion of artistic fulfilment.' Indeed not, Herr Fellmann. One can, for example, have an extremely consistent and praiseworthy attitude to art, yet still compose badly—namely, if this attitude floats freely above the work as its ideology without reaching the work itself, while the work is internally inconsistent and fails to meet the demands levelled at the author's work by that same attitude. Berg showed this in a polemic on Pfitzner, much too little known, published in *Anbruch* some years ago. The compelling arguments against Pfitzner are not, however, based on the fact that he is a 'Romantic'—the expression remains as nebulous as 'minstrel'—but that the quality of the compositions falls short, and only an insight into the compositional inadequacy can support judgements on the overall stance. This is the case if it transpires that the material used by the 'Romantic' Pfitzner, for example, no longer permits the leitmotivic-chromatic approach to music drama that he applies to it. But compared with so vague and materially uncontrollable a notion as 'contemporariness', which remains stuck in such abstract and in fact Romantic categories as that of the minstrel, even Pfitzner's outmodedness would be preferable—had it produced better music. In other words, stylistic critique can only grow from a critique of the concrete object, not skirt around it at a distance that mistakes itself for superiority and ideological authority, yet is actually based on nothing except an ignorance of the contextual problems in the work itself.

'The creator of *Der arme Heinrich* was as little able to move beyond himself as the creator of *Gurrelieder* and *Pierrot lunaire*.' Since when is it the artist's duty to 'move beyond himself'? Is this idea of self-transcendence, with its background of a mythology of death from Schopenhauer's and Hartmann's conception of the unconscious, not itself the epitome of Wagnerian Romanticism? When Schönberg composes, he does not hold Romanticism in one hand and the New Objectivity in the other, kneading each mass until the one absorbs the other—and if it is the folk-objective one all is well, but if it is the solitary constructivist one then all is not well. Rather, in every work, he finds a complex of musical *problems* that he investigates and attempts to solve in as suitable and controlled a fashion as possible—using a control that was not only invented by us evil intellectuals and constructivists, but was equally familiar to Schubert, whom the minstrel-composers so like to invoke. It is only repressed today because it bursts open, from within the *actual music*, the secure space of social communication in which today's minstrels make themselves comfortable, regardless of whether their works are composed correctly or not. A 'tragic artist's existence'? We are not such Romantics at all, Herr Fellmann; if our music needs time then we will wait, and know very well that—for social reasons—the waiting time will be longer than in the past, but otherwise attempt to produce something vaguely enduring, and to cook our musical dishes with such care and good ingredients that they will eventually find someone who enjoys their taste. Whether we are the tragic ones or those making a very perishable music, which incidentally has no more of an audience today than ours does (for both our audiences have been snatched away by talking films)—we shall leave the settling of that matter to the Romantic aestheticians, who presume to teach us the new health code while still speaking in the jargon of *Tristan* and not even noticing it.

'The reaction to the harmonically analytical and thus disintegrative work of Schönberg, who was a very great influence on the Russian . . .' Well, the influence of Schönberg on Stravinsky was never actually very substantial. Admittedly, Stravinsky freed his harmony from tonality in Schönberg's sense in some works—only a few, and lesser-known ones—though tonality almost always remains latently in effect in his music. Aside from this, however, Stravinsky did not adopt a single one of Schönberg's compositional methods, and the change in the harmonic surface in the latter's music might be its most conspicuous aspect to the layman, but it is purely contingent on much more deep-rooted compositional changes that took place. And what of his harmonically analytical, and thus disintegrative, work? If one takes Fellmann at his word, all harmonic analysis would be destructive, and Riemann would be exposed as a cultural Bolshevist—something in which even Fellmann is surely not interested. He uses the term 'analytical' to refer not to musical insight, only to a musical technique, without making clear what is actually being analysed: as a composer, Schönberg did not 'analyse' music but strengthened the individual scale degrees in the harmonic fabric to such an extent that they could no longer be held together by the tonal schema and necessitated a different one. In other words: for reasons of compositional coherence, he replaced simple overtone relationships with more complicated ones on a large scale. To quote a passage from an earlier text:

Others speak of 'disintegration' with reference to the mere material, which they think of as immutable and natural, as if the simpler overtone relationships were written in the stars. Even if they did, what happens to them is decided by humans; history, in art and elsewhere, proceeds as the destruction of the merely existent, which passes itself off as natural in order to keep the changing consciousness at bay, which comes from a better nature than the existent itself.[4]

'They also ignored the biological laws governing musical development, and overlooked that the aim of art is ultimately not to provide practical evidence to support a theory for connoisseurs and committed fanatics'—which biological laws do you mean, Herr Fellmann? Can the notions of the living and the organic even be applied to the sphere of artistic works, which are constructs and not creatures? Is it not simply a case of the norms of a particular period being presented as 'biological'? Norms that changed, not simply because they became outdated but because the problems arising in works of art could no longer be overcome within the old framework—works of art originally based on the same norms now being negated by the work? I refer to this relationship as the *dialectic* of art, an idea I must hold on to for as long as the interwoven nature of these problems forces me to. Those who start from an understanding of the dialectic of art, and cling to that insight even if such insights are concealed by an ideological smokescreen—discrediting these people as 'committed fanatics' is too easy. But that is simply how it is in the polemics directed at New Music: those who abandon it are supposed to prove that it is no good, and those who keep at it are branded relentless fanatics, without any questions as to the possible basis for their

4 See Theodor W. Adorno, 'Musikalische Aphorismen no. 25', in *Gesammelte Schriften*, VOL. 18, *Musikalische Schriften V* (Frankfurt a. M.: Suhrkamp, 1984), p. 28.

insights. Background knowledge is assumed by all art, and if this insight has become so exclusive in the case of New Music, this is the fault of society's structure, not the speculating artists.

'With the catchword "atonality", it (the audience) appeased its conscience without realizing that this atonality is not an invention of the present day. A vacuum came about, entirely of its own accord and through a natural process, between artistic production and demand.' Fellmann says nothing about this natural process. Though I do not deny this process as such, it hardly strikes me as natural, nor does it contribute to its explanation to use the phrase 'of its own accord'. The answer I have sought to offer to the question of why the new art is so hard to understand is precisely the one Fellmann omits to supply; here, as an 'excursus' to Fellmann, I must append my complete essay. One will certainly find the difference between a 'natural' and a historical process dealt with sufficiently there. Fellmann is right to say that atonality is not a modern invention but the result of a historical-dialectical process. His reference to atonality as a 'catchword', however, has the style of a catchword itself. I shall take the liberty of quoting myself once more:

> [T]he bourgeois reactionary knows that there is no such thing as music without tones, atonal music; more informed persons say that everyone means something else by the term, hence it is of little use. One cannot escape the impression that so many people wish to battle against the word 'atonal' because they think they can do away with the matter through terminological discussions. The expression is not as bad as some make out: it distances itself emphatically from what has been and from any confusion with what has been.[5]

5 See Adorno, 'Atonal Intermezzo?' in this volume, p. 222.

Lastly: Fellmann claims 'the human being' as the ultimate authority in the evaluation of art. The statement that art can only be judged by humans is a truism that already requires a lack of inhibitions to utter in the first place: this, with all the will in the world, is all that can be extracted from it. For 'the' human being is an entirely abstract category that takes on different historical manifestations, and from whose abstract purity one cannot derive any criteria of *content* for art or any other phenomenon of historical human life. 'The' human being that does not understand modern music and rejects it is not the human as a natural being, which cannot be crystallized as such in the first place: it is as much a product of history as the human being that *does* understand modern music, and differs from it only in its historical backwardness. Therefore, one should not invoke the human being and rely on the pathos of a generalized concept where highly particular answers are called for, answers that cannot be concealed by this general-human mask in any case. One should, rather, investigate the concrete problems of art and those of the social process, and seek to understand how art and society intersect—in reality and in the individual detail. This will be of greater use to the human being: the true human being as it appears in history.

1932

No one would see the palette of a painter and immediately take it for a painting. No one would be so quick to declare this painting, which is none, a failure. And least of all would anyone rebuke the painter for arranging the colours he planned to use for a painting on his palette in a careful, considered fashion. On the contrary: it would be considered useful for the selection and allocation of colours on the palette to be carried out quite consciously, and according to what the painter required of the picture he intended to paint.

The situation is very different in music. As one cannot hold its material in one's hands or buy it like the painter's colours, and as one rarely sets eyes on the musician's palette— although he requires one no less, and must arrange the material for a work in advance just like the painter—no composer is safe from a confusion of the palette with the painting as soon as some aspect of his 'palette' becomes visible to the public. If the palette then looks sober and pragmatic, or too little like a painting (for which it is mistaken), one will quickly hear voices calling the painting sober and practical or meaningless. Even if one has managed to distinguish between the palette and the painting oneself, this confusion nonetheless has dangerous repercussions. As music is considered a purely inward art whose inspirations come, without any effort from the artist, directly from the depths of his soul or from heaven, some will hold it against him if they can tell that this is not quite the case. And they proceed to avenge the destroyed illusion: why does he need a palette in the first place? It can only be because heaven and inwardness have abandoned him. So he is not an artist, only a craftsman or a mathematician. Away with him, away with the palette, away with the picture! The mere fact that it was painted using a palette is already suspicious. Let us return to heaven!

This is the sort of resistance found everywhere against the twelve-note technique developed by Schönberg and, with certain modifications, adopted by the entire young Viennese School. For it is really nothing other than, and above all no *more* than, the palette. It is a particular allocation of material: one composes *with* it. Only after this is done does actual composition begin, with all the urgency and all the joy that has always characterized it. If a composer had nothing but a twelve-note row with all its transpositions, inversions and retrogrades (it is the retrogrades—'crabs'—that horrify people most!), and lacked the ability to shape the music through the power of his imagination, the twelve-note technique would be of little use, and he would produce the same dreary, academic boredom as some crusty conservative with his triads. The twelve-note technique is not a recipe for composition; one should not fear that it might transform the 'man in the street'[1] into a Beethoven with the aid of a slide rule or a logarithmic table. A few schoolmasters have tried their luck with the twelve-note technique; to no avail.

Admittedly, one might now ask: 'So why use the twelve-note technique in the first place? First you are mathematicians instead of composers, and then your mathematics turns out to be useless; it does not even guarantee that you will compose well. Then you might as well give up altogether—certainly the

1 English in the original. [Trans.]

technique, and best of all composition too. They never had it in the old days either, and we still like the music from back then better than your useless contrivances. We don't need you!'

But wait! It does help us in various ways. It does not relieve us of the effort of composing, but at least of having to produce our compositional material ourselves first—like a painter who had to squeeze out cochineal beetles and cook indigo before he could begin his work; for we would indeed have to do so otherwise. Certainly, the composers of the past did not need any twelve-note technique. But the musician's material was different: it was already preformed, and tradition offered him a reliable palette: *tonality*. The artist, however, in this as in other respects, is not as free as the audience imagines in its idealization and longing: he cannot choose his material at liberty, but is bound to whatever his own historical moment offers him. No one who chose to work with tonality today could ever achieve the same effects as the tonal masters. The material has changed so much that nothing would emerge except forced pastiches—or dull, lifeless epigonal works; he would be unable to conjure up the power of Beethoven through the old tonality. Or do any of those falling back on the material today have that power? No, the old palette has dried up; we must produce a different one.

But, as was said earlier: the composer is not 'free' but, rather, dependent on the material as it necessarily and bindingly presents itself at that historical moment. So he will not be able to put together his palette freely and cheerfully; that historical condition of the material, according to its most advanced state, must rather be represented in the arrangement. And what about the twelve-note technique? Is it really a free-floating mathematical device—or does it have an internal *historical* justification?

Here lies the reason for its necessity. For that is precisely what characterizes its nature: it does not dictate the material for composition haphazardly or according to abstract rules, without any connection to the state of that material; rather, all its rules, even those forms so often disdained as 'mathematical', are no more or less than the concise and binding expression of those laws that the compositional material itself is asserting to composers today. Simply put, the compositional ear can tell as much nowadays as back then what is 'right' and what is 'wrong' in a piece of music; the difference is that it is becoming harder for the non-musician to establish the same. In addition, it is no longer sufficient to demand a resolution of dissonances, as all manner of other laws are now more important, ones that—let it be quite clear—*also* applied in the past, but whose significance was concealed by the most primitive of harmonic considerations. The twelve-note technique, however, is the epitome of these laws developed in the material of today: not for the speculating eye but, rather, the vigilant ear—no less than the laws of tonality in former times.

If, then, it is stipulated that a 'prime form', the starting material for the themes, should contain all twelve notes of the chromatic scale, this is simply a systematic expression of the fact that, following the total chromaticization of our musical material, the living *ear* immediately perceives any recurrence of a note before the presentation of the other eleven as an imbalance—as *'wrong'*—and that the theme must therefore be formed in such a way that this disturbance is avoided. If, furthermore, *everything* is fashioned from this row, it reflects the circumstance that, with tonality no longer sufficient to structure a composition, that structure must be based on the unique form of the particular theme—but then rigorously: that nothing may remain thematically 'fortuitous', and everything must instead be developed from the same substance if the music is to gain the same cohesion previously bestowed upon it automatically by tonality. The technique of Brahms, with its strict economy of motivic use, essentially developed this already, and it is in this respect more than any other that twelve-note music is connected to the great classical tradition. Lastly, the fact that melody *and* harmony are based on the same rows, this only proves that today, with the rules determined by the individual work, not a presupposed system of coordinates, it can no longer be the case that melody is 'individual' and harmony merely an external frame of reference. Rather, both come freely and in unity from the same centre: the original composition *conception*.

Such is the nature of the palette. And in the end, it is more than merely a palette: just as it is demanded by the conception of the work, the individual work, it in turn affects the composition of the work through the rigour of its selection. But is this any different to the painter's palette? And could the trained eye not already discern something of the artistic intention in the arrangement of colours on the palette of a great painter—just as the purity and rigour of the picture testify in turn to the purity and rigour of the palette?

c. *1935*

THE DEVELOPMENT AND FORMS OF NEW MUSIC

The only way for me to approach the task of saying something about the development and forms of new music in fifteen minutes is by pointing to certain aspects of the situation now, one year after the death of Schönberg. 13 July 1951 marks the caesura in the history of New Music. Not only did Schönberg create it, discarding a tonality that had become drained, its possibilities all exhausted; not only did he gain complete freedom of control over the resources of music and simultaneously develop the powers to shape that unbound material—he has also remained its true master to this day, and in the force and integrity of his mastery become one of the great composers, preserving tradition in the energy with which he, its heir, remodelled it. It is time to draw attention very emphatically to the latter in particular, Schönberg's compositional brilliance, because there is a danger of demoting him to a mere pioneer, reformer and inventor of a system. Every one of his works confronts the artist with that same imperative formulated by Rilke in his 'Archaic Torso of Apollo': 'you must change your life'. If one can speak of some clear tendency of development in music, instead of deftly sensing which way the wind is blowing, then it lies in this imperative: to compose with absolute consistency and the utmost responsibility. This responsibility extends so far, however, that even consistency and integrity of form must be sacrificed if it demands so.

This imperative comes only from Schönberg's work itself, however, not his much-discussed stylistic history—just as, in his book *Style and Idea* (published in English), he emphatically advocated the concept of a musical idea unfolding from its own logic against a notion of style imposed upon the works from above and without. Today, one encounters such phrases as 'Schönberg, the father of twelve-note music'. Whoever has a serious interest in learning about the development of New Music would do well to place no trust in such odious clichés and, indeed, to leave the twelve notes to themselves, and instead attempt through faithful and attentive listening to gain a sense of the fabric of Schönberg's music and that of his closest pupils, Berg and Webern. I can think of no better pieces to recommend for this purpose than those which marked Schönberg's breakthrough to New Music; those which still retained a connection to conventional music, but whose inner constitution already contained everything that was essential to him. No one could say that one needs to be familiar with any system to listen to them; but whoever truly understands them will automatically come to appreciate the later pieces, which use note-rows for the sake of their own compositional organization, not simply for purposes of reform. I shall therefore name some of those works that I consider not only keys to Schönberg's development, but to that of New Music itself—and which, though they mostly use tonal resources, have not actually been absorbed into the repertoire any more than his twelve-note works. I am referring to the songs Op. 6, which perhaps form the best introduction to the music that was new by its very nature, the orchestral songs Op. 8, the two string quartets Op. 7 and Op. 10, the Chamber Symphony Op. 9 and, lastly, the George songs Op. 15, which were the first example of pure atonality but retain a clear simplicity of structure throughout. Allow me to add that nothing demonstrates Schönberg's creative ambition more compellingly than this group of compositions, which combine the freshest spontaneity of musical intuition with the richest capacity for abstract construction.

It is not without reason that, after being invited to speak about current developments, I have drawn your attention to a single composer and to a group of works written between forty and fifty years ago. For the fate of this composer and his work illustrates the nature of musical development today, and indeed how questionable that notion has itself become. Only recently a composer of some repute was able to declare unashamedly in a public discussion that he did not understand Schönberg's late works; and it is indeed a sign of the times that as soon as people do not understand something, they feel they are supported in their incomprehension by the naïveté currently in demand everywhere, and even pride themselves on it. I doubt that said composer understands what Schönberg wrote fifty years ago any better. He is not alone to blame for this, however, but more generally the development whose notion I questioned. Today, the old, but previously latent social contradiction that human consciousness was not keeping up with the development of the objective spirit in its own culture is now appearing openly everywhere—the cultural failure that laid the anthropological foundation for the barbaric upheavals and outbursts of recent decades. In music, this rupture, which was already beginning to become apparent around the middle of the nineteenth century, has taken on subterranean depth. For reasons I cannot analyse here, the vast majority of people are not even hostile—those were better days—but completely uncomprehending and indifferent towards the objective inner development of music. But because art concerned with the artistic content itself, not its effect, also suffers from this; because it threatens to waste away in a specialist culture, and ultimately in the designing of musical wallpaper patterns; because not only philosophers, but also artists need first of all to live, and the *horror vacui* robs them of their productive power—because of all this, we are now faced with the paradoxical, though by no means unique circumstance that composers (and not only those without talent) become defeatists of their own cause, namely that of immanent artistic development. Those who were left behind have elevated their regression to an aesthetic programme for their own activities, and whoever does not play along is viewed as an old-fashioned individualist whom they can slaughter on the turned tables. Because the extreme intellectual and spiritual demands placed upon the listener by the musical work that is finally emancipated, mature and divested of all infantile appeal are barely met with any response, they have decided to discard those demands, denigrate more highly organized music as unnatural, and enter a pact with the dominant condition among listeners, which is relentlessly strengthened by the commercial interests of the culture industry. As, however, the path of the objective spirit, the logic of the matter, is governed by a necessity that cannot be escaped through subjective whims, and as none of the generally binding and accessible artistic values invoked by that self-righteous naïveté are so present in the current order of things that they could be drawn upon simply and unthinkingly, those restorative attempts—as sanctimoniously as they might hide behind the phraseology of eternal bonds and sounding being—not only bear the hallmarks of simplification and regression, but also have a profoundly helpless and mask-like quality.

That is why it is so difficult to speak of any wholesale development of New Music; on the one side, there are unpopular people making an effort to swim against the tide and follow the tendencies of the music itself by pushing it further; while on the other, there is the compact majority, evident in its rawest and most brazen form in East Germany, which denounces this tendency of development as loss of substance, formalism, decadence and the like, trumpeting a more or less cleverly designed path backwards as a higher, collectively supported form of development. In contrast to past oppositions, even that between Brahms and Wagner, it is barely possible to subsume these two tendencies under a single concept of development. I am not unaware that Schönberg's and Stravinsky's interests overlapped at one point; nor that, especially in the first twelve-note works, for example from Op. 25 to Op. 31, Schönberg's impulses show certain analogies with neoclassicism (though one should not overestimate the importance of his recourse to 'older' forms). On the whole, however, the artistic motives of Schönberg's school are radically incompatible with the aims pursued by such composers as Stravinsky and Hindemith, in spite of their shared origins. But the more recent softening of neoclassicism into a semi-literary, semi-dilettantish universal style, that is viewed as 'development' in most of today's compositional work, no longer has anything at all to do with an unfolding and intensification of artistic productive powers. All criteria dissolve into dreary approximation, and the liveliness of free enterprise adapts to the mindlessness dictated by totalitarian systems of both varieties. The supposed will to a new order, this rampant fear of chaos, is nothing but the brutality of insecurity, which prohibits the expression of any opposing human impulses.

No membership of a particular school is a guarantee against this kind of development, however. Just as any insight can turn into delusion if it becomes rigidly entrenched, even consistent musical progress can, once systematized, be twisted into absurdity. The weakness of the artistic subject, which no longer takes it upon itself to craft a de-qualified, de-structured material in freedom and thus reconcile it but, rather, follows the maxim 'build a wall around us, said the pious little mother'—this aesthetic renegade mentality can find shelter as easily in twelve-note music as with simple, sincere masters and toccatas with wrong notes. Among the symptoms suggesting that the current state of music is much more desolate than during the crisis twenty or thirty years ago, which caused widespread horror, perhaps the worst is the behaviour of those young people who consider themselves avant-garde but rely blindly on rows and retrogrades, missing the true achievements of Schönberg's compositions and losing the ability to distinguish between what is meaningful and what is senseless in music; they content themselves with an entirely abstract and thus superficial and deceptive concept of correctness.

If the notion of musical development is to be more than an empty historical slogan, it is vital to admit unreservedly to all these negative elements, which are by no means restricted to a single artistic camp, to do away with all belief in magic formulas and fetishes and use the discipline of such critique and self-critique to acquire the freedom already inherited, so to speak. It is peculiar to this freedom, however, that it cannot be possessed; it is fulfilled only through intransigence and resistance. It will no longer be able to rely on ready-made forms. One can, however, see something of such an emancipated language in the great, authentic works of New Music. It would be musical prose, yet saturated with all the experiences of the binding methods of former times; a language in which the dynamism of the sonata would be combined with the integral unity of polyphony; one so wholly imbued with the developmental spirit that not a single development section, and thus no sonata or fugal schema, would any longer be required. The last instrumental work completed by Schönberg is entitled *Phantasy*. It would perhaps be not entirely wilful to take that title as a programme for the development and form of a music that, in spite of all, would still be possible. Here, the word 'phantasy' has a twofold meaning: in musical tradition, it refers to a work devoid of all surface systems, formed freely from artfully balanced sections. In an artistic sense, the concept of fantasy, of imagination, refers to a genuinely free music: the image of something that has not yet been, of possibility, which rises as high above mere being as art in its weightlessness has always intended but so far has not been able to achieve.

1952

If one attempts to gain an overview of the musical situation at a given time, this is hardly based on an appropriate perspective. One presumes an overall tendency of historical movement in the musical realm and wants to draw a conclusion. But the question 'Where do we stand?' ignores all too easily the one phenomenon in which art has crystallized since time immemorial: the individual, concrete work. The habit of thinking in broad historical perspectives, forgetting the binding, determinate manifestations that give rise to those perspectives in the first place, results in a blindness to values, an inability even to experience an artistic construct as such, in a nimbly classifying arrangement into various directions and, ultimately, in an administrative approach to art. If, instead of lingering, one simply wishes to know where things are heading, one is closing one's eyes to the decisive element: what music is in itself. Today in particular, when even the field referred to as 'New Music' displays an absence of any general binding style, all categorical reflections on New Music and its state will inevitably be skewed. The fact that it contains some good works and a great many bad ones does not make it any different from traditional music, and any attempt to claim an opposition between two independent historical worlds of music is as fruitless as a blindness to the fundamental aspects that have changed. One major difference is that in earlier periods, for example the seventeenth and eighteenth centuries, bad music was cloaked by conventions and not immediately identifiable as such; this, at least in part, is the cause of today's rampant predilection for what, using a thoroughly inappropriate analogy to visual art, is termed 'Baroque' music. On the other hand, the disintegration of a firm binding tradition and the inadequacy of conventional schools of craftsmanship in the face of liberated productivity are scarcely less disorienting. But the criterion used to distinguish between good and bad modern music is itself often an expression of confusion—not only among listeners but also among critics. Good modern music is said to be that which speaks to people, music that can be followed by listeners and 'gives them something'; and bad music is that which one does not understand, which does not present any tangible context and which one cannot get anything out of; or music that one finds provocative and ugly. The immediate effect, often based on uncomprehending and therefore incomprehensible performances, is equated with the music's quality. But the upshot of this is usually that the music of 'moderated' modernity, i.e. that which somehow swims with the tide of the new but makes sure to cater to the established listening habits and expectations of the audience, is considered good, self-assured and even especially human and sincere, while composers who follow the historical state of the musical material and their own consciousness through to its conclusion, eschewing any effects that do not follow from the demands of that material itself, are maligned as intellectual and abstruse. That which is honest and capable of resisting the industry is vilified, while that which is weakly and follows the maxim 'modern, but not too much' is rewarded for such conformism by being affirmed as vital, fresh and communally minded.

By no means is it the case that all 'radical' music, which is very unjustly equated with twelve-note music today, is good and all other music bad. But one simply cannot pass judgement on a composition if one does not move beyond the pleasant or unpleasant impression it leaves. Certainly, any music that has not engaged seriously with the standards of radical modernism as represented by the Viennese School of Schönberg, Berg and Webern will scarcely be of value. But it is not simply a matter of mindset. What drove that school to its innovations and its collision with musical conformism was, rather, its unbending consistency—nothing else. There were also other innovations, to be sure: the works of the young Stravinsky, for example, above all *Le Sacre du Printemps*, are full of them. But these innovations were restricted to partial aspects; they concerned the harmony or the instrumental sound, but left other aspects entirely unchallenged. This is clear as day in *Le Sacre*: rudimentary tonal motivic cells are presented over multi-note harmonic complexes, then repeated and shifted around. Melody and harmony contradict each other. After eliminating the tonal chords and functions in the harmonic department, the formal progression of the piece is brought about by the crudest of means, namely unbroken rhythmic movement—at best varied through irregular accents. The question of the connection between the parts and the whole does not even arise; all elements are articulated by a stamping that is imposed on them purely from without. This formula was simultaneously responsible for the success of Stravinsky and his imitators and offensive to a compositional school that listens carefully to itself, and seeks to achieve objectivity—if at all—only by following the laws of its own fabric.

Hence, radical music, in the work of its significant exponents, achieved the emancipation of the musical material from tonality, to which music owed its evolution into great art but which was subsequently exhausted by that same great music. It achieved this in all aspects: harmony, sonority and melody, but also in the development of polyphony and the conception of forms. Many works, not least Schönberg's, strike an ear concerned with smoothness and obvious surface connections as ruptured. The only reason for this, however, is that he no longer created the context through such easy means as simply letting the music run on in time but, rather, developed it in each piece by establishing in which direction the sounds themselves want to move, and by allowing a single, determinate, specific form to breathe. So if harmony and melody tend towards equivalence in twelve-note music, if chords and the connections between them are fundamentally derived from the same row as the horizontal level—melodies and individual voices—this is not based on arithmetic but simply the need to do away with the divergence of the horizontal and the vertical at which all great music since Bach has laboured away.

If one wished to offer a crude description of the current situation, one could probably say that something of such ideas established itself in the consciousness of the responsible composers of the post-war generation. Twenty-five years ago, the music festivals, which already resembled exhibitions of commodities and placed more emphasis on compromise than selection according to quality, were dominated by neoclassicism and its folkloristic supplements. Stravinsky and Hindemith provided the models of all the concerti, toccatas and suites, modified with unbearable monotony, which were both archaic—for all their wrong notes and metric games—and 'up to date'[1] in their manner, often with an air of gratuitous irony. This changed after a while: deliberate boredom ultimately proved too boring for the more talented purveyors. It may be a factor that the two protagonists of neoclassicism, Stravinsky and Hindemith, have meanwhile progressed to full-blown classicism: they recognized the conflict between the objectivity they employed and their subjective-modern traits, and consequently

1 English in the original. [Trans.]

opted for pure pastiche, a primitive quotation of the past, or for academic harmlessness. This approach did not find many followers. Its sterility was too blatant, and to a generation that had lived through the fear and catastrophe of recent European history, this artificial naïveté and splendour was simply too irreconcilable with their own condition.

Instead, the Viennese School, at best tolerated as a sort of oddball German group at the former music festivals—rehearsals had led to open conflict between Schönberg and the directors of the International Society for Contemporary Music—seemingly established itself internationally. Though the three great Viennese composers are dead, and left behind no heirs in their own city (which never showed them much appreciation), there are groups of twelve-note composers not only in Germany but also in France, Italy and North America. Apparently, Schönberg himself was not especially pleased about his late triumph. When Darius Milhaud spoke to him in California shortly before his death, telling him of the universal interest in the twelve-note technique among young composers, he reportedly answered with the question: 'Yes, but are they making music with it too?' To an extent one can hear the inventor speaking here, worried about something that he views as his private property yet which is so important precisely because it is more than mere invention. At the same time, Schönberg's jest shows a concern that touches the heart of the present condition: the danger of neutralizing the productive impulses of New Music, something that would suit the state of society only too well.

'Twelve-note music' and 'dodecaphony' are no less popular expressions today than 'existentialism'. They seem to be equated quite readily with radical music per se, and wrongly so. A great deal of the music produced by the Second Viennese School and composers associated closely with it in its heroic years, from 1910 until the middle of the 1920s, including the most inspired and spontaneous works, was not written using the twelve-note technique. The technique itself, however, is widely understood. It is fundamentally wrong to speak of a 'twelve-note system' that, following Cocteau's basic formula, purports to follow chaos with order, a replacement for the exhausted, liquidated tonality of the past. Tonality articulated music in an immediate speech-like manner comprehensible to all through a reservoir of harmonic formulas and the corresponding structural aspects. The twelve-note technique does nothing of this kind; it takes effect behind the scenes, not—or hardly—in the manifest sonic phenomena. Whoever attempted to discern and remember the basic row of a twelve-note piece in the same way as the tonic key of a traditional composition, or indeed its 'theme', would be on the wrong track. It is precisely because people repeatedly confront New Music with the wrong expectations, which are then inevitably disappointed, that there is so much resistance. Overall, the twelve-note technique is no more or less than the universal expression of the technical experiences—and in art, this always includes the prohibitions—that shaped New Music. The less it was able to bind itself to a general idiom that would integrate its different aspects, the more urgently every composition needed to bring forth a coherent structural context from within itself and develop into a self-sufficient microcosm. The technique of 'developing variation', which had grown under the protection of tonality since Viennese Classicism and, in tonal music, found its most consistent representative in Brahms, already served this purpose. The twelve-note technique gives it a central role: it is a procedure of total variation that tolerates neither a note that is 'free', i.e. independent of the respective starting material, nor conversely any recurrence of a given element without transformation. It aims to establish rigorously the idea of unity within diversity in music. Within such an undertaking, tonal elements would sound external and heteronomous in relation to the actual construct. They are frowned upon in twelve-note music, unless the construction of the rows themselves, as occasionally in Berg's works, permits tonal enclaves.

Because the twelve-note technique absolutizes the principle of variation, however, the principle known in traditional music as 'thematic work', because everything that goes on becomes thematic work, thematic work ceases to be the content of composition; it becomes its precondition. Composition is intended to be liberated precisely by pushing back all the things at which music once laboured away—everything characterized in the eighteenth century as 'learned', in contrast to 'galant'—in a process that is, in fact, complete before the compositional act itself even begins. The twelve-note technique is thus not a musical system but, rather, a pre-ordering of its material; something that takes place on the palette, not the painting. This predisposition of the material is only justified in artistic economy where it is necessary, where there is something to organize in the first place. Otherwise, it would degenerate into a mere exercise and become fetishism. Artistic means can only be such in proportion to the artistic aim, the 'composed' object that is intended to result. If, for example, the variations of the note-row are manipulated for the sake of a music so simple that it would happen without such techniques, these techniques lose both their function and their right to exist. The crudeness of the musical content contradicts the circumstances that are brought about, and which usually only highlight that crudeness all the more garishly. The twelve-note technique only gained a meaning from the polyphonic, in every sense extremely complex compositional approach of the Viennese School—only in something truly manifold does one sense the need for a clamp to hold it together as firmly as does the twelve-note technique. It cannot be isolated from the anarchic, chaotic element of expressionism and free atonality that conditions it. It is not an absolute.

That, however, is how it is misrepresented today. The generation that has embraced it, and which perhaps experienced too much chaos in real life to look it in the eye aesthetically, is being seduced by order as such with no consideration for what is being ordered. In this sense, twelve-note music took over the legacy of its opposite—run-down neoclassicism. It tempts its followers with promises of security. It calms the composer's fear that he is on his own and must listen, with nothing to support him, for what the work itself demands at each moment. People suppose that it makes composing easier; that it serves to abolish what it is meant to prepare, namely compositional freedom. A young American composer, when asked why he adopted the twelve-note technique, replied that he had not known when composing which notes he should use for the melodies and harmonies whose approximate outlines he envisaged; now he had his basic row and its permutations to tell him. One can be sure that the notes he used to fill the emptiness he perceived in his own music were not the right ones but merely a substitute for the work and effort of active critical listening. There is a barbaric anartistic element that lies within these artificialities. Not only semi-dilettantes lose their head in this manner; even highly talented composers achieve little when they use the twelve-note technique for purposes that have no connection to its original idea. Thus Luigi Dallapiccola, for example, unquestionably one of the strongest talents of the middle generation, uses it within a traditionally music-dramatic, very Italian language whose drastic nature does not even require such an organizational principle, and probably deteriorates as soon as it relies upon it. In Berg's work too, the twelve-note technique was simply one means of articulation among numerous others, and was combined with traditional elements. In his music, however, the element that gives the twelve-note technique its substance, namely thematic variation, is developed to the highest degree and integrated meaningfully into the twelve-note procedure. Among countless young composers, however, Schönberg's technique is simply misused to conceal the absence of any true compositional cohesion; the frailty of the compositions is clear enough. The excuse that everything is in order by the rules of the game is sophistic and mechanical.

Such symptoms are especially evident in opera, which, after all, is confronted most directly with the question of audience effect, and is thus under the greatest pressure to compromise. An avant-garde is on the defensive that not only draws the most rigorous conclusions from the twelve-note technique, which it views as binding and self-evidently justified, but also attempts to go further and apply that constructive principle to a much greater extent than the mere preformation of pitch material through a given sequence of intervals. Among the practitioners of this music, which is so indebted to Schönberg, one finds a certain anti-Schönbergian climate, a form of rebellion against the father figure that, paradoxically, accuses him of excessive freedom, subjectivity and expression. It is no coincidence that Pierre Boulez gave a manifesto-like essay the title 'Schönberg est mort' ['Schönberg and Death']. What is fundamental, however, lies in the very thing from which these composers want to escape. There is an element of arbitrariness to the twelve-note method itself and the definition of its rules, but especially the restriction of the constructive principle to the regulation of intervals, while other musical dimensions such as rhythm and dynamics are not affected. The twelve-note technique stops short of the ideal of 'integral' composition unquestionably following from the principle that every note is strictly determined. Closely tied to this is the fact that the actual musical language of Schönberg's late works, their compositional means, consistently refer back to traditional music and tonal relationships, and are thus not entirely in keeping with the preformation of the pitch material which discards these resources of musical language. Schönberg self-assuredly ignored this contradiction and indeed simply 'made music' with his rows, composing much as any of the great composers dealt with their material. Webern already seems to have been irked by this; he tried, at any rate, to close this gap between the musical language and the rows in most of his later twelve-note works from the Symphony onwards. He sought to make all musical events correspond to the structure of the row and its various manifestations, renouncing an incredible amount of what one had previously understood as composition. Late Webern combines an undreamed-of density of twelve-note relationships with stark compositional simplicity, in a fashion comparable to the paintings of Mondrian. This reduction often made his music 'pointillist' [*punktuell*]; but even the barest of those constructs contain barely a note that does not have some highly precise and convincing meaning, however skeletal. It is against such musical sense that the rebellion of this group of young composers—highly diverse within itself—is directed; it includes Boulez in France, Stockhausen in Germany and Maderna and Nono in Italy. Objective construction is now supposed to encapsulate all elements mathematically, in particular rhythmic ones; the aim, to put it drastically, is the liquidation of composition in each composition. A concrete idea of the sounding result becomes irrelevant, as do the musical language and anything resembling a semantic context. These composers hope to partake of some cosmic essence by driving out the subject. The same aversion to expression found in the archaically anti-Romantic tendencies of neoclassicism becomes yet more extreme among its antipodes. Some have compared their aims to the cybernetic efforts of science and industrial automation; they are so automatic in their realization that, as E. I. Kahn put it, a form of 'robot music' is beginning to emerge.

Here, the concept of musical progress is transformed into its opposite. Pure material consistency regresses entirely to the anartistic, to the mere physics of sound—and indeed a number of German pointillists have turned to electronic experiments. The increasing resemblance between artistic method and science, even though art can never become science, makes the purpose of the whole, of the music's existence, questionable, and converges with the question with which Halldór Laxness confronted poetry:

> I was shown all the pictures of Buchenwald . . . one can no longer be a poet. One's emotions freeze. One can no longer control one's emotions when one has seen a photograph of those withered skeletons; and those dead, gaping mouths. The love life of the trout—little red rose on the meadow—*Dichterliebe*—all finished, over, done. Tristan and Isolde are dead; they died in Buchenwald. And the nightingale has lost its voice, because we have lost our hearing; our ears died in Buchenwald.

But an awareness of the impossibility of absolute construction is beginning to develop among those composers themselves: Stockhausen has admitted a threshold of 'indeterminacy', and an eminently talented composer such as Boulez seems capable of casting off his self-imposed shackles and, drawing on all the experiences gained through ascetic discipline, writing convincing music. The musical situation is a bottleneck in which one cannot remain, but which can also not be avoided, and from which nothing emerges unchanged. Even in the strongest compositional forces, in spite of everything, one sees the realization of that human freedom shining through for whose sake modernity began to break open the musical material, and which alone can reconcile us with the violence that music took upon itself. It cannot escape the curse of reality, and knows no other hope but the unassuming one contained in reality itself.

1955

If one is to speak about the current state of music in Germany—whose key is composition—in the space of a few pages, there is no room for a discussion of individual composers or schools. One should rather identify the specific nature of the German situation. Fifteen years after the fall of Hitler, the question is no longer whether Germany has been able to join in the international scene, whether composers are keeping in mind the tradition of modernity in their own field, whether they have escaped the condition of barbaric simplification and have the necessary technical means at their disposal. The difficulty of reaching a concise formulation is due, rather, to the remarkable similarity that has developed between the styles of different countries, as has long been observed in the visual arts. Among the work that merits serious consideration, there are no longer any national trademarks that distinguish countries from one another, no musical dialects of the kind that had developed in the course of late Romanticism. One should not, therefore, look for the specifically German quality in the immediate style but, rather, in the way composers approach the meanwhile generalized material. This is complicated by the fact that the musical direction considered a German and Austrian speciality for twenty-five years, until the outbreak of the Third Reich, namely consistent atonality and its systematization in the twelve-note technique, spread through the whole world after the Second World War. It was this, through its rational principle of construction, that made national styles disappear. The internationalization of music is a function of that German evolution of musical material that, together with the ideal of comprehensive motivic-thematic work, extends far back into the German tradition. Most of the connections can be personally identified. Webern's pupil René Leibowitz taught Schönberg's technique in Paris, creating such an awareness of its necessity that, in France, it experienced its first reception outside of the Germanophone world. Conversely, the further development of Schönberg's technique into the 'serial' method, the incorporation of every conceivable musical dimension into the constructive process, was initiated in Paris by Messiaen, and its effects subsequently came back to Germany, in particular through Boulez. It was, admittedly, already foreshadowed by Berg's technique of thematic rhythm and Webern's late style.

In this country, both the older academic traditions and the 'New German School' of Wagner's followers have meanwhile died out, as if the petty-bourgeois reactionary culture of the Hitler era had filled the subsequent generation with a shame that made it suspicious of anything that had been on top during those twelve disastrous years, including Richard Strauss. In organizational terms, this meant that the Allgemeiner deutscher Musikverein [General German Music Society], which had been a carrier of Wagnerianism in particular, did not resume its work after the war. The centre of modernity in Germany has also shifted away from the International Society for Contemporary Music, however, which had provided many impulses between the wars. Stravinskyan neoclassicism, which previously dominated its programmes to such a great extent, has all but died out in Germany; perhaps because it was opposed so vehemently by theoretical criticism. In addition, the monotony that characterized Stravinsky's music for three decades may have disappointed young musicians as much as Hindemith's development in his later years. Only a few older composers, for example Karl Heinrich David, still remain in that realm; aside from that, neoclassicism is now found only in the depths of archaist folk and youth music which wrongly calls itself 'young music'.

The extent to which twelve-note music has spread, however, is a source of some consternation. Having lost both conventional tonality and the pseudo-objective formal imitations of neoclassicism as support structures, a great many young composers are no doubt lured by the phantom of security in twelve-note rows. They take something as a 'system', a form of substitute tonality, that is in reality simply a tool for the constructive organization of unruly material. Countless twelve-note pieces are so primitive in their actual compositional substance that they would not even require such a means of representation, which is only justified when it holds together complex events, especially polyphonic ones. When Darius Milhaud told the aged Schönberg shortly before his death of the international triumph of the twelve-note technique, he reportedly answered: 'Yes, but are they composing with it too?' There is indeed an unmistakable tendency to adopt the problematic aspect of the twelve-note technique— the mechanical element that exempts composers from compositional effort, and is often empty and clanging—without honouring the duties and implications of the method; and, above all, without the spontaneous musical impulses and tensions being strong enough to make the manipulation of the rows something more than a game, something that provides the certainty that every note, every colour, every rest is derivable from the same basic material and therefore correct. The fetishism of the row, a sort of second-order faith in the raw materials and trust in mere technical agreement, becomes a substitute for what is composed; the means replace the ends.

This danger is international. If one is looking for the best thing about what is being produced in Germany today, it perhaps lies in the way in which the most talented and responsible composers there react to it. They recognize, explicitly or implicitly, the duty to operate with the liberated and thoroughly organized material in such a way that the composition is fully appropriate to it. The core of the serial minimum is made the source of a fully articulated musical language. By submitting unreservedly to the material and its tendencies, instead of imposing twelve-note procedures on the composition, composers hope to find the meaning within. This is exemplified by electronic music, which does not simply 'use' electronic sounds but, rather, attempts to deduce compositional structures from the nature of those sounds. The experiments with the principle of chance, stimulated theoretically by Stéphane Mallarmé and practically by the American John Cage, are at once related and opposed—they seek to remedy the brute force of the mechanical by taking their submission to this principle to the point of a self-effacement of subjective compositional intention.

The specifically German quality can probably be identified in the fact that people here are not composing with rows, series or electronic sounds as a medium to control at will but, instead, strive to make the entire compositional structure follow without intervention, as it were, from such conditions. Here, it is the advanced German music of today, represented in particular by Stockhausen and his Cologne circle, that goes to the extreme: by the internal shaping of the material as much as by loosening it, two opposing tendencies that, as has long since been noted, converge. It is hardly far-fetched to suppose that this tendency to go to the extreme, both in the wonderful and the questionable, is a German one. The German contribution to the music of today would therefore be, as it was fifty years ago, that of radicalism. The necessary conclusions are drawn uncompromisingly from the results of material development. Everything that lives on in the musical language as the rudiment of an older obsolete material is eliminated. Music would rather break away from language, hoping to create a new one in the process, than tolerate incongruities and impurities in the medium.

One cannot yet foresee where such consistency will lead when it is no longer driven by conflict with an opposing resistant musical substance. So far, the most important results of this conception are works by Stockhausen such as the chamber piece *Zeitmaße*, *Gruppen*, written for three orchestras in order to incorporate the spatial dimension of composition, the meanwhile famous electronic piece *Gesang der Jünglinge*, and, most recently, *Kontakte* for electronic sounds, piano and percussion. But the German tendency towards extremes is rearing its head even in the moderate schools that survive, for example in the music of Carl Orff. A neoclassicist by provenance and disposition, he drives the simplification and reduction of musical means so far that composition itself is liquidated in favour of designing dramaturgical aural scenery. Of course, the restorative content of such efforts is diametrically opposed to what the Cologne and Darmstadt avant-garde is aiming for.

Total determination converges with chance, in the sense that thoroughly constructed music is as alien to and incommensurable with the subject as random events. It would certainly be naïve to overlook the fact that constructive objectivity, the radical preformation of the material, inevitably refers back to the subjectivity that carries it out. It is beyond doubt, however, that total constructivism, as a taboo on the subjective need for expression, stirs up opposing forces in the composers; the passionate engagement with chance is their expression. Some of the most talented German composers, on the other hand, suffer so terribly under determinism that they attempt to break free of it; the foremost of these is Henze. In such works as the opera *König Hirsch*, however, this attempt led not to the longed-for realm of freedom, a true 'musique informelle' but, rather, backwards: to compromise. The laments about the compulsion of constructivism can become a mere pretext to withdraw into the more comfortable bondage of convention.

The platitude that the musical situation is open, and the direction of overall development undecided, merits all the more suspicion—because asking what is historically stronger and prevails is by no means identical to asking what is better. Nonetheless, the thesis of the unresolved situation is more valid than thirty years ago, namely during a period when those with insight could not fail to recognize the superiority of Schönberg and his school over the moderated modernity of the time. Today, such categories as musical sense, intelligibility of context and the concrete logic of constructs in their sensual manifestation have been called into question; not simply because these standards cannot be met but because there is a growing suspicion that they may be no more than a harmonious illusion. For the matter at stake is whether music, and art in general, is able to survive its illusory character without negating its own concept. What is currently taking place in German music derives its force from the fact that it takes this question to its limits. The answer will scarcely be found in the music alone but in the entire social constellation. The antagonisms of contemporary composition, however, express the real state of affairs all the more faithfully the less the music concerns itself with it.

1960

The analogies between contemporary painting and music are self-evident. In both fields, the conventionalized formal language of bourgeois society, which had congealed into a second nature, has disintegrated. Its antithesis is the effort of the aesthetic consciousness, as unconscious as it may be, to shatter the context of delusion created by ideology and reach the true essence. The abandonment of similarity to the object in visual art corresponds to the abandonment of the structural schema of tonality in music. They had served the same purpose: to measure the individual work of art against a standard that lay outside of its own formal laws and was affirmed by society, to turn its in-itself simultaneously into a for-others. When this function and the immanent demands of the construct diverged entirely, obedience to this dictate was refused. Viewed from a certain distance, the lines of development were parallel. An anarchic, revolutionary period, classified by systematic mindlessness as a mere transitional phase, described as Fauvism and Expressionism in the one medium and free atonality in the other, was supposedly followed by a manner of new order: Cubism, New Realism and Classicism, as well as the twelve-note technique. The old view of the asynchronicity seems obsolete. With the growing integration of society, the manifold resistance against its rules of play has also become more uniform; music no longer lags behind painting. Wagner, who had already envisaged a form of synchronization of all the arts that foreshadowed the totalitarian administration of society, still showed that asynchronicity nonetheless. Twenty years after developing approaches in *Tristan* that had been anticipated by the techniques of Impressionist painters, his opinion of Renoir—whom he had, in fact, allowed to paint him—was akin to Kaiser Wilhelm's opinion of sewer art. And the visual element in Bayreuth was indeed regressive and trivial.

The relationship changed radically with the advent of expressionism. The programme of Der Blaue Reiter, led by Klee, Marc and Kandinsky, also incorporated music by Schönberg, Berg and Webern. The boundaries separating different talents were no longer respected. Schönberg, precisely in the decisive revolutionary phase of his development, painted with considerable ability, and his pictures show the same pairing of expressive force and objective hardness that characterizes his music. Feininger carried out serious and intensive musical work. Of the younger composers, Berg and Hindemith had a specific visual talent, and Berg, a friend of Loos and Kokoschka, liked to say that he could just as easily have become an architect as a composer. The affiliation of the arts around 1918 was due not so much to any intentional synchronization or all- encompassing monumentality as to a rebellion against reification, which had revealed itself even in the compartmentalization of the objective spirit's zones. It is contrasted with the unmediated vitality of human expression, which it forces to redeem, pervade and humanize everything that is alien and object-like. Schumann's old Romanticist programme, in which the aesthetic of one art is also that of the others, is finally realized by expressionism. It considers the material, indeed the sphere of aesthetic objectification itself, insignificant alongside the pure self-articulation of the subject.

Many of the analogies between the later developments in both spheres can be historico-philosophically explained by the fact that one cannot maintain a position of pure subjectivity, that a consciousness which is for itself must inevitably divest itself for the sake of its own truth. It remains questionable, however, whether those analogies really show such an authentic equivalence in the different fields as is argued by a cultural and intellectual history that self-assuredly follows the 'major' tendencies without examining the discipline of the actual production. The mere fact of the joyful agreement among the aesthetic arbiters that there was initially chaos, but that this was essentially a form of tunnel that one only needed to enter in order to find the light of a new, preferably secure and generally binding order at the other end, should arouse our suspicion. It is precisely when art is not simply an articulation of subjectivity but has to undergo the ordeal of a confrontation with something opposed to it—if it is not simply to remain in a state of vain fortuity—that the artist must not ignore what the specific nature of the material through which he experiences that opposition and its demands means for the work. For this meaning is not mere subjectivity as such in its abstract state but, rather, what results from overcoming the conflict between the subject and its opposition. The simple differences, between both the different materials and the individual historically developed arts, cannot simply disappear in the unity of subjective expression, nor in the parallelism of developmental traits. Analogous formal tendencies inevitably have different, possibly even opposing, meanings in the temporal art of music and the spatial art of painting. Music, being essentially non-pictorial, necessarily changes the meaning of formal elements that, however indirectly, are gained by abstraction from the objective realm. A musical surface is fundamentally different from the surface of a picture— because timeless motion knows no surface, because the formation of musical surfaces was borrowed from painting to begin with and functions entirely differently in the musical continuum and that of painting.

The correspondences between the music that is quantitatively dominant today and certain visual tendencies are, in fact, substantially a result of music's adaptation to painting. It is uncertain whether the Schönberg of around 1910, the initiator of musical expressionism, was influenced by radical painters in his decision to break with tonality, or whether—as seems quite likely—the technical development of his own problems would equally have exceeded the boundaries of tonality without such connections to painting. There is no doubt, however, that the origins of New Music in the Western style can be found in painting. The more or less accurate generalization that France is the country of great painters and Germany the country of great music can be attributed to the fact that painting itself, an ordering of the spatial world controlled primarily by humans, fitted better into the continuity of rational, Roman and civilizatory elements in the Western world than music, which—for better or for worse—contains an unfathomed, chaotic, mythical aspect. Nietzsche in particular was aware of this contrast. Something of that still remains, even if one knows that within the totality of culture the different elements have become interwoven, that Impressionist painting, for example, became the vehicle of protest against the object-centred rational order despite its technical spirit, while music became binding in human terms precisely through its own development towards rationality. If one views the overall development under late capitalism as a progressive enlightenment and rationalization, however, this largely amounts to a triumph of the spirit of painting over that of music. In France, where the productive powers in music—perhaps precisely because they had always been socialized—were not as developed as in Germany, music was forced to cling to painting in order to reach the general level of artistic development at all.

This was practised from the 1890s on by Debussy, who, with indescribable tact and the sharpest awareness of the specific qualities of musical material, transferred the achievements of the great painters to that material without ever descending to merely painterly, derivative composition. This involved far more than simply the analogy between lighting and the inclusion of more distant overtones, or the technique of sound dabs, especially doubling in seconds, which was related to the impressionist comma. Debussy elevated an intention otherwise known only from the salon music of the nineteenth century to an aesthetic level. His pieces, rarely of extended duration, no longer contain any progression. One could say they have been removed from the flow of time, that they are static, spatial. In the famous *Feux d'artifice*, at the end of the second book of preludes, for example, the sequence of individual sections is, by the standards of 'development', fortuitous: their temporal succession is not a substantial constituent of the form but, rather, corresponds more to a tastefully contrasting juxtaposition of coloured surfaces. If, in the spirit of philosophical positivism, memory and expectation are eliminated, and we acknowledge only what is respectively the case, then, in its flirtations with physics, Debussy's music—as much as it might be one of 'atmosphere'—does justice to this by seeking to evade the darkness of inner meaning and temporal dialectic in favour of vivid simultaneity, in so far as music's contingency on the passing of time permits this at all.

Stravinsky adopted this exact intention from Debussy— except that he eliminated the blurred, internally mediated quality of Debussy's music, the last trace of the musical subject, so to speak. By stringing together complexes that are starkly separated, yet lack any sense of time either in themselves or in their relationships to one another, he founded that musical style which, looking first of all to Picasso, declared itself first a form of musical cubism, then neoclassicism. The history of modern music's development—in so far as it includes the majority of composers—the much-vaunted transition from dissolution to supposedly new forms, would then stem from a pseudomorphosis of music towards painting. Music was not simply stimulated in certain respects by painting; it followed painting in its very structural constitution.

The turn towards objectivity, which is viewed on all sides as progress in modern art, has brought the element of play to the foreground. The subject, which can no longer be sure of its status as the creator and substance of the work of art, but more as the executor of what is necessary for the matter at hand, no longer posits itself in the traditional sense or as bindingly as before, and no longer expresses itself with the same naïveté. Because such objectivity is in turn experienced largely as one instigated by the subject, however, not one stemming purely from the matter itself, it cannot present itself as directly objective to the same extent as in the classicist tendencies that emerged repeatedly through the centuries. Stravinsky took over the masquerade, the game that admits to being one and underlines it, from Picasso. Its function, however, is radically different in the two cases. First of all, there is the difference of temperament: the painter sticks his tongue out at the bourgeois spirit of personality, development, inwardness and responsibility, proclaiming liberty as one who has all the elements of space at his free disposal. Stravinsky's game, on the other hand, mockingly degrades freedom to powerlessness from the outset, before denouncing it with cynical earnestness. This, however, reveals the true divergence between the media of new painting and New Music. We know that Picasso refused to join Kandinsky in severing all ties with the representational. Even at the height of cubism, the constructions were made from fragments of the object world. This was not the hesitation of the reactionary; rather, it expressed the profound knowledge that anything visible remains tied to similarities with the visible world—

because, in its literal and metaphorical organization, the eye that constitutes the image is identical to the eye that perceives a space and which, by virtue of its nature, man has always tended to dominate in the same manner that Picasso's controlling eye takes to the extreme. This dictates the limit of the artist's freedom. The playful, clown-like element, art's self-subjection to irony, means the retention of freedom both in the face of such onerous contingency on the object and the attempt to deny that contingency. Even the traditional painter's gaze, which is characterized by an agreement with the things he paints and could, in a certain sense, almost be viewed as the defining characteristic of talent, still mirrors something of the stubborn practice of nature's domination. Painting can break free of this only if it ceases to take its object-like heaviness, and its dominion over it, quite so seriously. Thus the clown's acts seemingly take the domination of the material world to the limit in order to reinstate the being: he provokes laughter in equal measure at himself, the world and domination. This domination is overturned: once it loses its grip upon things, it no longer does harm to that which is. Picasso's game is the withdrawal of the power he himself asserts. His pictures outdo the reification of reality in order to refute it.

Music, however, lacks any bond to the objective world from the outset: the ear does not perceive objects. Therefore, it neither needs to dissolve objectivity, as something heteronomous, nor to withdraw its control over objects. If it becomes a play of masks, it does not negate its problematic relationship to an other, but only to itself. Picasso leaps clear of both the contingency on a heterogeneous continuum and the arbitrariness of the subject. In Stravinsky's case, irony itself becomes something a-musical, something heteronomous— the affirmation through music of something that music itself is not, namely conventions: it renounces its own freedom. Picasso's playfulness is concerned with the greatest possible reconciliation by aesthetic means of subject and object, while Stravinsky's serves the opposite of reconciliation, namely the elimination of the subject and the triumph of the crude, violent objectivity in which the ego crosses itself out. Hence, Stravinsky's historicism, his fetishization of cultural corpses where Picasso still manages to call the fetishes of primitives affectionately into the kaleidoscope of subjective freedom. It is hardly a biographical-psychological coincidence that for Picasso, neoclassicism—which incidentally also brought him closer to the market—remained, more than any other of his phases after the break with representational similarity, a mere episode, whereas Stravinsky has clung doggedly to his restorative tonal exercises for the last thirty years, without allowing his fauvist past to seduce him even once into experimenting. It would be inconceivable for a path to lead from Picasso to something like representational realism or a mischievous bourgeois rehash—not even of Ingres, whom the master had cultivated for a time. Stravinsky, however, has meanwhile—albeit by a somewhat roundabout path—become the god of provincial conservatorians, who think they can freely and uncritically produce toccatas and canzonas of a pre-Bachian character, and delude themselves that they have overcome subjectivism simply because they are not subjects. Cubism, which was perhaps the first general category of new painting, may have been rendered obsolete in Picasso's later works by an infinite wealth of concrete shapes; but his successors were fortunately spared that pharisaic simplification which poses as art based on transcendent bonds. One could contrast this with a comparison between Kokoschka and Schönberg. Kokoschka's work, in Austria, probably shows much the same pseudomorphosis towards music as music does towards painting in the West. The dynamization of the visible phenomenon, and before that the attempt to capture the unconscious temporal stream of experience in a portrait, is more genuinely native to music than painting, and it is no coincidence that Kokoschka's poetry has exerted a very strong attraction on the musical avant-garde. If, however, one compares Kokoschka's paintings of that kind with directly related music from Schönberg's or Webern's expressionist phase, one will hardly be able to shake off the impression that, in the quasi-documentary communication of a purely internal state, the musician is superior to the painter in his power of objectification, and indeed proves more 'modern', to the same degree that in the West, conversely, Picasso's painting is superior to Stravinsky's music, which simultaneously bows to it and perverts it.

All forms of fixed consensus must be disabled, even if they apply to the new art itself. Hence, the thought that phenomena and developments which coincide in their concrete approach may have different, even contradictory, meanings in painting and music respectively. To highlight the relationship through exaggeration: when music resembles painting through a deconstruction into geometric complexes, it adopts a spatial law that is literally external to it and then blindly subordinates itself to it. In painting, on the other hand, a reduction to spatially pure forms is as native to the material as it is to the subject. So here the process of reduction is aimed at freedom. One could say that music which seeks to resemble modern painting inevitably descends into the violently reactionary character of an order imposed from without while, conversely, an approach to painting that clings to subjective dynamism succumbs to Romanticism—and it is no coincidence, incidentally, that Kokoschka's models came from the early nineteenth century, for example Delacroix's portraits of other artists. Picasso's counterpart is not Stravinsky, who transposes him but, rather, his antipode Schönberg. The latter's principles of construction crystallized from the specific problematics of music, not from the will to bring about some united artistic front through literary programmes. It would seem that the insertion of expression into construction in Schönberg's most recent works and the undermining of the image's shape with shock-like fragments of the human face in late Picasso (since *Guernica*) indeed relate to the same core of historical experience. The unity of modern art, its emancipation, the idea of complete freedom, is most aptly encapsulated in the statement '*Les extrêmes se touchent*'.

c.*1950*

ON THE CURRENT RELATIONSHIP
BETWEEN PHILOSOPHY AND MUSIC

I

The crisis of music, which scarcely needs to be pointed out, concerns more than the difficulties of consistent and meaningful musical shaping, more than the increasing commercial rigidity and levelling out of musical life, and more than the divide between autonomous musical production and the audience. Rather, all these problems have grown to the point where quantity has turned into quality. The right of music—all music—to exist in the first place is becoming questionable. This should not be mistaken for one of those overly methodical attempts at doubt, where one can already hear the imminent 'however' as soon as they begin; it is, rather, confirmed by any sense of experience that is not inclined to accept the mere existence of the industry as its justification. One need only randomly turn the dial on a radio: even if one manages to evade the endless uniformity of pop songs, be they the cosy or the disdainful kind, and find some serious music—or, as it is known in the sphere of informed barbarism, 'classical music'—the mere fact that it takes its place amid the monotony as one category among others means that it in turn appears, even in its difference, as simply another facet of that monotony. The very first sound tells us: 'serious music', just as the first note played by an organ sends us the signal 'religion'. With this classification, appended in advance of the actual phenomenon, it already ceases to be what it claims to be: something in itself. It becomes a mere being 'for-others', and culturally faithful attempts to save it do more to encourage the tendency than to alleviate it. By making the existing division of intellectual labour its own business as well, the Third Program only contributes further to the neutralization of culture.

While music, omnipresent and inescapable, installs itself as a tangible part of life, as one standardized consumer product among others, divesting itself of anything that would go beyond the service and deception of the customer, it becomes comical. The pathos that is native to it, even in the utmost degradation—to say nothing of its autonomous manifestations, works that follow only their own laws—the echo of the cultic element even in its most secular forms, contradicts its increasing wear, its ubiquity, the commodity character that it has universally assumed in society, and this contradiction provokes laughter. When, in one of the incomparable film farces of the Marx Brothers, an absurd sequence of events suddenly leads to the showing of an opera scene with tragic arias, illustrated by the clumsily grandiose, old-fashioned gestures of the singers, the effect is the demolition of the tragic stage—and indeed, the clowns immediately set upon it and bring the scenery crashing down. But all this does is to highlight, through garish caricature, an aspect of music that is in fact inherent in all its manifestations. It is only faith in education and cultural ideology that prevent people from mentioning it otherwise, yet it is precisely the deadly seriousness of cultured posturing, which clings obstinately to the music's dignity, that involuntarily contributes to its ridiculousness. The grotesque untruth and discrepancy of such a sight as the zealously emotional oratorio singer in coat tails, or the certified positivity of a full choral sound, already begins in the gloom of the basses, the wastefulness of the violins or the veiled remoteness of the horn in great symphonic works, and only compositions that ascetically refuse to take part in all of this are granted a period of grace. A music that needs only to begin in order to define itself as an exception to standardized life, as an elevated extreme, contradicts the claim automatically staked by its mere presence through its ever potentially palpable, but meanwhile also complete integration into the typical everyday routine of a false life.

Composers face the agony of choice. They can turn a deaf ear and carry on as if music were still music; or they can practise the same levelling out on their own account, turn music into normality, and maintain, as far as possible, a certain level of quality. Alternatively, they can oppose the tendency by resorting to extremes, with the prospect of either being drawn in and levelled out after all—as one can already witness with Kafka—or withering away as a speciality. The highly uncomfortable situation of composition today stems from the decline of music's *raison d'être*, the undermining of its very possibility. This, admittedly, communicates itself in the decline of criteria, in the loss even of a tradition that could be experienced negatively, and in technical, intellectual and social disorientation. If, in the works of Webern, one of its most significant representatives—and therefore one practically unknown outside of the smallest circles—contemporary music contracts into mere moments and obeys the command to fall silent, which is even greater than the composer's insistent formal will, this demonstrates how the music's inner fabric reflects its relationship with the conditions of its existence. A music that remains true to itself would rather not be, would rather fade out—in the most literal sense, as indicated so often in Webern's scores—than betray its essence by clinging to existence. The suspicion once voiced by Eduard Steuermann is justified, namely that music, at least great music, which idea

extends from Bach through Beethoven to Schönberg, is an
ephemeral category tied to the bourgeois era and destined to
be forgotten—just as a jazz athlete no longer even understands
what all that was about, rejects serious music as 'corny',[1] as an
old-fashioned mixture of naïveté and extravagance; and, no
longer content to pride himself on his ignorance, even declares
it openly in the name of the world spirit.

If philosophy now attempts to penetrate to the heart of
this condition, it will almost inevitably be confronted with the
question of what music actually is. One need only describe
the character of the crisis with one of the figures of speech
common today, for example 'radical jeopardy', to create a climate of cosy unease. The desired response to radical jeopardy
is to be mindful of the being of the jeopardized person as such,
and one can wager that, at the end of such considerations,
music's own state of jeopardy, sinister and comforting at once,
will transpire as its true essence. The obstacle to all epistemo-
logical reflections on the validity and identification of such
fundamental questions of origin, however, is the impossibility
of pointing to one single category that could be used for a direct
definition of its meaning, that is to say the basis of its right to
exist. One could add that the emergence of a highly enigmatic
element can be observed in all music. It is not resolved by the
psychological question of why music exerts such an arousingly
strong effect but is, rather, connected to the fact that one simply
cannot name any general aspect which goes beyond the description of music and reveals music's meaning and justification. If
one comes close enough to music to become estranged from
it, meaning that one no longer identifies its occurrence automatically with its justification, it becomes incomprehensible
whence it gains the dignity bestowed upon it in our culture.
This is why many of a positivist ilk—and Nietzsche was not

1 English in the original. [Trans.]

so far removed from their views at times—denied any such dignity, at least in music's being-in-itself, and reduced it to a system of subjective projections and conventions.

The banal but not easily refutable distinction between the musical and the unmusical confirms the specific riddle-character of music. The fact that certain music quite simply does not speak to whole groups of people who are not aesthetically unreceptive, that they cannot get anything out of it, while there is barely anything analogous in visual art or poetry—this is certainly due largely to the constitution of these people, especially their childhood; it does seem to indicate, however, that the essence of music is not as unambiguously given as that of other artistic media, and hence does not compel the recipient subject to the same degree. If music, as Schönberg said, expresses something that can only be expressed in music, it takes on a cryptic and at once emphatically fortuitous quality. It is still undecided whether the question of the *raison d'être* of all that is image and not reality is a dead end; for presumably all art eludes precisely that immanent framework of legitimation which demands for the existent to show its identification, that very *raison d'être*. In the end, the *raison d'être* of all art is to reject the *raison d'être*, that is to say the justification of its own existence, according to the standards of self-preservation (however sublimated). There are many indications that any fundamental question as to the essence of an art remains futile, or leads to the mere repetition of the fact that it simply exists, because the question itself belongs to the same realm of identificatory instrumental rationality that is suspended by art. If philosophy—as it must repeatedly attempt, and as art itself demands that it attempt—were able to determine art's *raison d'être*, art would indeed be entirely absorbed by cognition and thus obsolete in the strict sense.

It is particular to music, however, that through its isolation from the visually or conceptually determined, objective world, it highlights, in fact almost urges the riddle-character; in both language and visual art, it is concealed. Language constructs are always lent a certain semblance of 'transparency' or comprehensibility by their participation in the medium which is also the medium of cognition, regardless of how far that which emerges as a poem's meaning may differ from its substance—what Benjamin calls 'the poetized' [*das Gedichtete*]. In visual art, the riddle-character is reduced through the medium's constitution in the same external sense that also conveys the objective world to us. Even in the associations of abstract painting, the relation to the concrete merges with the art's substance. While such aspects may ultimately heighten the irrationality in the non-musical arts by concealing it, it is part of the very phenomenon in the case of music, and thus perhaps also offers a perspective for overcoming it. But in any case, to recall the two familiar options of musical aesthetics, the purported joy in sounding forms in motion is much too thin and abstract a principle on which to found a highly organized art. If it were enough, there would be no difference between the kaleidoscope and a Beethoven quartet except for the mere materials. On the other hand, the component of expression, which has been recognized as the corrective for Hanslick's principle, is too ambiguous and undefined in every one of its individual manifestations to constitute the substance of music by itself. All music inherently possesses what words in language only gain when distorted through concentration. It looks at its listener with empty eyes, and the deeper one immerses oneself, the more unfathomable its real purpose becomes—until one learns that the answer, if there can be one, lies not in contemplation but in interpretation: that one can solve music's riddle only by playing music correctly, namely as a whole. Its riddle dupes the observer by seducing him into hypostatizing something as being that is in fact a process, a becoming, and into elevating a behaviour to the level of human becoming.

Music is concerned not with meaning but with gestures. In so far as it is language, it is like the notation in its history— a language of sedimented gestures. One cannot ask what meaning it communicates; for the central issue in music is how gestures can be immortalized. Thus the search for the actual meaning of music, as it is supposed to reveal itself in the rational proof of its *raison d'être*, transpires as a delusion, a pseudomorphosis towards the realm of intentions into which we are seduced by music through its resemblance to language. As a language, music is concerned with the pure name, the absolute unity of object and sign, which in its immediacy has been lost to all human knowledge. In the utopian, and at once hopeless efforts at naming lies the relation of music to philosophy, to which it is incomparably closer in its idea than any other art for that very reason. But the name appears in music only in the form of the pure sound, separated from its bearer, and thus the opposite of any bestowal of meaning, any intention towards sense. Music does not know the name—the absolute as a sound— directly, but, if one can view it in this way, attempts its invocatory construction through a whole, a process; for this reason, it is simultaneously woven into the very process in which categories such as rationality, sense, meaning and language apply. It is the paradox of all music that, as an effort to attain that non-intentionality for which I have chosen the inadequate word 'name', only unfolds precisely through its participation in rationality in the widest sense. In the role of the sphinx, it fools the observer by constantly promising meanings, even granting them intermittently; but they are only means to the death of meaning in the truest sense, and therefore music is never exhausted in them. As long as it was kept within a reasonably closed traditional context, such as that of the last 350 years, this insoluble aspect, namely that everything implies meaning but nothing actually intends meaning, could be concealed. Within that tradition, music's existence was accepted, and music asserted itself as something completely natural (except in the most overwhelming experiences of amazement). But today, as music is no longer controlled by tradition, its riddle-nature comes to light as weak and meagre, a mere question mark—whose outline, admittedly, becomes distorted as soon as one demands that it should declare what it is actually communicating. For the name is no communication of an object.

This emergence of music's riddle-character tempts us to ask about its being, while the process that brought it to that point forbids the question. For music does not possess its object, it does not hold power over the name but, rather, dwells on it—and, precisely in doing so, aims at its own demise. If music were to achieve for a moment what the notes revolve around, this would mean its fulfilment and its end. Its relation to that which it does not want to depict but, rather, to invoke is therefore an infinitely mediated one. It is no more privy to the name itself than human languages are, and the theodicies of music as a manifestation of the divine, which are especially popular at the moment, are blasphemies; for they afford music the dignity of a revelation because, as art, it is nothing but the secularly captured form of prayer—which, in order to survive, must reject its content and hand it over to the idea. In this effort to attain that to which it is simultaneously denied access, then, music is by necessity infinitely mediated within itself. It has no being that could be cited by any who might be tempted by the riddle but, instead, draws the name closer through the unfolded totality, the constellation of all its aspects. The simple being of music, something that could be pinpointed by some primal question if it only managed to do away with enough layers of concealment and inauthenticity and immerse itself unwaveringly—this is a mirage, no different to the being with which philosophy, weary of its laborious mediations, hopes to reassure itself. What such a mode of interrogation treats as a mere epiphenomenon, an occlusive and accidental ingredient from which the true essence must be extracted, is precisely the unfolded life of music, in which its truth is located and in which its essence is determined in the first place. Only by virtue of its historical traits can music develop a relationship with the unattainable. Without historical mediations, taken as a pure principle or primal phenomenon, it would be entirely impoverished, abstract, and insubstantial in the truest sense of the word. When, in a moment of fleeting association, the clip-clop of horses' hoofs becomes audible as 'meaning' for three bars shortly before the end of the first movement of Beethoven's sonata *Les Adieux*, this passage, beyond all words, tells us that this most ephemeral quality, the intangible sound of disappearance, holds more hope of return than was ever revealed by reflections on the primal essence of the sound in search of a shape. Only a philosophy that truly managed to secure, to their innermost core, such micrological figures from within the construction of the whole would come into contact with the riddle-character without flattering itself that it could resolve it. But whoever presumes to unlock the secret of music as such directly, through the magic spell of primal words, will merely be left with empty hands, tautologies and statements that can at best provide formal constituents—if music has something like a formal *a priori* at all—but which are eluded by the very essence that is usurped by the disposition of language and the concern for music's supposed origins. What Hegel expounds in *Phenomenology of Spirit* (1807) in his critique of *prima philosophia*, of all absolute first principles, applies especially to the relationship between music and philosophy. Nowhere could the statement that what is first, the starting point, is not synonymous with the truth, be more valid than in that art whose most elevated works are justified because their truth emerges only in the final bar—in Hegelian terms, as the 'result'. For this truth, the emptiness of its beginning becomes the motor for its own form.

There has been no shortage of attempts to 'interrogate' the pure being of music, that is to establish a musical ontology. Considering the poverty of the blanket statements about music to which such attempts must restrict themselves, as much as their authors might protest and extol their abstractions as particularly concrete, it is not difficult to conceive something of this kind. Some have sought, for example, to spin out the essence of music from the claim that musical space and musical time form a single continuum absolutely separate from empirical space and empirical time; or also the notion, closely related to this, that music is a language *sui generis*. It is particular to all such hypotheses that they remain in the greatest and vaguest generality, without actually gaining the *a priori* truth they claim through this caution towards everything they consider contingent and ephemeral. The demarcated status of music is common to all art: the phenomenologist Donald Brinkmann defines the delimitation of the aesthetic from the natural by referring to the special aesthetic sphere as one that is free from spatio-temporal facticity. This definition is itself of a historical nature, the secularized legacy of the magically separated cultic realm—almost a form of disempowered sorcery, and thus woven into the overall dialectic of enlightenment. The special aesthetic sphere, not being an *a priori*, cannot by any means maintain itself *a priori*, and the historical movement of all art takes place not least through the instability of the aesthetically pure. This is obvious in the case of literature. But even in music, which only took that separation to the extreme, and by no means monopolized it, one can repeatedly find semantic implications that are not themselves part of the aesthetic image-character—from the echo of march and military music in the great symphonies, which contributes to their power, for better or worse, to the real, extra-aesthetic shocks and emotions whose documentation gave rise to the new formal language of music. Nonetheless, the theory of music as an enclave is specifically true to the extent that what is 'said' by music, if there is such a thing, evidently resists translation into other media far more strongly than other art; or perhaps in so far as music supplies the prototype of untranslatability, which only subsequently becomes fully evident in other artistic spheres. Schumann, that great musician so shamefully neglected by the mindless pre-classical collectivism of today, made the once-famous statement that the aesthetics of one art is also that of any other. It is no coincidence that Romanticism developed this programme, which was subsequently taken to the point of absurdity in the *Gesamtkunstwerk*, starting from music; it was music that resisted the apparent unity of overall aesthetic development most stubbornly. With the increasing integration of bourgeois culture in the nineteenth century, Schumann's demand must have seemed urgent if one was to avoid the verdict of insufficient education and provincial, insecure craftsmanship. Nonetheless, it is precisely the historical extra-territoriality of music that points to an element which cannot simply be integrated, and provides the dialectical ferment of music in the overarching process of development. But this element, precisely as one with an antithetical effect on the process of pan-European Enlightenment, cannot be removed from that process—and above all, as one of the temporal art's essential qualities, not from its formal constitution. Even if one remained at the level of the most general characteristics, the ownness of musical space and musical time would merely be due to the negation of the empirical which its limits serve to keep out, and it is precisely through such polemic that empirical space and empirical time return in the inner constitution of music itself. In order to understand this, one must cast an eye over the specific complexion of music from different periods. Musical time is only truly musical—i.e. not simply the measurable time of a piece's unfolding—when it is a concrete way of conveying something successive that both depends on the musical content and determines it. But this musical time varies so completely from one type to the next that its overarching idea would have to be restricted to the most external level, to chronometric unity. Even someone who rejected formulaic analogies such as 'static music', an expression propagated by neoclassicists, could not fail to see that the varieties of temporal consciousness conveyed by the musical content in a vocal work by Palestrina, a fugue from *The Well-Tempered Clavier*, the first movement of the Seventh Symphony, a prelude by Debussy and a quartet movement by Webern restricted to a mere twenty bars are completely different. But this already shows how little a musical doctrine of invariance, which purports to secure the essential as something lasting, actually gains hold of it. For the music of Webern and Bach, the temporal experience that is specific to each and characterizes its fabric is a more essential aspect than the fact that both unfold in time, or even that musically arranged time does not coincide with chronometric time in either case.

Just as the temporal form of all music, its inner historicity, varies historically, this inner historicity is always simultaneously a reflection of the real, external one. Pure musical time, in its difference from the other kind, stands in the same relation to it as the echo to the reflected sound. The truly dynamic developmental time of music, whose idea crystallized in Viennese Classicism, that time in which being itself was made a process and simultaneously its result, is not simply genetic; rather, in its substantial nature, it is the same time that characterized the rhythm of emancipated bourgeois society, which interpreted its own play of forces as stability. The kinship between Hegel's logic and Beethoven's compositional methods, which can be revealed in the actual details, and is all the more significant because, unlike the case of Schopenhauer and Wagner, one can absolutely exclude any notion of influence,

is more than mere analogy: it is based on the historical constellations, which in both cases constitute the organon of
truth. And the stance of philosophy on musical objectivity, i.e.
the attempt to answer by conceptual means the riddle question
posed to the listener, requires determining the nature of such
constellations by reaching the innermost core not only of the
technical procedures but also of the musical characters themselves. Only through such mediations, not in the immediacy
of the pure question of being, can the tools of thought come
closer to what music is in the first place. And it would be of
little help to modify, for example, the attempt at a musical
ontology by extricating oneself from the supposed quagmire
of the ephemeral and declaring historicity itself the essence of
music, which is precisely what the immanent processual character of highly organized Western music tempts us to do.
Rather, the time that is immanent in all music, its inner historicity, is real historical time reflected phenomenally. One can
indeed suppose that its attempt to gain possession of the absolute consists in precisely such intellectual sedimentations of
real time. Developing this idea would be the task of an elaborated philosophy of music based on Beethoven's work as it lies
before us, in the light of the musical-logical and real historical
process that has affected the work no less than society.

   The historical movement in which the essence of music,
supposedly the most irrational art, is located has a part in clarifying this; it turns from something merely existent to something of the spirit. And only then does it find its truth, the
critical truth, in relation to existence. This movement, however, is synonymous with the progress of its reflection within
itself, the mastery over the merely natural, in short: with its
increasing subjectification and humanization. Referring to the
process as the genesis of a language simply means looking at
the same state of affairs from a different angle. The ontological
definition of music as a language *sui generis* is thus either so

abstract that it says nothing except that there exists an articulated connection with its own 'logic' between the individual musical facts, as Harburger attempts to show in his book on metalogic; or that definition once more amounts to classifying a fundamentally historical tendency, in fact virtually the *entire* historical tendency of music, as an invariant. As stated above, one of the favourite methods of today's ontologists is to deal with the historical dialectic that, in its authentic Hegelian formulation, had resolved the question of being, by absorbing history within being and celebrating ephemerality with solemn gestures as everlasting. The specific language-character of music lies in the unity of its objectification, or perhaps reification, with its subjectification—just as reification and subjectification are never mutually exclusive but, rather, mutually dependent as opposite poles. As Max Weber shows in his posthumous sociology of music, music's language-character has increased since music became part of the process of rationalization in Western society. This character is of a twofold nature: on the one hand, it causes music to change—through its control over the natural material—into a more or less fixed system whose individual aspects have a meaning that is both independent from the subject and open to it. All music from the start of the Baroque period to the present day is connected as a single 'idiom' largely given through tonality, and its power still continues to be felt in the current negation of tonality. What is termed 'musical' in common parlance relates precisely to this idiomatic character, to a relationship with music in which the musical material has, by virtue of its objectification, become second nature to the subject. On the other hand, however, the legacy of the pre-rational, magical and mimetic also survives within the language-like aspect: through its development into language, music has asserted itself as an organ of imitation—but, in contrast to its early, gestural-mimetic impulses, it is now a subjectively mediated and reflected imitation, the imitation of what takes place within human beings. The process of music's development into language simultaneously means its transformation into convention and expression. In so far as the dialectic of the enlightenment process consists essentially in the irreconcilability of these two aspects, however, this dual character places all Western music in a state of contradiction. The more—as language—it takes hold of and reinforces expression as the imitation of something gestural and pre-rational, the more it simultaneously—as the rational means of controlling it—works towards its dissolution. The current crisis, the endangerment of music's right to exist, results primarily from the relationship between those two aspects. Here, the objectivity of signs has dissolved; music ceases to be an idiom, it ceases to represent a stable tradition through traditional forms. But this disappearance of the objective element is accompanied by that of expression, even though it was precisely the intensification of expression that initially caused the objectively traditional side of musical language to be negated. Contemporary music is faced with an aporia: after dissolving the idiomatic element for the sake of pure, unreified, immediate expression, it has now lost control of that same expression. In the end, the natural material emerges from the dialectic in a dangerously pure state. The more music adapts to the fabric of language, the more it simultaneously ceases to be language, to say anything, and its estrangement is only completed with its humanization.

Among the motifs of a possible future that can be observed in music today, its emancipation from language is certainly not the least significant, the reinstatement of its sonic, non-intentional essence, so to speak—of precisely what the concept of the name was meant to outline, however inadequately: overcoming music's control over nature through the process of its completion. It is not superfluous, however, in a situation where the crisis of musical expression has become a pretext for mindlessness, and where a way of thinking that has dispensed with subjective reflection seeks to derive ontological primacy from that very fact, to point out that music cannot succeed in emancipating itself from language by wilfully abandoning the characters it has developed through language and taking supposedly pre-lingual structures as its model, imagining that being will speak through it if the subject stops talking and instead contents itself with poorly quoted ornaments. The truth that enables music to go beyond language is not the residuum left after the gullibly masochistic self-effacement of the subject; it could only be attained if the subject were also positively sublated in post-lingual music. There is no shortage of testimonies to this possibility. It can scarcely be realized from the perspective of music alone, however, but only in an altered relationship between it and society. Music cannot bring about such a relationship at will, for example by adapting to human consciousness; it would have to develop within society itself, not for the sake of art. One can, however, tackle the current musical crisis as a crisis in its lingual nature. It sometimes seems as if, compared with the latent, never explicit yet always palpable possibility of music, its movement towards language—with all its triumphs—were a form of world- historical damage; as if the dignity of the greatest music, the late works of Bach and Beethoven, resulted from music going beyond its own linguality, just as, by comparison, Hölderlin's late poems strive to exceed the sphere of lingual meaning. At this extreme, which is admittedly reached through technique, especially through integral polyphony—in those abrupt moments when the language of music as such becomes visible in all its nakedness and defencelessness, and ceases to be language precisely as a result of this, lies the relevance of the great late works for the music of today. The only tradition in which it can place its faith is the fragmentary tradition of artistic edifices in which music abandons all faith and all tradition.

II

Reflecting on the current relationship between philosophy and music leads to the realization that the timeless essence of music is a chimera. Only history itself, real history with all its neediness and its contradictions, constitutes the truth of music. What this means is that philosophical insight into music cannot be gained through the construction of its ontological origin, but only from the perspective of the present; this alone permits the recognition of all those concrete and contradictory aspects that were only potentially manifest in earlier phases. As the truth of musical works itself unfolds in time, it is no metaphorical exaggeration—nor the commonplace reference to the 'living I–you relationship' between subject and object—to say that Beethoven can be understood far better by examining that aspect which, as the construction of an antagonistic totality and ultimately its suspension, emerges from it today, than by restricting one's view to the historical preconditions and immediate intentions that once gave rise to the work. What becomes visible today in his work, and equally in Bach's, is not the product of a more or less dissipating intellectual history; rather, it is determined in all its details by the state reached by compositional procedures today—procedures that drastically develop those laws of construction encapsulated by Beethoven's or Bach's works throughout the nineteenth century. Only the most advanced creative work can shed light on the entire genre.

It follows from this that an analysis of the current state of music should itself contribute as much towards philosophical insight as, conversely, that philosophical reflection is inseparable from the current situation of music. The explanation of a few elements must suffice. Our thoughts will inevitably be directed towards Schönberg, the master of New Music—assuming it is still permissible today to use the title of 'master', originating from the sphere of craftsmanship and shamefully misused in Wagnerian ideology. It should be used not only to compensate for at least a small part of the injustice done to Schönberg through wilful ignorance and conformism up to the last moment of his principled life. Let us emphazise, however powerlessly, what the general consciousness will one day also be unable to dispute, provided that the idea of the invalidation of great music does not indeed prove true with catastrophic rapidity. Schönberg was—and once again we lack the appropriate words, for they have all been appropriated and worn out by the industry of cultural celebrities—the true musical force of our time, and above all: a great composer. It is time to resist the formulaic phrases that are used to deal with him. In most cases, they simply amount to critics projecting their own inability to understand Schönberg's unprecedentedly organized art, an art finally emancipated from musical stupidity, onto it as an accusation, possibly even claiming that it failed to keep up with the spirit of the age or its collective demands because of its advanced nature. People deal with Schönberg's earlier works and their richness by labelling them with the music-historical cliché of a late-Romantic imitation of Wagner; one could just as easily dismiss Beethoven as a late-classical disciple of Haydn. It is impossible to untangle the nonsense of all these statements, concocted from a mixture of pharisaism, philistinism, incompetence and resentment. Anyone who has an ear for musical quality, and does not make any spontaneous experience impossible by subscribing to the neoclassicist ideology, need only look at one of the works from the period of Schönberg's breakthrough, such as the Second String Quartet or the comparatively straightforward Op. 6 songs, and they will no longer be talked into adopting the verdicts of the compact majority. Turning against this compact majority, however, also involves self-correction. For the *Philosophy of New Music*, whose dialectical method could not fail to address Schönberg, has occasionally been adopted by open or disguised musical reactionaries for this reason. This was only possible because the book does not obey its own principle as strictly as it should have. In certain sections, instead of devoting itself unreservedly to the experience of the works throughout, it treats the material as such and its movement—primarily the twelve-note technique—almost abstractly, without reference to its crystallization in the works themselves. This may have revealed aspects of the historical tendency that could not have been identified as finally in specific works. Nonetheless, this unwittingly supported the misconception that Schönberg was a mere reformer or forerunner, one who provided a more polished and coherent set of tools, but whose own works should be treated as unappealing textbook examples. The decisive aspect, the interpretation of Schönberg's compositions, was still given too little attention. This resulted in the impression that music was to be completely absorbed by cognition. But, while an attempt to achieve penetrating insight is irrefutably demanded by the music itself, music's concretion defines its limit; without this limit it becomes, to quote Kafka, a light and cheerful trip, the automated self-movement of the concept. Schönberg, who was scorned as an intellectual but, with all his rational intellect, belonged—for better or worse—to the category of naïve artists, often decisively changed the general tendency of style and technique precisely through the individual work, incommensurable with stylistic labels. In terms of compositional procedures, one could point to the inevitable ruptures in his late works, in which, perhaps for the last time, he struggled for expression and inserted it into his constructions with allegorical severity. But these ruptures, as in every significant late style, are themselves the instruments of historico-philosophical truth. The endeavour begun by Schönberg still proves itself in the harrowing works of his last years, in which the power of the once-lucky hand seems to be waning, and in which precisely this sense of yielding, of letting go, comes to serve expression; and it proves itself in the fact that, to use a Hegelian expression once again, each new step in his work brought the emergence of new immediacy. No one present at the premiere of the *Dance around the Golden Calf* from the opera *Moses and Aaron*, the performance that, only a few days before the master's death, marked the first occasion on which a twelve-note work of his had brought him complete outward success, could have remained unmoved by its vivid and drastic nature—one could almost say its simplicity of effect. That of *A Survivor from Warsaw*, a companion piece to Picasso's *Guernica*, is no less powerful; here, Schönberg achieved the impossible, namely to stand up to the horror of the present in its extremest form, the murder of the Jews, in a work of art. For this alone he would already deserve the gratitude of a generation that disdains him—precisely because one can hear the tremors of that unspeakable horror, which everyone is already trying to forget, in his music. If music is to avert the threat of its invalidation, the loss of its *raison d'être* discussed above, it can only hope to do so if it achieves what Schönberg achieved in *A Survivor from Warsaw*: by confronting complete negativity, the utmost extreme, which makes manifest the whole constitution of reality.

It is precisely by considering Schönberg's specific compositional achievement in his last works that something can be gained for philosophical insight. Here, one can draw on the concept of musical space as developed especially in Ernst Kurth's psychology of music. This musical space is no more a manifestation of pure being than musical time; it comes about in the collective implications of all music, the character of something that embraces groups of human beings, which was gradually transferred to sound as such. The phenomenon can only be described with analogies but is very precisely perceptible: it is unmistakable, for example, in Bruckner's symphonies.

The spatial quality is evident in the harmony and instrumental sonorities; these two musical dimensions, after all, consistently evolved in parallel during the nineteenth century. Through the critique of tonal harmony, in which the spatial awareness had sedimented itself, so to speak, such that certain chord connections and especially certain modulatory relationships seemed to directly constitute musical space, this spatial awareness had now been eliminated in a fashion not unlike the abolition of spatial perspective in modern painting. Musical space had revealed itself as a historical phenomenon that would not survive the necessary emancipation of music from all sustaining collectivity. If one listens with unbiased ears to early works of free atonality, for example the especially aggressive third piano piece of Schönberg's Op. 11, one is confronted—if one can circumscribe it thus—by a feeling of spacelessness, of two-dimensionality. Among the shocks this music thrusts upon the listener, one of the fundamental ones is undoubtedly that it refuses to draw the listener in; it denies him a sense of being embraced. It sounds, to exaggerate somewhat, like a beating. This probably explains the oft-noted impression of snubbing the listener in the works of his expressionist phase. In some of Schönberg's late works, as most recently in the *Dance around the Golden Calf*, one observes that without borrowing any of the traditional methods for creating musical perspective, he established a new type of musical spatiality—purely through the disposition of colours, the art of multilayered instrumentation taken to the utmost extreme. It remains to be seen whether this amounts to musical space genuinely being gained anew, or simply to an artful reproduction of the past form; nor is it clear how the collective pathos that presents itself in such spatiality justifies itself. But the technical content points beyond some statements made in *Philosophy of New Music*. The section on the twelve-note technique was still too reliant on its origins in the thesis that every musical dimension is an aspect of its own, largely independent of the others. This was used to assess the situation of the individual dimensions in the integral compositional technique of today. But it seems as if nowadays, precisely because all dimensions of composition have been reduced to the common denominator of internally consistent construction, one is interchangeable with another. As is well-known, Schönberg was already speaking of *Klangfarben-melodien* forty years ago. An analysis of the instrumentation in early songs by Berg showed that the process of orchestration has a formally constitutive effect, that it either clarifies the purely musical context—commonly viewed as a drawing of sorts—or even posits it in the first place. This now applies in a much more general sense. If instrumentation indeed proves as spatially constitutive as it is in Schönberg's biblical opera fragment, this means nothing less than that instrumentation can be used as a substitute for harmony, which had previously been used to create a sense of depth. This would deal with the charges of 'randomness' directed at twelve-note harmony, in the sense that those functions which were fulfilled adequately by harmony in traditional music, without any need to descend into blindness and wilfulness, are now being achieved by other compositional means.

But this refunctionalization of individual material dimensions in their state of uniformity, as brought about by the twelve-note technique, also extends to the heart of the technique—namely polyphony, whose requirements gave rise to the entire process. It bears repeating that in the recent history of Western music, counterpoint and harmony are correlative notions. One generally deems counterpoint good if it makes sense harmonically while displaying full autonomy in the simultaneous parts. The critics of twelve-note music claimed that the triumphant counterpoint of the late Schönberg, in a sense, made things too easy for itself, by dispensing with the corrective of the harmonic context. This danger is undeniably present in some pieces of his, especially such early twelve-note ones as the Wind Quintet. One should not impose a verdict from above based on this, however. The philosophical interpretation of music in particular should be careful not to perform what Schönberg referred to in the title of a text as the 'death dance of principles'. One of his statements was that good counterpoint can only really come about if one forgets about the harmony. This formulation is as trenchant in its paradoxical simplicity as Schönberg's pronouncements always were when they concerned actual musical matters. He was the last person who would have recommended the sort of wild, unthinking use of counterpoint sometimes practised by young composers in the name of linear counterpoint. But the density of relationships between several simultaneous voices—whether through similarity or through contrast, but primarily through its binding, thematic-constructive interconnections—can certainly reach such a level of intensity that the question of harmonic progression becomes unimportant; similarly, in the greatest works of polyphonic instrumental music from Bach's late period, the force and unity of voice leading does not (as is the case today) eliminate the chord scheme of figured bass, but at least makes one forget it. Hence, it is not only colour, but also—and even more so—counterpoint, the true medium of New Music, that is capable of taking over the legacy of harmony and, on the basis of its own law, overcoming harmonic randomness. In the light of such achievements, which by no means stem from the rules and system of the twelve-note technique but, rather, arise from the configuration of the works, the technical work of art is perhaps not as hopelessly doomed to failure as the *Philosophy of New Music* suggests. Its organizational principles need not remain external to the musical events, provided that it indeed establishes a binding context purely from within itself. Directing one's attention at the compositions themselves not only corrects some of the mistakes that result from merely observing the tendency of the material; it also reveals that for all the danger of violence and self-estrangement in the most advanced music—the only kind that truly counts—the possibility of binding, compelling works of art is greater than the false superiority of aloofness would suspect. This, however, relates to the more philosophical question of music's *raison d'être* in the current situation. For there are a number of convincing indications that the self-dissolution of this *raison d'être* through the process of aesthetic rationalization, the increasingly drastic contradiction between the complete purposiveness of the work in itself and its equally complete purposelessness in the reality of social existence, may not have the last word. Now, as a consequence of that very rationalization, the most advanced musical works are already releasing forces that will perhaps eventually be able to heal the wounds inflicted upon works of art by rationalization and perfection.

Admittedly, only the most advanced will achieve such healing. Sedlmayr has cast doubt on the validity of 'deeming Schönberg the only pure level of music in our time, and viewing everything that has moved on from there as degenerate and reactionary, for example the new works of Hindemith or Stravinsky'. He believes that 'a genuine need is expressed in them, and that here, as in many other things, a form of "third way" is being sought, even if, in comparison to Schönberg's œuvre, those composers admittedly have nothing credible or similar to show, only poor compromises.' As untenable as strictly exclusive philosophical thought may be, and as thoroughly as one must contest all totalitarian claims made by aesthetic schools, which can always descend into violent sectarianism, Sedlmayr's pluralism nonetheless remains questionable. The third way he desires does not constitute anything new in contemporary music, no addition of fresh musical characters. Rather, the products of the third way in fact show precisely that sterility with which ordinary critics charge advanced music, calling it—with overly hasty historical foresight—a dead end instead of taking a look at what is actually being realized in it. In order to set themselves only slightly apart from convention, without bearing the burden of going all the way, the composers of the third way restrict their innovations to *one* dimension of the material: normally that of 'rhythm', to a modest degree also harmony. In all others, however, they content themselves with the forceful repetition of something long past—a repetition that is never substantial, only modified to take on some distinctive character. Through the specialized restriction of their approach, the grotesque consequence of modern labour division, the products of these schools show an obstinate similarity amongst themselves, and lead to the type of festival music that has now been afflicting exhibitions of modern music with boredom for nigh on thirty years. The possibilities one can identify in Schönberg's last works, i.e. the new fluidity of composition through the functional changes in the musical dimensions, which had previously been rigidly separated, are denied to the moderate school because they have not worked towards that uniformity, instead accepting the conventional distinctions between rhythm, melody, harmony and counterpoint uncritically. Therefore, they cannot truthfully use one as a substitute for the other. Crudely put, they have not paid the price without which music, which has become problematic to its very core, has no hope of rescue. It would be futile, however, to speak with the greatest pathos about the danger on the one hand, while believing on the other that it could be overcome by ignoring it: that shakes off the burden, insists self-righteously on one's own carefreeness and simplicity, and exempts oneself from the effort without which the pressure on music, which has meanwhile reached an immeasurable level, can simply not be dealt with. The reason for stressing this is not to make one school right and the others wrong; but one cannot turn a blind eye to the fact that fascism continues to have an effect on the German intellectual climate, thanks to the widespread inclination to reject mentalities and tendencies that attack existing habits of thought and emotion, be it as negativistic or as already being a thing of the past. Instead, people opt for warmed-up cultural artefacts, or non-committally cryptic efforts that are themselves restorative in their innermost substance. The communist protectors of culture, on the other hand, ever close to the people, are best pleased with the situation. It is what psychoanalysis, which is suppressed according to the same schema, refers to as defence mechanisms: people are too uncertain of the positivity of continued existence after Armageddon, and probably also too much bound by unconscious feelings of guilt, to let in anything that might endanger their precarious security. All those arguments that are at the ready as soon as the concern is to evade the pain and negativity from which no truth can be separated today are nothing more than acts of self-defence. It is because they only serve their own purpose, never engaging with the matter itself, that they are so powerless and meagre. The charge aimed at New Music in its advanced form, namely that it has no relation to human beings or to reality, inverts the true state of affairs. Only by remembering what one is loath to admit can one develop a relationship with the reality of this life, which could be revoked at any time. Something that plays along with reality, however, and even condescends to justifying the purpose of its thusness, is only fit to distract from it, and is nothing more than ideology in the strict sense, social illusion and false consciousness.

In stating all this, we are by no means preaching a higher form of optimism or pretending that music, or any other art, could bring in order the things that conceal the nature of reality, and whose unwavering recognition is the foremost task of art today. To return to specifically musical matters: it is uncer-

tain whether those extremely stimulating aspects of Schönberg's late works and his technique can genuinely be viewed
as the first signs of a higher form of immediacy, one that positively cancels music's pseudomorphosis towards language.
They may themselves even be restorative, albeit in the most
sublimated sense: as attempts to cling to music as language,
even in the de- lingualization of the material. The fact that
many of those who listened to the *Dance around the Golden
Calf* were delighted by the powerfully operatic character of
this ballet music does, at least, make the idea of such restoration plausible. It should be taken all the more seriously because
there is something absurd about the notion that music today
could be saved through its own strength—while it can, at the
same time, scarcely be saved in any other way than through
its own strength. Speaking with younger physicists, one often
encounters the sentiment that compared with quantum
mechanics, Einstein's theory of relativity is essentially classical
physics. Schönberg's achievement, which does not coincide
with Einstein's only in chronological terms, may one day similarly be ranked as 'classical music'—not in the sense found in
the culture industry's sphere of influence, but rather the sense
of Schönberg's deeply buried, yet nonetheless strict allegiance
to the Viennese School of variational-thematic work. The conventional separation of the traditional from the innovative element is probably too mechanical in any case. Stable tradition
is hardly ever a straight, unbroken, self-assured continuation
or succession; this is claimed only by the traditionalists who
invoke tradition because they have none. Rather, tradition—
as stated by Freud in a very profound passage from his late
work on Moses and monotheism— always means forgetting.
It asserts itself by discarding the recent past, not in the con-
servation and continuation of achievements, the protection of
property. Schönberg was able to assert tradition substantially
against its erosion through mere imitation only by discarding

all superficial elements of Viennese Classicism, from the chordal formulas and modulatory equilibrium to the full, sustained sound and the balance of form through the sonata reprise; only because he occasionally even sacrificed the principle of thematic work that was so natural for him as a quartet composer. Because he and his school shattered the Classical-Romantic facade, he became able to realize the ideal of the liberation—or emancipation, as he himself called it in his final book—not only of dissonance, but of music itself, as prefigured by Beethoven and Brahms. Only through this emancipation was it possible to conceive of the ideal of a pure, thoroughgoing construction of music in all its aspects, the ideal to which the deepest impulse of tradition points.

Schönberg's principle of the thoroughgoing construction of the material, the integral composition striven for by his school, clashes with the linguality of music. The more its characters validate themselves purely through their contexts, their mutual relationships, the less can one ascribe to it the character of saying. Because, in his last works, Schönberg did not content himself with the liquidation of music's lingual aspects and their replacement with pure internal coherence but, rather, attempted to turn music into language once more, he is facing the charge of restoration. In other words, his attempt at integration did not go far enough for some young composers. It is indeed true that Schönberg's rationalization left the shaping of rhythms, and largely also the forming of melodies, to the composer's free imagination. So, as in traditional music, there is room for the 'individual idea', for a shaping of musical elements that is not bound by the material. This is why Schönberg is attacked, not only by the neoclassicists, as too subjective. It is precisely his music's likeness to humanity, the aspect in which he still communicates—in however mitigated a fashion—with tradition, that is viewed as a residue of wilfulness by the objectivist zealotry that emerged from his school. The French composer Boulez, for example, a student of Messiaen, worked out a system in which rhythmic relationships are rigorously incorporated into the totality of the construction. Ultimately, one could say that all sound-psychological parameters of music—pitch, tone, intensity, duration and timbre—are turned into an inventory, and all the possibilities they allow are systematically combined to produce contrasts and constant variation. The ultimate goal is for them to neutralize one another. The intention, not entirely unlike Stravinsky's, is to produce a form of static equilibrium. The music that results, and which, like some of Webern's late works, sounds as if it consisted only of dissociated individual notes, leaves an abstruse impression; and no doubt the atmosphere that some listeners still felt in it would, according to the underlying theory, be a mere misunderstanding. But one cannot rule out the possibility that comprehension reached its limits. Someone whose powers of musical perception are profoundly music-lingually formed may be able to recognize the extinction of the lingual element in music, but not to spontaneously make the transition to a music cleansed of all language. In the meantime, however, the abstruseness of the object seems more probable. One is reminded of an aspect that must be mentioned all the more openly because it is by no means limited to music, but can be sensed to some degree in almost all present intellectual and artistic movements: the element of the apocryphal, trivial and comically odd, the particular category that is suddenly inflated into a totality. The problem of twelve-note music probably requires that one account to oneself for this murky sediment, which may ultimately even be the cause of the peculiarly wide appeal some twelve-note music has lately been having. Though one must view this music as the fulfilment of an irresistible tendency in the material itself, it is equally true that the rationalist decree—Schönberg placed great value on having invented, not discovered the twelve-note technique—has something infantile about it. In the musical context, the connection between progress and regression developed in general terms in the *Dialectic of Enlightenment* does not follow only from the consequences of twelve-note music; there is already an element of tinkering, of faith in the philosopher's stone and the taste for roulette in its origins, like a shadow of the legitimation it draws from the progress of the compositional method. Someone who, almost thirty years ago, came from a background of free atonality and encountered Schönberg's first twelve-note works will recall not only an admiration for their ingenuity but also the impression of that madly apocryphal quality that is so deeply related to anything systematic. This aspect was later forgotten, and Schönberg's entire œuvre from the second half of his compositional career could easily enough have exposed itself as the endeavour to dominate that apocryphal element after all through musical self-reflection. But today, with the existence of an entire twelve-note school, it is erupting anew, and fitting in splendidly with the general regression of consciousness. The theologically intended passage in Kierkegaard's *Stages on Life's Way* (1845) in which he describes how, in the place where the yawning abyss of the wolf's glen once lay, there is now a railway bridge from which one can cast a fleeting, pleasant glance downwards, condemns the twelve-note composers sprouting like mushrooms everywhere. The hope that the new musical means would elude the absorption that perverts them was a vain one. The contagious willingness to dispense with autonomy and seek shelter under a roof, however riddled with holes it might be, has brought the twelve-note method its keen disciples. How carefully Webern, in the Op. 5 quartet pieces, handled the new multi-note chords; he was in such awe of their power that he would not have turned them into common currency for a single moment. He held on to each chord, only fearfully letting it go to make room for the next sound. One should compare this with the courage that results inevitably from the progress of composition, but which has long since ceased to cost anything. Today's composers use these sounds as if they were simply the triads they were invented to oppose. They act as if they were in control, but this is not a blessing. The more carefree such attempts are, the more emphatically the fortuitous element at their heart, the apocryphal quality of the self-imposed rule, emerges. In most cases Schönberg's row technique is adopted, but without that infinitely rich, complex and articulated structure of composition whose realization is the only measure of the technique's value. Often, for example in the one-act opera by the unquestionably talented Dallapiccola that was premiered in Frankfurt, the twelve-note technique is reminiscent of what is known in mathematics as overdetermination: musical events of drastic simplicity whose cohesion is guaranteed by traditional means, and which do not require the twelve-note procedure, are subjected to the row principle in addition, almost from without. The systematized avant-garde, divided into schools and their leaders, has become no less resigned than the conformists who simply write what people want to hear. When twelve-note schools claim a certain exclusivity, for example compared with neoclassical tendencies, and refuse to make concessions to the audience's comprehension, this is not due to radicalism—which precisely those who rely on the simplified and infallible system lack—but rather to that absurd element of blind force in the system which is driven to the surface by the turmoil. Relentless self-reflection—the technical and spiritual forms are the same in this case—is what is needed in New Music more than anything else if it is not to contribute in unsuspecting zeal, through the very thing it views as development, to the destruction of that *raison d'être* of all music for whose rescue it was once willing to endure hatred and defamation. What was foreseeable in philosophy one hundred and fifty years ago is meanwhile also true for art—especially music, whose essence, as that of an unfolding truth, is so closely related to philosophy: the critical path is the only one still open. This critique, however, does not consist in the critical stance of the consciousness towards works that are alien to it; rather, it becomes manifest as that which it has secretly always been: the formal law of the works themselves.

1953